MW00581847

SOULSTEALERS

SOULSTEALERS

The Chinese Sorcery Scare of 1768

Philip A. Kuhn

Harvard University Press

Cambridge, Massachusetts

London, England

This book is printed on acid-free paper, and its binding materials
have been chosen for strength and durability.

Library of Congress Cataloging-in-Publication Data
Kuhn, Philip A.
Soulstealers: the Chinese sorcery scare of 1768 / Philip A. Kuhn.
p.   cm.
Includes bibliographical references.
ISBN 0–674–82151–3 (alk. paper)
1. Bureaucracy—China—History—18th century.   2. China—Politics
and government—18th century.   3. China—History—Ch'ien-lung,
1736–1795.   4. Witchcraft—China—History—18th century.   I. Title.
JQ1508.K84   1990
951'.032—dc20
90–32807
CIP

For Mary

Acknowledgments

Chinese colleagues have contributed to this book from beginning to end. Wei Qingyuan of Chinese People's University and Ju Deyuan of the First Historical Archives initiated me into many documentary mysteries while they were in Cambridge as guests of the Harvard-Yenching Institute, and again later while I was pursuing this research in Peking. Their friendship and courage have inspired me throughout my work. Tai Yi, Wang Sizhi, and others at the Ch'ing History Institute, Chinese People's University, offered warm hospitality and intellectual guidance. I owe a special debt to the directors and staff of the Chinese archives, particularly Yan Yunsheng and Xu Yipu (Peking), and Ch'ang P'i-te and Chuang Chi-fa (Taipei). That China has opened her great repositories of Ch'ing documents to researchers from all nations must rank as one of the great events in the history of modern scholarship. We are only beginning to realize its significance for our understanding of the human condition.

The National Academy of Sciences' Committee on Scholarly Communication with the People's Republic of China provided financial support for my work at the archives during 1984. My colleagues at Harvard's Fairbank Center for East Asian Research, along with the staff of the Harvard-Yenching Library, were always encouraging. My assistant, Elaine Mossman, was particularly helpful and resourceful. I cannot adequately thank the generous friends who read the manuscript carefully and extensively: Prasenjit Duara, Lillian M. Li, Lin Man-houng, Susan Naquin, Evelyn S. Rawski, Nathan Sivin, and

James L. Watson. During her two years at the Fairbank Center, Beatrice S. Bartlett shared with me her profound knowledge of the Ch'ing communication system. Many others helped me solve particular problems: Daniel Bell, Peter Goldman, R. Kent Guy, Arthur Kleinman, Patrick Tai (who ingeniously programmed my database), Pei-yi Wu, and Judith Zeitlin. The project could never have been completed without the able assistance of Chiang Yung-chen, Han Ming, Kam Tak Sing (who worked out the transcriptions of Manchu names), Luo Lida, Beata Tikor, Diana Wang, and Yang Jeou-yi. I am grateful to Pat McDowell for preparing the maps and to Olive Holmes for preparing the index. The editorial work of Elizabeth Gretz, of Harvard University Press, was consistently insightful and sympathetic. Although all these friends saved me from many errors, those remaining are entirely my own fault. My wife, Mary L. Smith, by critical reading and staunch encouragement, has earned the dedication of this book many times over.

P.A.K.
Ipswich, Massachusetts
January 1990

Contents

MAPS AND ILLUSTRATIONS

The Chin-shan temple complex at Ch'eng-te. From *Ch'eng-te ku chien-chu* (Peking: Chung-kuo chien-chu kung-yeh ch'u-pan-she, 1982), 124. *75*

The Tibetan-style potala at Ch'eng-te. From *Ch'eng-te ku chien-chu* (Peking: Chung-kuo chien-chu kung-yeh ch'u-pan-she, 1982), 293. *75*

A soul-calling ritual. From Henry Dore [Henri Doré], *Researches into Chinese Superstitions* (Shanghai: T'usewei Printing Press, 1918), V, facing p. 473. *100*

Two builders' curses and an antidote. From Wu Jung and Chang Yen, comps., and Chou Yen, ed., *Lu-pan-ching chiang-chia-ching* (Shanghai: Sao-yeh shan-fang, 1909), chap. 4. *106*

A beggar makes a scene in front of an official's palanquin. From *Tien-shih-chai hua-pao* 73/*chia*.9 (Shanghai, 1884–1889; reprint, Hong Kong: Kuang-chiao ching, 1983). *116*

Governor Funihan's memorial of November 13, 1768 (detail), on the prosecution of soulstealing suspects, with Hungli's rescript at left. From *Chu-p'i tsou-che* 860.12, Ch'ien-lung 33.10.5, First Historical Archives of China, Peking. Reproduced by kind permission of the First Historical Archives, People's Republic of China. *180*

PROVINCIAL ADMINISTRATION IN 1768
Central and Eastern China

-·-·-·- Provincial Boundaries
ппппппп Grand Canal
ᴧᴧᴧᴧᴧᴧ Great Wall

Sheng-ching

SHENG-CHING

Ch'eng-te (summer)

Peking

Pao-ting

Taiyuan

CHIHLI

Tsinan

SHANSI

SHANTUNG

KANSU

Yellow River

Wei River

Yellow River

Kaifeng

Sian

Area of Detailed Map

SHENSI

HONAN

ANHWEI

KIANGSU

Nanking

Soochow

HUPEI

Anking

Lake T'ai

Wuchang

Hangchow

SZECHWAN

Yangtze River

CHEKIANG

River

Lake Tung-t'ing

Lake Po-yang

Yangtze

Changsha

Nanchang

HUNAN

KIANGSI

Foochow

KWEICHOW

FUKIEN

Kweiyang

Kweilin

KWANGTUNG

Canton

KWANGSI

0   100   200 miles

☐ Imperial Capital

○ Seat of Governor-general

△ Seat of Provincial Governor

LOWER YANGTZE REGION

Showing Soulstealing Incidents, Spring, 1768

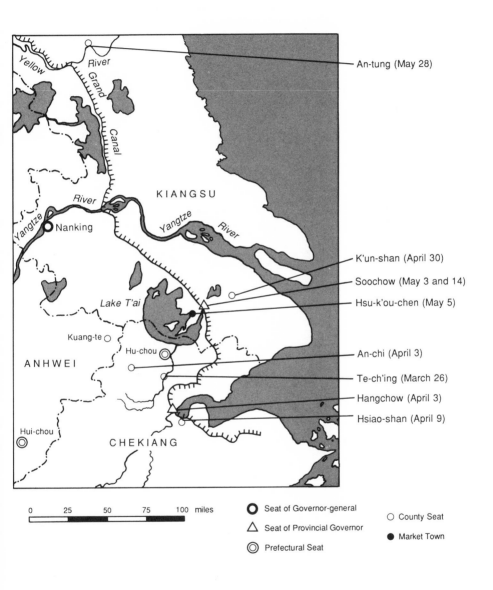

An-tung (May 28)

K'un-shan (April 30)

Soochow (May 3 and 14)

Hsu-k'ou-chen (May 5)

An-chi (April 3)

Te-ch'ing (March 26)

Hangchow (April 3)

Hsiao-shan (April 9)

Yellow River

Grand Canal

KIANGSU

Yangtze River

Nanking

Yangtze River

Lake T'ai

Kuang-te

Hu-chou

ANHWEI

Hui-chou

CHEKIANG

| 0 | 25 | 50 | 75 | 100 miles |

○ Seat of Governor-general

△ Seat of Provincial Governor

◎ Prefectural Seat

○ County Seat

● Market Town

SOULSTEALERS

CHAPTER 1

Tales of the
China Clipper

In the year 1768, on the eve of China's tragic modern age, there ran through her society a premonitory shiver: a vision of sorcerers roaming the land, stealing souls.[1] By enchanting either the written name of the victim or a piece of his hair or clothing, the sorcerer would cause him to sicken and die. He then would use the stolen soul-force for his own purposes. What are we to make of this hysteria that affected the society of twelve great provinces and was felt in peasant huts and imperial palaces?[2] Were the conditions of the age (seemingly so prosperous) sending warnings about the future that could be sensed only in the guise of black magic? Men and women of the eighteenth century—before the West arrived in force—were already creating the conditions of China's modern society. In the light of what the Chinese have experienced since, it would not be surprising to find that their eighteenth-century ancestors perceived these conditions as phantom images of fearsome power.

Though we say that we cannot see the future, its conditions lie all around us. They are as if encrypted. We cannot read them because we lack the key (which will be in our hands only when it is too late to use it). But we see their coded fragments and must call them something. Many aspects of our own contemporary culture might be called premonitory shivers: panicky renderings of unreadable messages about the kind of society we are creating. Our dominating passion, after all, is to give life meaning, even if sometimes a hideous one.

Loading dock at a silk plantation in Hu-chou, Chekiang Province.
A Westerner's impression from the nineteenth century.

The Masons of Te-ch'ing

The silk district of Chekiang Province, "one vast rich and fertile mulberry garden," is a virtually flat floodplain, laced with creeks and canals and studded with residual hills, which appear to a visitor "as if they had been thrown out as guards between the vast plain, which extends eastward to the sea, and the mountains of the west."[3] A century before the time of our story, the inhabitants were already so committed to the silk industry that "no place was without mulberry trees, and in the spring and summer not a person was not engaged in sericulture." Day and night, wrote a seventeenth-century observer, the inhabitants worked to harvest the raw silk, "which they produce to pay their taxes and rent, and on which they rely for clothing and food." So wholly dependent were they on the silk market that "if ever it is unprofitable, they have to sell their houses and property."[4] In the midst of this thoroughly commercialized district lay the county seat of Te-ch'ing, some twenty miles north of historic Hangchow. The river Nan-t'iao, on its way northward to Lake T'ai, ran right through the walled city. In 1768, the thirty-third year of the reign of Hungli (Ch'ien-lung),[5] fourth monarch of the Manchu Ch'ing Dynasty, the water-gate and bridge in the eastern side of the city wall had fallen to ruin and needed rebuilding.[6]

Magistrate Juan hired the mason Wu Tung-ming from Jen-ho, the neighboring county. Wu and his crew began, on January 22, the heavy work of pounding the great wooden pilings into the riverbed. The water was running high, and the men struggled at their task.[7] Nevertheless, pilings were sunk by March 6, and Wu's men began to install the new gate. By the twenty-sixth, Wu was running low on rice to feed his men and made the ten-mile journey to his home town, the commercial center T'ang-hsi on the Grand Canal, to buy a fresh supply. When he arrived home, he learned that a stranger had been asking for him: a peasant named Shen Shih-liang, who proceeded to seek Wu's help in a curious and frightful project.

Peasant Shen, aged forty-three, lived in a family compound with two sons of his deceased older half-brother.[8] These harsh, violent men tormented him, cheated him of his money, and even beat and abused his mother. Without hope of earthly remedy, he besought the powers of darkness. At the local temple he filed a formal "complaint" with the King of the Underworld by burning a yellow paper petition before the altar.[9] In February, Shen heard of a promising new remedy: travelers brought news of the Te-ch'ing water-gate project. They had heard that the masons needed the names of living persons to write on paper slips, which could be nailed onto the tops of the pilings to add spiritual force to the blows of the sledgehammers. This was called "soulstealing" *(chiao-hun)*. Those whose soul-force was thus stolen would fall ill and die. With renewed hope, Shen had written the names of his hated nephews on slips of paper (since he himself was illiterate, he painstakingly copied them from an account book kept by his nephews in connection with a commercial fishing venture). Now producing the rolled-up slips of paper, Shen asked mason Wu: What about it? Do you practice this technique?

Wu would have none of it. He knew that masons, along with carpenters and other builders, were commonly thought to have baleful magical powers (as I shall explain in Chapter 5). He was also,

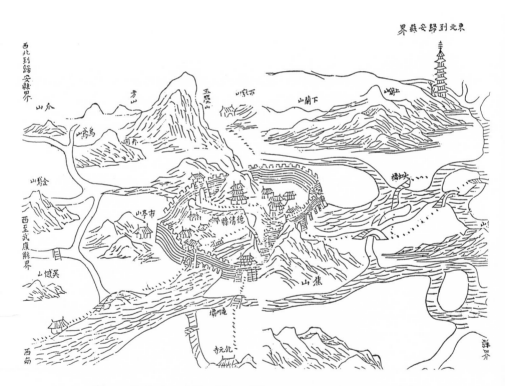

The walled city of Te-ch'ing. Water-gates can be seen at right and lower left of the city.

no doubt, aware of the kind of rumors peasant Shen had repeated, and feared that he might be implicated in this hated practice of soulstealing. He quickly summoned the local headman and had Shen brought to Te-ch'ing for questioning. Magistrate Juan settled the matter by having Shen beaten twenty-five strokes and then released. Mason Wu's misadventures with sorcery, however, were not over: he was soon to be implicated in an outbreak of public hysteria.[10]

One early spring evening, a Te-ch'ing man, Chi Chao-mei, had been helping with funeral arrangements at the house of a recently bereaved neighbor. On his way home he had a few drinks, and he was relaxed enough by the time he reached his house that his uncle suspected him of having been out gambling and began to beat him. Smarting and fearful, Chi fled the house and walked the twenty-odd miles to Hangchow, the provincial capital, where he thought to support himself by begging. After midnight on April 3, he found himself before the Temple of Tranquil Benevolence near the shore of Hangchow's fabled West Lake. A bystander grew suspicious of Chi's Te-ch'ing accent, and when Chi acknowledged his origins, a crowd surrounded him. One man shouted, "Here you show up in the middle of the night, and either you're about some thievery, or else it's because you people in Te-ch'ing are building a bridge and you've come here to steal souls!" The crowd quickly turned ugly and set upon the outsider, seizing and pummeling him. Off they dragged him to the house of the local security headman.

The headman tied Chi to a bench and threatened to beat him if he held back the truth. The bruised and terrified Chi now concocted a story that he really was a soulstealer. "Since you're a soulstealer," shouted the headman, "you must have paper charms on you. How many souls have you stolen?" Chi said he had indeed had fifty charms, but that he had thrown forty-eight of them into West Lake. He had used the other two to cause the deaths of two children, whose names he proceeded to invent.

The next day Chi was taken to the constabulary, and from there to the yamen (government office) of Ch'ien-t'ang, the metropolitan county of Hangchow Prefecture (located in the same city). There Magistrate Chao asked where Chi had obtained the charms, and who had told him to steal souls. Chi had heard the usual rumors about the bridge project in Te-ch'ing, that the pilings had been hard to sink, and that the masons needed names of living persons whose soul-force could lend power to their hammers. He had also heard that

Constable leading a prisoner, who is carrying
his own sleeping mat and a fan.

the contracting mason was Wu something or other, and that his given name had the ideograph *ming* in it: "It was Wu Jui-ming who gave them to me." Mason Wu *Tung*-ming must by now have been thoroughly dismayed by the hazards of his calling, for he was forthwith haled into the Ch'ien-t'ang County yamen. Luckily, Chi's perjured story was quickly exposed when he failed to pick Wu from a lineup. Put to the torture, Chi now admitted that his whole story had been concocted out of fear.

The sorcery scare in Chekiang had by now sparked several unpleasant and bizarre incidents. In addition to the affairs of Shen Shih-liang and Chi Chao-mei, there had been the matter of Wu's co-worker, mason Kuo, who, on March 25, had been approached by a thirty-five-year-old herbalist, Mo Fang-chou, who sought to entrap him into placing a paper packet on a bridge piling so Mo could ingratiate himself with the authorities by turning in a soulstealer. The furious mason had seized Mo and dragged him to the county yamen, where the would-be informer was beaten and exposed in a cangue (a heavy wooden stock placed around the prisoner's neck) for his trouble.

These irksome cases moved the provincial authorities to hold an inquiry in which accusers and accused alike could be questioned, thus to make an end of it. Governor Hsiung Hsueh-p'eng ordered the local prefect to convene a court with the magistrates of Ch'ien-t'ang and Te-ch'ing counties. Chi again failed to identify Wu in a lineup. The authorities searched Wu's home secretly and found no sorcerer's paraphernalia. Magistrate Juan had already made discreet inquiries among the bridge-workers and found no evidence that persons' names had been intoned while the pilings were being driven. Sorcery indeed! Herbalist Mo, peasant Shen, and even the unfortunate Chi Chao-mei were exposed in the cangue at the Hangchow city gates as a warning to the superstitious multitude. After all, nobody had been shown to have sickened or died on account of soulstealing; on the contrary, public credulity had damaged civic order. Such was the agnostic summary later offered to the Throne by Yungde, the succeeding Chekiang governor.[11] But fear of sorcery was not so easily exorcised from the public mind.

The Hsiao-shan Affair

On the evening of April 8, 1768, four men, marked as Buddhist monks by their dark robes and shaved heads, met at a rural teahouse

Scene at the entrance of a county yamen in the lower Yangtze region. The convicts in cages are being left to die of starvation. At lower right are two convicts wearing the cangue.

in Hsiao-shan County, Chekiang, just across the river from Hangchow. All were based in Hangchow temples and were wandering the nearby villages to beg alms. Sketches of these men may be drawn from their own later testimony.[12]

Chü-ch'eng (this was his dharma-name, assumed when he was tonsured as a monk), aged forty-eight, lay surname Hung, was a native of Hsiao-shan County. When he was forty-one, after his parents and wife had all died, he entered a temple in Hangchow called Ch'ung-shan-miao, where he assumed the tonsure.[13] There he shared a teacher (master, *shih-fu*) with the younger monk Cheng-i, and the two addressed each other, in the conventional clerical "family" way, as elder and younger brothers. Chü-ch'eng had not, however, reached the next stage of monastic life, that of ordination. Because his temple had no means of supporting him, he went begging in his native county, where we now find him.

Cheng-i, twenty-two, a native of Jen-ho in Hangchow Prefecture, lay surname Wang, was Chü-ch'eng's "younger brother." Because he was a sickly child, his mother had him tonsured at the age of nineteen at the God-of-War Temple outside the city gate. He later studied alongside Chü-ch'eng at Hangchow, but like him did not receive ordination. He joined his "elder brother" to go begging across the river in Hsiao-shan.

Ching-hsin, aged sixty-two, was from the Grand Canal city of Wu-hsi in Kiangsu Province; his lay surname was Kung. At the age of fifty, after his parents, his wife, and his children had all died, he journeyed to Hangchow to take the tonsure at a small Buddhist retreat, where he then resided. Later he was ordained at the monastery called Chao-ch'ing-ssu. In the course of his travels to study at various monasteries, he met the monk called Ch'ao-fan, whom he later invited to join him as his junior acolyte.

Ch'ao-fan, forty-three, from poor and mountainous T'ai-p'ing County in Anhwei, lay surname Huang, was Ching-hsin's acolyte. He had been tonsured at eighteen at a local temple. Later he received ordination at the Tzu-kuang-ssu monastery, whose location is unknown but was probably in Hangchow. He went to live with Ching-hsin in 1756.

The great cultural and religious center of Hangchow had attracted all four: two had forsaken lay life because family deaths had left them alone at what in eighteenth-century China was considered old age. Two had been tonsured in youth: one because of sickness (an eco-

遊方僧

A wandering Buddhist monk, in an eighteenth-century
Japanese impression gleaned from Chinese merchants at
Nagasaki. The stubble of hair betrays a degree of
indiscipline that would not have been tolerated at
an established monastery.

nomic liability to his family), and the other for reasons unknown. Two bore the government-mandated identity papers (ordination certificates) and two did not. Now all four were pursuing the most common outside occupation of monks: begging. Apart from the spiritual benefits of begging (a demonstration that they had renounced worldly concerns), their monastic homes lacked the means to support them. We do not know exactly the extent of the catchment basin of Hangchow mendicants, but Hsiao-shan was right across the river from the city, and at the teahouse the four decided to set forth together there the next day. Chü-ch'eng and the elderly Ching-hsin would spend the day begging in the villages, while the juniors would carry everyone's traveling boxes to the old God-of-War Temple near the west gate of Hsiao-shan City.

Making their way along a village street, Chü-ch'eng and Ching-hsin saw two boys, aged eleven or twelve, playing in front of a house. One saw Chü-ch'eng's name inscribed on his bronze begging bowl and, to the monk's surprise, recited the ideographs aloud. "So, Mr. 'Official'—you can read!" chuckled the delighted monk. "You study a few more years and you'll certainly get an official post. What's your name? After you've become an official, don't forget me," he added, hoping to please the youngster so he would fetch his parents from the house to give alms. The boys paid no attention. Seeing no adults around, the monks gave up and resumed their progress.

A few minutes down the road, a frantic couple came running up behind them. "Why did you ask our child's name?" they wailed. "You're a soulstealer!" Once a sorcerer knew a victim's name, who could say what incantations he could work upon it? Chü-ch'eng explained that they had come only to beg. "What's 'soulstealing' about saying a few words to your child because he could read?" Agitated villagers quickly crowded around. Some had learned that these days "soulstealers" were coming around from far places, casting spells on children so that they sickened and died. "These two are bad eggs for sure!" The mob, angrier than ever, tied them up and searched them roughly. Finding nothing, they began to beat them. As the hubbub drew a larger crowd, some shouted "burn them!" and others, "drown them!"

In the crowd was a local headman who managed to quiet the furious peasants but shrank from handling so serious a matter himself. He therefore took them to the imperial post station (the nearest agency of the official establishment) to be questioned. The monks were searched again, but no proof of soulstealing could be found. (What would such proof consist of? Books of sorcery? Tools of magic?) Just to be sure, the literate child was brought in, inspected, and found to be in good health. Nevertheless the distraught parents, trusting in the omnipotence of the written word, demanded that the post-station clerk draw up a formal document stating that all was well. This responsibility the clerk was unwilling to assume. Instead, he wrote up a memorandum for the county authorities. Soon the magistrate's attendants came to haul Chü-ch'eng and Ching-hsin away to the fearsome county yamen of Hsiao-shan. There the two monks found that their companions, too, had been arrested and had been interrogated under torture.

It was persistent rumors of "soulstealing" that had brought Cheng-i and Ch'ao-fan to grief. In surrounding counties, public fears were running high. In Hsiao-shan, Ts'ai Jui, a county constable (*pu-i*), had been instructed by his superiors to arrest "vagrant monks" from outside the county who might be responsible for "clipping queues." A sorcerer with the right "techniques" could say incantations over the hair clipped from the end of a man's queue and so extract the soul of its former wearer.

Lurking in the background, unmentioned by anyone connected with the monks' case, was the *political* meaning of hair: the queue, worn behind a shaved forehead, was the headdress of China's Manchu rulers. It was also universally prescribed, on pain of death, to be worn by Han Chinese males as a symbol of allegiance to the ruling dynasty.

Patrolling outside the city's west gate, constable Ts'ai heard street-talk that two monks from "far away" with strange accents were lodging in the old God-of-War Temple. As Ts'ai later reported to the magistrate, he then entered the temple and began to question Ch'ao-fan and Cheng-i. Getting no satisfaction, he began to search their baggage. From Ch'ao-fan's he pulled clothing, a bronze begging bowl, clerical robes, and two certificates of ordination. In Chü-ch'eng's, which he had to break open with a stone, he found *three pairs of scissors*, a pigskin rain-cape, an awl, and *a cord for binding a queue*.

An excited crowd gathered. "What's a monk doing with this kind of stuff?" These fellows must be up to no good. There were cries of "beat them up" and "burn them!" Constable Ts'ai, as he continued in his report, summoned his courage and told the mob to keep out

The queue and the shaved forehead. At a barber's stall, a man is having his forehead shaved in the prescribed manner.

Courtroom scene. A prisoner is interrogated with the aid of the leg crusher. The clerk at left records his confession, while prisoners kneeling at right await their turns.

of this; since Ch'ao-fan was a "real monk" (as shown by his certificates) there was no basis for arresting him. Cheng-i, however, not only lacked an ordination certificate (meaning he was only a novice, a status readily obtainable) but also had with him Chü-ch'eng's traveling box and its suspicious contents. Bound in chains, the young monk was taken off to the yamen. Ch'ao-fan found his way to the yamen to lodge a protest, but was then arrested himself and brought with the others before the magistrate.

In the great hall, Chü-ch'eng and his companions, chained hand and foot, knelt before the county magistrate, who sat at his high desk flanked by his judicial secretaries.[14] The questioning began: "How many queues have you clipped?"

The terrified Chü-ch'eng protested that he had clipped none. The magistrate then presented Chü-ch'eng with the evidence constable Ts'ai had brought in: *four* pairs of scissors, one cord for binding a queue, and two short pieces of braided hair. "Are these, or are they not, evidence of your queue-clipping?" Chü-ch'eng answered that three of the scissors had belonged to his dead son, who had been a leather-worker. The fourth he knew nothing of. The queue-plaiting cord had, he said, been used to bind his hair in the days before he had taken vows and shaved his head. Afterward, he had no use for it but kept it with his gear. For the braided hair, he offered no explanation.

An unsatisfactory confession, this, from a prisoner whose guilt was presumed in advance. Now began the customary courtroom torture. Attendants dragged Chü-cheng over to the *chia-kun*, or "pressing beam." We are not told whether this was the regulation ankle-press, a device for crushing the ankles by slow degrees, or an equally fearsome instrument that inflicted multiple fractures of the shinbones. A nineteenth-century observer describes the ankle-press as "a sort of double wooden vice" consisting of three upright beams, of which the outer two functioned as levers:

> The chief torturer gradually introduces a wedge into the intervals, alternately changing sides. This mode of forming an expansion at the upper part, causes the lower ends to draw toward the central upright, which is fixed into the plank, by which the ankles of the victim are painfully compressed, or completely crushed. Should the unhappy sufferer be resolute from innocence, or obstinate from guilt, and submit to the consummation of the horrid procedure, his bones are ultimately reduced to a jelly.[15]

Overwhelmed by the pain, Chü-ch'eng eventually declared that all charges against him were the truth. Still the magistrate was not satisfied, because the agonized monk's story was not sufficiently coherent. Twice more the *chia-kun* was tightened, but with no better result. Ching-hsin now underwent the same torments. After three days, the magistrate had something resembling admissions of guilt from all four monks. The maimed prisoners were sent, probably in the regulation wheeled boxes used for transporting prisoners, some twenty miles eastward to the Shao-hsing prefectural yamen, the next rung in the official ladder, and again interrogated. This time, since Chü-ch'eng's bones were already broken, the presses were not used. Instead, his lips were slapped ten times with a wooden switch. Cheng-i was again subjected to the *chia-kun*. Ching-hsin and Ch'ao-fan were by this time seen as less promising culprits and were spared further torture.

By now the testimony was more confused than ever, and the pris-

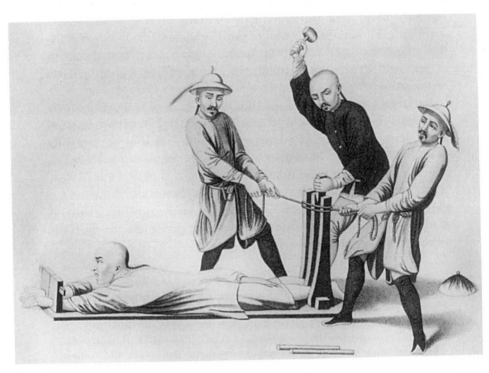

The ankle-press at work.

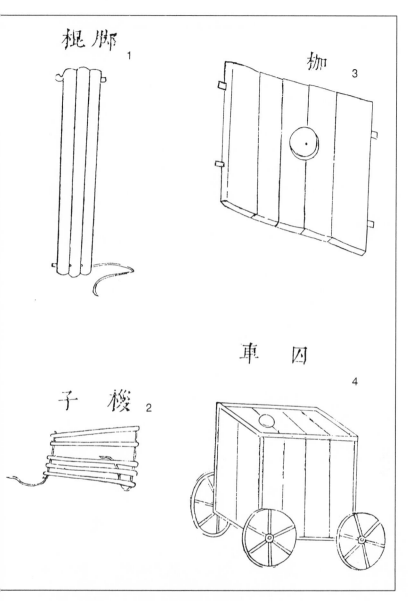

Various authorized torture ("punishment") implements:
(1) the ankle-press;
(2) a device for squeezing the fingers;
(3) the cangue;
(4) a prisoner transfer cart.

Court in session at a provincial yamen. The governor and his aides are reviewing cases forwarded from the

oners were sent on up the ladder: this time to their final place of torment, the provincial judge's yamen in Hangchow. There something surprising happened.

Ever since their first encounter with the Hsiao-shan authorities, Cheng-i and Ch'ao-fan had stubbornly clung to the story that constable Ts'ai had arrested them falsely, because they had refused him money. This was a story common enough in local society. Yet who would believe these ragged monks? Could the public hysteria about sorcery be wholly groundless? And what of the concrete evidence Ts'ai had produced from Chü-ch'eng's baggage? At neither the county nor the prefectural level were the monks believed. Now the provincial judge, Tseng Jih-li, pursued the same line of questioning:

> *Judge Tseng:* Chü-ch'eng, you're a beggar-monk, so you naturally have to beg for your vegetarian food. But how come you had to ask the name of someone's child? This is crystal-clear proof of your soul-stealing. When you made your first confession here, you wouldn't admit that you had asked the child's name.
>
> *Chü-ch'eng:* . . . That day, at the county yamen, I said I had asked his name, so the magistrate kept asking about soulstealing. The attendants gave me the *chia-kun* three times, and my legs still haven't healed. I was really scared, so when I arrived here and Your Excellencies questioned me, I didn't dare say anything about asking the kid's name . . .
>
> *Judge Tseng:* . . . If there wasn't solid proof that you did these things, how come the crowd was so angry that they wanted to burn you or drown you?
>
> *Chü-ch'eng:* . . . When they saw the parents had grabbed us, they all suspected we were soulstealers, so they shouted about burning and drowning us. Really, that was all just guff. Later, when the headman took us to the post station, the crowd all went away . . .

Officials at the grand provincial yamen were apparently less inclined to coddle police underlings than were officials at the county, who depended on the likes of constable Ts'ai to carry on their daily business. As the prisoners cowered before the provincial judge, Cheng-i repeated his tale of attempted extortion. Ts'ai Jui, he insisted, had told them that day in the temple that he had been ordered to arrest "vagrant monks" and would let them off only if they paid him the "customary fee." Cheng-i had answered, "We're beggar monks. Where are we going to get money to pay you?"

Something about Cheng-i's story struck Judge Tseng as plausible. Men like constable Ts'ai were not professional police, but belonged to the general category of local underlings known as "government runners" *(ya-i)*. They performed many distasteful and demeaning local jobs such as torturing suspects, serving summonses, "urging" the payment of taxes, and running miscellaneous errands around the government offices. Those who, like Ts'ai, did police work were considered to be of "mean" status and not permitted to sit for civil-service examinations. They were paid little and had to support themselves by demanding "customary fees" from all commoners whom they dealt with. Some "runners" were not even on the official rolls, but were destitute men who had attached themselves as supernumeraries to others. These received no pay at all and simply preyed upon the public. It was commonly said that runners were a low lot and had to be kept in check, yet few officials could do so because the runners' services could not be dispensed with.[16]

Now constable Ts'ai was brought forward and made to kneel. Though Judge Tseng probed at his story, Ts'ai clung firmly to it, and was left kneeling for the rest of the day. At last the exhausted man realized that the game was up. Indeed, he now confessed, he had demanded cash. When the monks balked, he proceeded to search their baggage: "Where did these things come from? Now if you don't fork over several strings of cash, I'll take you to the county and say you're queue-clippers."

With the discovery of the compromising scissors and queue-binder, the stakes rose. As the shouting match grew louder, the inevitable crowd gathered. Amid the hysteria, Ts'ai sensed more trouble than he could handle. He persuaded the crowd to disperse by arresting Cheng-i and dragging him off. Instead of taking him directly to the county yamen, however, he brought him and the incriminating baggage to his own home, located in a blind alley which backed onto the city wall. He was followed by the irate Ch'ao-fan, who demanded his traveling box. "I'll give it to you only if you bring in those two other monks," said Ts'ai. Ch'ao-fan, fuming, set off for the yamen to protest.

Constable Ts'ai's confession went on. Once safely in his own house with the chained Cheng-i, he said, "Now that everyone's gone, just cough up a few strings of cash, and I'll be glad to let you escape." But the outraged monk insisted that he was going to file an official complaint. Ts'ai started beating him, but without result. He realized that he was in serious trouble unless he could make the queue-clipping charge stick. Unfortunately, there was only one lock of hair in Chü-ch'eng's box; furthermore, it was straight hair and did not really resemble a clipped queue-end. So Ts'ai found an old lock of hair in his own house, went out in the alley where Cheng-i could not see him, and carefully braided it. For a bit more evidence, he cut some strands of fiber from his own hat fringe and braided them up to resemble two little queues. This hastily concocted evidence he placed in the monk's traveling box along with his own pair of scissors (making a total of four), and marched his prisoner off to the magistrate's yamen.

There, even under torture, Cheng-i clung to his extortion story. But the magistrate sagely pointed out that there was obviously no bad blood between constable Ts'ai and Cheng-i, the two being total strangers, so Ts'ai could have had no motive for framing him. On this basis, the case had gone up through the prefectural court without being suspected.

Now that Ts'ai had confessed to the frame-up, however, Judge Tseng turned the case back to the Hsiao-shan County authorities. The constable was beaten, exposed in the cangue, and finally let go— perhaps a more circumspect guardian of public order. The monks were freed, each with 3,200 cash to sustain him while his broken bones healed.

Popular hysteria and petty corruption had nearly resulted in a serious judicial error. Courtroom torture had elicited confessions, but these were compromised by the accuseds' complaints before higher authorities. Once the case reached the provincial level, the bias against the accused was balanced by the worldly-wise skepticism of high officials far removed from the pressures and temptations of grubby county courtrooms. A case of sorcery? More likely, the usual nuisance of a credulous rabble abetted by greedy local police ruffians and incompetent county authorities: a case the province was now happily rid of.

Yet the tide of public fear was stronger than Judge Tseng and his colleagues knew. The same day that Chü-ch'eng and his friends were arrested, persons elsewhere in Hsiao-shan had beaten an itinerant tinker to death because they believed that two charms found on him were soulstealing spells. Officials later discovered that they were conventional formulae for propitiating the Earth deity. The unlucky tinker had been carrying them while cutting trees in his ancestral cemetery. A week earlier in An-chi County, which bordered Te-ch'ing, the epicenter of sorcery fears, an unidentified stranger with an unfamiliar accent had been roped to a tree and beaten to death by villagers on suspicion of soulstealing.[17]

Within a fortnight, rumors of soulstealing in Chekiang had spread to Kiangsu. Soulstealing (by the queue-clipping method) was believed to be practiced by itinerant beggar-monks from Chekiang, who were entering the neighboring province to practice their loathsome craft. The local authorities were alerted. Likely suspects were quickly found.

The Beggars of Soochow

In Soochow, an ornament of China's most elegant urban culture, seat of the governor of Kiangsu, China's richest province, on May 3, 1768, local constables seized an old beggar of "suspicious" appearance. The charge was clipping queues for the purpose of soulstealing.[18] Local authorities did not, however, allege an association between queue-clipping sorcery and the political symbolism of the queue.

The ragged creature who was dragged into the constabulary on that May morning was Ch'iu Yung-nien, a native of Soochow Prefecture. Ch'iu, fifty-eight, was an unemployed cook who had turned to begging "along the creeks and rivers." By April 26, his wanderings had brought him to Ch'ang-shu, a county seat just south of the Yangtze, where he took lodgings at a rooming house. There he met two unemployed men who, like him, had taken to the road in order to survive: Ch'en Han-ju, twenty-six, an unemployed "maker of dusters and hat fringes," whose home was Soochow; and Chang Yü-ch'eng, forty-one, formerly a peddler of dried salt fish. Chang was the only one from outside the province, having wandered all the way from Shao-hsing, Chekiang (a journey of 120 miles along the Grand Canal). These three marginal men, cast off by the "prosperous age" of the mid-Ch'ing, found that they were all heading south toward Soochow, and on May 2 set out together.

By the next day they had reached Lu-mu, a teeming commercial district north of the Soochow city wall, on the banks of the Grand Canal. While his companions begged in a pawnshop, Ch'iu squatted by the roadside. There he was seized by constables from the Soochow garrison, accompanied by two constables from the Ch'ang-chou County yamen. He was found to be carrying a knife and some paper charms. As the constables questioned him, a crowd gathered. Among the bystanders was a ten-year-old boy, Ku Chen-nan, who told anyone who would listen that earlier the same day he had felt his queue tugged, but could not see who had done it. That was enough for the police. Beggars Chang and Ch'en were quickly found and imprisoned with Ch'iu. The three were tortured with the *chia-kun* in the usual manner. Confronted with the incriminating evidence found on him, Ch'iu insisted that the knife was for making "orchid-flower beans" for sale. The paper charms (each imprinted with "great peace," *t'ai-p'ing*) he would paste on doorways in the market streets and then ask for handouts. All three steadfastly denied the crime of queue-clipping. The boy, brought in and questioned, repeated his story:

> I'm ten years old and I study at the County Academy. On the third of May, as I was going home, walking north, someone gave my queue a yank from behind. I turned right around, saw someone running away. My queue had not been cut. Later I was told that the constables' post had arrested some men and I was ordered to go there and identify them. When it happened, I was walking along and the person was behind me. I couldn't see his face. The man wearing black here, Ch'en Han-ju, looks sort of like that person, but I can't identify him for sure.

Later, the suspects were brought to the county yamen, where they were tortured again with the *chia-kun*. Ch'en stated that he knew nothing about "stupefying people" or clipping queues: "The kid even says he can't identify me. When I was at constabulary headquarters, they tortured me with the *chia-kun*, so I don't dare lie to you. My legs still haven't healed. Also, the constables searched me thoroughly and didn't find anything illegal. Even if you torture me to death, I couldn't tell you anything. I beg you to spare me more torture."

In the end Magistrate Tu had to let them go. His final report stated that the three men were

> persons of no fixed abode, who got together to beg. They are definitely not respectable types. However, having put them to torture, there is still no hard evidence of queue-clipping. Ku Ch'en-nan could not identify them positively. The paper charms seized at the time of the arrest, we have found, are not things for stupefying people, and nobody has made complaints against these criminals.[19] Apparently these men are not guilty of queue-clipping. We have now released Ch'en, Chang, and Ch'iu to return to their home jurisdictions, there to be placed under the supervision of the local security authorities. We shall continue to search for the real criminals.

But the public temper was so disturbed that Magistrate Tu could not consider the case closed. On May 9 he posted proclamations that read, "We have found that there are queue-clipping criminals per-petrating illegal and harmful actions." Investigations were con-tinuing. Though the beggars' guilt had not been proved, persons who might have suffered at their hands were urged to come forward without fear of harassment, in case the criminals had been lying.

One prisoner, it turned out, could not be released. The two county policemen who had made the original arrests (and who were held responsible for the prisoners throughout their custody by the county) reported on May 5 that criminal Chang had contracted a high fever and could not eat. Magistrate Tu ordered immediate medical care, and physicians were summoned. A jail death meant irksome paper-work, a possible investigation, and a fine to be docked from the magistrate's salary, should he be found guilty of negligence or mis-treatment. Chang's condition worsened, the police reported; by May 20 he was near death. The physicians found his pulse weak, his skin hot and dry, and his tongue yellow. Herbal medicines were admin-istered without effect, the report continued, and the patient died that night.

That a beggar died in jail surely surprised nobody. Although Ch'ing jails were probably not much worse than contemporary jails elsewhere, they tested even the stiff upper lip of a British prisoner who was confined briefly in the Board of Punishments' jail in 1860:

> The discipline of the prison was in itself not very strict, and had it not been for the starvation, the pain arising from the cramped position in which the chains and ropes retained the arms and legs, with the heavy drag of the iron collar on the bones of the spine, and the creeping vermin that infested every place, together with the occasional beatings and tortures which the prisoners were from time to time taken away for a few hours to endure,—returning with bleeding legs and bodies, and so weak as to be scarce able to crawl,—there was no great hardship to be endured.[20]

A Chinese literatus who spent a year in the same prison (1712–13) described the treatment of his fellow inmates: "Their ordinary stan-dards of sleeping and eating are disregarded, and should they fall ill, no doctor or medicine is provided. That is why they so often meet their death."[21]

The file of the late beggar Chang in Soochow was now meticulously furnished with testimony to certify the cause of death. Depositions were obtained from the police ("we by no means mistreated him"), from a fellow prisoner (the police "by no means mistreated him"), the county doctor ("an incurable illness"), and the coroner ("died of disease"). A coffin was provided at county expense, and his native county was notified in case relatives wanted to claim the body.

One criminal dead, two more released for lack of evidence: hardly a memorable piece of judicial work. Yet Magistrate Tu must have felt relieved that a troublesome matter had been disposed of. Though he was obliged to protect himself from later charges of negligence by issuing a public proclamation about queue-clipping, there was no reason to hold beggars Ch'iu and Ch'en. A silly and trivial business. Superstitious rumors among ignorant commoners. A pesty child who was probably imagining things anyway. A dead prisoner—but prisoners died all the time. A cause of future trouble? Most unlikely.

An Incident at Hsu-k'ou-chen

Monk Ching-chuang lived and worshiped at the Dharma Cloud Temple in Hu-chou Prefecture, Chekiang Province, just down the river from the scene of mason Wu's encounter with sorcery.[22] In the spring of 1768, it was time to replenish temple supplies (devotional materials such as incense) in Soochow and to visit relations and friends there. Along with six companion monks, Ching-chuang hired boatman Yao to sail them to the metropolis along the eastern shore of Lake T'ai. Ching-chuang and his acolyte, Ta-lai, carried with them a string of 1,000 copper cash, and others carried cash in varying amounts. They set sail on May 4 (the day after the beggars' arrest in Soochow) and, on the afternoon of the following day, anchored at the lakeside market town of Hsu-k'ou-chen.

Monk Ching-chuang and the boatman went ashore to buy food and stopped to rest at the Hsu-wang Temple. A fisherman, Chang Tzu-fa, entered the temple and asked whether Ching-chuang was from Hu-chou. Fearsome rumors had recently convinced local folk that monks from Hu-chou were coming to clip people's queues. Was Ching-chuang one of these? Fisherman Chang threatened to seize him and find out. Ching-chuang and the boatman fled out the door. His suspicions confirmed, Chang pursued them in full cry. The market crowd swirled around the pair and began to pummel them, seriously injuring boatman Yao.

A constable who ran to investigate seized Ching-chuang's belongings and searched them, along with the rest of the baggage on Yao's boat, but found no suspicious items (queue-clipping equipment such as scissors, or powders for stupefying victims). Still, with the crowd so ugly, he could not let the monks go. He put Ching-chuang, the boatman, and the original accuser Chang onto the boat with all the other monks to take the lot to the assistant magistrate's yamen at Mu-tu-chen, on the river route to Soochow.

The boat docked at Mu-tu-chen after dark. Taking monk Ching-chuang with him and leaving the others on the boat, the constable went ashore and headed for the yamen, stopping on the way to report to the local constabulary barracks. Finding the assistant magistrate out, he brought his prisoner back to the barracks. By that time the crowd in the local market had learned that queue-clipping monks had been arrested, and a noisy mob had gathered at the dock. Local rowdies, led by T'ang Hua and Li San, had discovered that there were still some monks aboard the boat. The terrified suspects and their boatman were dragged ashore and brought to the constabulary. Later that night, persons unnamed boarded the boat and helped themselves to the travelers' money and clothing. Yao's boat was wrecked. Now the constables feared major trouble at Mu-tu-chen if the suspects were held there any longer. In a second hired boat, the miserable group were taken to Soochow that very night for interrogation by the magistrate of Wu County himself.

For want of firm evidence of queue-clipping, the county magistrate determined that Ching-chuang and his companions were monks going about their lawful business. Furthermore, fisherman Chang should be held responsible for starting the whole affair. The monks, not satisfied at merely being released, went over the magistrate's head and filed charges at the office of the prefect to seek recompense for their lost money and clothing. The prefect responded by ordering the Wu County magistrate to seize fisherman Chang and compel him to make restitution, even though he himself could not be shown to have stolen anything.

The Bureaucracy: Managing Sorcery

The hysteria that spread over east-central China in 1768 was cultured in a rich broth of local sorcery beliefs. Details varied from region to region, but the common ingredients were these: the human soul can, under certain conditions, be separated from the body of its owner; one who obtains another's soul can use its force for his own benefit; the stealing of a soul (soulstealing, *chiao-hun*) can be brought about by sorcery, either by reciting spells over some physical entity that has been detached from the victim's body, such as a man's queue-tip or a woman's lapel, or by placing the victim's written name on or under a piling that is to be driven into the ground and/or calling the victim's name while driving such a piling; the victim may be stupefied by dusting or blowing a powdered drug *(mi-yao)* on him, so he cannot resist being clipped; victims are very likely to be male children; victims will sicken and die.

In a patrilineal society with high infant mortality, the protection of children (particularly males) is one of life's highest priorities. Since the etiologies of most diseases were either unknown or misapprehended in Ch'ing times, sorcery could never be ruled out when a child fell sick. Sorcerers would likely be persons who customarily dealt with the supernatural (such as Buddhist monks or Taoist priests) and who might reasonably be supposed to possess means of manipulating otherworldly affairs (charms or spells, perhaps written down in mysterious books).

What did provincial bureaucrats really think of all this? Here are three possibilities. Bureaucrats may have believed that rumors that soulstealing sorcery was being practiced were pure bunk: no such activity was occurring. Or they may have supposed that though some malefactors might really be clipping queues or placing victims' names on bridge pilings, such practices were mere folk superstition, incapable of actually stealing souls. It is also possible that officials thought that sorcery not only was being practiced but in fact was, or could be, effective.

The way provincial officialdom handled the spring sorcery cases suggests that they felt awkwardly balanced between dutiful caution and agnostic scorn. When suspected soulstealers were brought before them, careful investigation had to follow. After all, a magistrate or provincial judge could not be seen to scoff at a crime so detested by the general public, particularly when sorcery in a number of analogous forms was prohibited by the penal code, as we shall see in Chapter 4. And of course there was always the outside chance that sorcery might really exist; who could certify that it did not? But the decisive factor was surely the potential for general panic. If evil men were *trying* to practice sorcery, they had already ignited dangerous popular fears and must be harshly punished. In the event, all the sorcery suspects were released for lack of evidence, and their accusers shown up as fools or perjurers. Judges must have risen from their courtrooms with discreet sighs of relief and retired to tea, confirmed in their scorn for the fears of the ignorant mob.

Were those fears put to rest? Not likely. Whether a judge was a believer or an agnostic, to punish the accusers, rather than the accused, made him look soft on sorcery. Whatever the mental state of particular bureaucrats, the official reaction to sorcery hysteria was to get the case out of the streets and into the courts. Public disorder in one's jurisdiction was an unmistakable sign of incompetence or neglect. It could break an official career even more surely than failure to fill tax quotas. Though a crowd might be mollified if a stranger were lynched, no official wanted such a blot on his copybook. Of course a suspected sorcerer could be prosecuted under the *Ch'ing Code,* which made certain occult practices a capital crime. But since all capital sentences had to be reviewed by the highest court in the realm and ultimately by the monarch himself, the evidence had better be good. If judicial inquiry turned up perjury or slander, the only recourse was to punish the accuser, free the defendants, and thus warn the public against irresponsible talk and lawless violence.

The costs of hindering the public's effort to protect itself against sorcery, however, might be considerable. Examples from other cultures show how deeply compromised are agnostic or unbelieving governments that prohibit antisorcery violence among their subjects. Navahos complain that not only do the white authorities forbid them to kill witches; they even "fail to punish people for the worst crime we know."[23] Modern governments in East Africa have suppressed popular antisorcery measures (such as the poison ordeal) at the cost of accusations that they "have aligned themselves on the side of evil."[24] From the standpoint of the state's public image, perhaps the cleverest solution is one reported from Uganda. Under the British protectorate, a law existed to punish those who "pretend" to be sorcerers (in order to threaten rivals or project a fearsome reputation). Here the state does not admit to believing in the substance of sorcery and maintains it is contending only with the pretense of it. Yet ordinary Ugandans fail to distinguish between pretending to be a sorcerer and actually being one; consequently, suspected sorcerers can be haled before civil authorities and jailed.[25] As we shall see, such agnosticism has some parallels in the antisorcery provisions of the *Ch'ing Code.*

Be that as it may, provincial bureaucrats must have considered that their courtrooms had worked quite smoothly in the cases of early

1768. The false charges against mason Wu and the machinations of
the corrupt constable Ts'ai had been exposed. In the Hsu-k'ou-chen
and Soochow incidents, those falsely accused had been released, and
the public had been duly warned against rash accusations. Though
lynchings of vagrant suspects would eventually come to Peking's
notice when the homicide convictions were automatically reviewed
by the Throne, there had as yet been no case of actual sorcery that
was worth troubling His Majesty about.

Yet fear of sorcery remained deeply embedded in the public mind.
Was there no protection against this scourge? How little the public
had been reassured! By June 21 the panic had broken out of the
lower Yangtze provinces and had spread five hundred miles upriver
to the prefectural city of Hanyang: there a large crowd at a street
opera seized a suspected soulstealer, beat him to death, and burned
his corpse.[26]

CHAPTER 2

The Prosperous Age

Sorcery panic struck China's last imperial dynasty, not during its waning days, but at the height of its celebrated "Prosperous Age" (*sheng-shih,* a conventional slogan that often adorned official documents as a talisman of benign rule). Sorcery's dread image was refracted through every social stratum. It overspread provinces with a total population much larger than the entire population of Europe at the time, and cost many lives and careers. Altogether, though, the damage to human life was slight compared to the great witch scares of sixteenth- and seventeenth-century Europe. Why the damage was so limited is as curious a question as why the scare arose in the first place.

That a whole society could envisage the threat, that lowly and lofty could sense the same emergency, suggests a cultural network densely twined. But the vision struck peasant, bureaucrat, and emperor in different ways, according to the preoccupations that ruled their several ways of life. The case suggests both unity and diversity: a nation in which events at the highest and lowest levels affected each other intimately, but in which society's prism refracted the soulstealing idea in various hues.

The Gilded Age of Hungli

The economic triumphs of the eighteenth century were founded on domestic peace. The last major fighting within China proper had ended in 1681 when emperor Hungli's imperial grandfather crushed the Rebellion of the Three Feudatories. The coastal frontier was secured in 1683 when Ch'ing forces conquered Taiwan. Peace nourished China's greatest period of demographic and commercial expansion, but the roots of this expansion dated from before the Manchu conquest. By the seventeenth century, new crops from the Americas (maize, sweet potatoes, peanuts, and tobacco, crops that could be grown on dry uplands) were already sown on the nonirrigable hillsides by settlers flocking to China's internal frontiers. By the late seventeenth century, the aggregate depopulation of the conquest years was already made good, and the stage was set for the population explosion of modern times. In the course of the eighteenth century, the population is thought to have doubled. To serve these growing masses, there emerged a dense network of rural markets. Not urbanization, but a proliferation of dusty (or muddy) local market towns put virtually every Chinese peasant in touch with regional systems of trade. Money was everywhere: silver from Spanish America promoted the free sale of land and labor. Commercial energy and population growth were creating a society that contemporary Westerners (whose industrial revolution was still in its cradle) considered vigorous and stable.[1] This is the society over which spread, in the early spring of 1768, the shadow of sorcery.

An Encouraging Story

Writing about eighteenth-century society has been a buoyant experience for Chinese historians, more inspiring than relating the decline and disruption, futility and weakness, of the period after 1800.[2] Eighteenth-century Chinese, whose genius for commerce and enterprise was sustained by firm and effective government, were admired by the world. The tone of social historical writing has been bright, even celebratory. Western historians too have caught the enthusiasm as they have explored this "new and higher form of economic activity."[3]

Researchers have indeed painted a flourishing economic landscape. The bustling eighteenth-century commerce had roots before the Ch'ing conquest: an expanded money supply, in both the silver and copper components of China's bimetallic currency, nourished an expanding domestic trade that overflowed the boundaries of China's major economic regions. Monetary expansion benefited from imports of precious metals and from their increased domestic production. Silver and copper streamed into China in exchange for her silk, tea, porcelains, and other products desired by the outer world. Exchange grew more efficient, farmers could specialize in cash crops, and handicraft industries grew rapidly. The government took advantage of all this liquidity to carry out major tax reforms.[4] This expansive scene, already visible in the late sixteenth century, was redrawn on an even grander scale as the nation recovered from the turmoil of the Ming collapse and Manchu conquest. The mild but persistent rise in prices that accompanied the influx of silver was generally good for economic growth: farmers could sell their grain more profitably and could pay their taxes more easily. Investors flourished in the long period of eighteenth-century inflation.[5] Such is our picture of a vigorous, bustling age. To understand the background of the 1768 crisis, however, it will be important to explore its effects on social attitudes, a subject we still know very little about. The place to begin is the region of the lower Yangtze, where the soulstealing crisis began.

The Society of the Lower Yangtze

The area known as Kiangnan ("south of the river") in east-central China formed the prosperous core of what we now call the lower Yangtze macroregion. On the provincial map, this core included southern Kiangsu, a corner of eastern Anhwei, and northern Chekiang.[6] It is in this setting, the most highly developed of China's economic regions, that the eighteenth-century commercial expansion is most often described. For three-quarters of a millennium it had been China's most prosperous regional economy. There most conspicuously were found the cash-cropping and the specialized markets so characteristic of China's late imperial economy. So specialized were these local economies, in fact, that grain production was much too low to sustain the population. As a result, a vast interregional grain entrepôt sprang up in Kiangnan cities and market towns. By the eighteenth century rice imports sufficient to feed between three and four million people a year were flowing from the upper- and mid-Yangtze provinces to the market towns around Soochow, Sung-chiang, and T'ai-ts'ang.[7] This rice made its way to grain-deficit areas all around east China. According to an early eighteenth-century observer,

Fukien rice has long been insufficient to supply the demands of Fukien. Even in years of abundant harvest much has been imported from Kiangsu and Chekiang. What is more, Kiangsu and Chekiang rice has long been insufficient to supply Kiangsu and Chekiang, so that even in abundant years they have looked to Hunan and Hupei. For several decades, rice from Hunan-Hupei has collected at the market town of Feng-ch'iao in Soochow Prefecture [just west of Soochow city]. By way of Shanghai and Hsu-p'u, this Feng-ch'iao rice makes its way to Fukien. Therefore, even though a year's harvest may be blighted, there will be no inflation of rice prices.[8]

In manufacturing, the basis of Kiangnan's wealth was textiles. Cotton products of the lower Yangtze reached a national market. Silk was the leading export product and clad the increasingly luxurious bureaucratic, scholarly, and commercial elites. These huge industries were built on the handicraft labor of millions of peasant families. So tightly was the peasant household bound to the marketing network in Kiangnan's highly commercialized society that no "isolated" or "cellular" local economies were conceivable (to cite an old misconception about village China). In its extreme form, this integration of village with market town meant a kind of slavery to handicraft work. For a swelling population to survive in this densely populated region on ever-smaller parcels of farmland, every family member was mobilized to produce for some niche of the market. As early as the fifteenth century, we find an account of such lives in the cotton industry:

> Cotton-cloth production is not limited to the villages, but also is done in the cities. At dawn the country women carry yarn they have spun into the city, where they exchange it for raw cotton; the next morning they come in with another load, without any respite. A [peasant] weaver can produce about a roll *(p'i)* of cloth a day, and some work all through the night without going to bed. After payments of taxes and interest, a farming family's resources are exhausted before the end of the year, and they rely for living expenses entirely on the cotton industry.[9]

Not only in highly commercialized Kiangnan but in less developed areas as well, intimate connections between village and market town formed the texture of late imperial society.[10] The suffusion of the late imperial economy by monetized silver and copper made possible—and in fact required—a constant flow of people to and from urban centers. Virtually every peasant household traded in a local market, and through it was linked to regional and even national markets. What this meant for China's premodern industry was that extensive, highly rationalized production could proceed without large-scale urbanization. Although large factories and urbanized work forces did exist in some regional metropolises such as Nanking, the more general pattern was of an intricate putting-out system, based on handicraft labor by the wives and children of land-poor farmers, who could participate in large production systems while still living in villages.

The Emancipation of Labor

The growth of commerce since the sixteenth century had been accompanied by a freer market in labor. Land tenancy tended toward long-term, contractual relations between landlord and tenant. In some areas, permanent tenancy rights (under a kind of dual-owner-ship system, in which surface and subsurface rights were held by different persons) had emerged by the eighteenth century. The hereditary status system of the early Ming Dynasty (1368–1644), in which millions of people were enrolled in special registers and com-pelled to work for the state in specialized occupations, was formally abolished soon after the Ch'ing conquest. Most important, the oblig-atory labor-service of all commoners (the corvée) was swept away in the tax reforms that began in the sixteenth century, by which land and labor taxes were merged and assessed on the basis of land. Instead, the state hired laborers to do its work. Indeed, by the eight-eenth century, labor-for-cash was the obvious and necessary basis of a commercializing economy.[11]

The spirit of formal equality—already so forcefully impelled by economics—was symbolized by the Ch'ing government's emancipa-tion of small groups of servile people in the 1720s and the enuncia-tion of a general policy of *commoner equality.* I emphasize this last phrase because eighteenth-century China remained a steeply hier-archical society, with towering heights separating the governing elite from the rest of the population. But though the numbers freed were very small, the symbolic achievement must have seemed worth the effort. By sweeping away "mean" *(chien)* status among the com-moners, the emancipation decrees apparently were meant to create a subject population uncluttered by specially disadvantaged groups. The proximate reasons for the decrees of the 1720s are still obscure. Nevertheless, the more general reason must have been related to the Manchus' distrust of the Han landlord elite (whose dependents these servile groups were) as well as a desire to express a kind of conqueror's "benevolence" in which the Manchu regime stood above a relatively undifferentiated mass of commoners—a scornful gesture at some long-standing Han social distinctions. Formal commoner equality was right in line with the despotic and rationalizing style of Injen, the third Ch'ing emperor and Hungli's father. The language of the emancipation decrees implied that lacking specific historical-legal reasons for servile status (such as penal servitude or a contract of indenture), all commoners were of equal standing before the mighty Ch'ing state. Writing about the despised Tanka (boat people) of Kwangtung, Injen pronounced that "they were originally ordinary subjects (*liang-min,* lit. "good [i.e., not polluted] commoners"), and there is no reason (*li*) to despise them."[12] Concludes a recent study: "Best of all," freedmen could now "take advantage of the expanded labor market and change employers if they wished."[13]

A free-wheeling labor market, the decline of personal dependency and servile status: these have great appeal to a twentieth-century Westerner, who associates them with Freedom and Progress. Yet their effect on the mentality of an eighteenth-century Chinese may have been somewhat different. No doubt they were appreciated by families struggling to survive on small parcels of land, who urgently needed to sell their excess labor power to fend off starvation. Landless men could hope to survive in a free market for hired farm labor. A few able and lucky outcasts might now rise from pariah status into the examination system (barred to "mean" groups) and thence into elite status. (A decree of 1771 dealt with such upstarts by ruling that only in the fourth generation after formal emancipation might a man legally sit for the examinations.)[14] With respect to servile groups, however, it may be wondered whether much "freeing up" actually occurred. Even half a century later, the serflike tenants in Hui-chou were having trouble asserting their imperially mandated freedom.[15] And one historian points out that provisions for cash redemption of servile status were in fact meaningless, for they were well beyond the resources of tenant farmers, and in any case "redemption" would leave them without a livelihood.[16]

Surely the underlying fact about "free labor" in the eighteenth-century economy is that it was sold in a buyer's market. In an increasingly crowded region like Kiangnan, "freedom" for the wage laborer meant the liberty to harness one's family to the kind of regime I have just described in the Kiangnan cotton industry. It meant the option to leave an oppressive landlord and take one's chances elsewhere. Liberty could also be found, presumably, in the labor gangs hired to work on government dredging projects, or on the docks of the maritime trading ports. But how many people could *not* find buyers for their labor in the growing economy of the age—and what happened to them?

Popular Consciousness of the Prosperous Age

Here indeed was a bustling economy. Its effects on social consciousness, however, are virtually unexplored. Take, for instance, social communication. The dense commercial networks so prominent in the eighteenth-century landscape put nearly everybody in a regular relationship to a market. Knowledge of regional and national events flowed with goods and people along the trade routes between villages and market towns, between local markets and regional entrepôts. The "back-alley news" *(hsiao-tao hsiao-hsi)* that Chinese of our day find so essential to supplement the government-controlled press was already well developed in late imperial times—and there is plenty of evidence that China's "back alleys" were, even then, linked to regional and national networks of information. News of opportunities elsewhere, as well as of dangers flowing from elsewhere, were the daily fare of the Chinese villager (to say nothing of the city dweller).

Hardest to estimate is what the Prosperous Age really meant to ordinary people. Attitudes about where life was leading, whether toward better conditions or worse, whether toward greater security or less, may have been rather different from what we would expect in a growing economy. From the standpoint of an eighteenth-century Chinese commoner, commercial growth may have meant, not the prospect of riches or security, but a scant margin of survival in a competitive and crowded society. Commerce and manufacturing enabled hard-pressed rural families to hang on, but only through maximum employment of everyone's labor. This scramble for existence in an uncertain environment may have been a more vivid reality in most people's lives than the commercial dynamism that so impresses us in hindsight.

Two large questions bear upon this late eighteenth-century consciousness: first, whether China's economic growth, however impressive in absolute terms, was able to offset the great increase of her population; and second, how the unevenness of that growth from region to region may have affected how people viewed the security of their lives.

Population, Prices, and Money

A steep rise in rice prices in 1748 set off alarm bells throughout the national bureaucracy. The effect on public order was immediate and disturbing: riots in Soochow and other lower Yangtze cities, which had become dependent upon rice imports from provinces upstream. But officials all around the empire were aware of the inflation in rice prices and its connection to population pressure. Ch'en Hung-mou, governor of Shensi Province, wrote that the inflation resulted from a long-term shift in the ratio between population and land. "It is certainly a result of population pressure . . . In all the provinces, the fertile land has already been brought under cultivation. Although there are still large areas of mountainous or marshy wasteland, the soil is so poor that it must be left fallow for two years after one year's cultivation."[17] An experienced official, Wang Hui-tsu, commented on what these conditions meant for his home county of Hsiao-shan (adjacent to Hangchow, and a scene of soulstealing panic twenty years later): "When the rice price was up to 160 copper cash for one peck, all the grass roots and tree bark were eaten. In places where there was powdery sand, people unearthed it to eat and called it 'Buddha's Sand,' though some died of it."[18]

This was no short-term problem; rice prices continued to rise during the second half of the eighteenth century. Yet their effect on local society was apparently buffered by a rise in the money supply. Beginning in the 1760s, the opening of silver mines in Annam by Chinese entrepreneurs, as well as a quickening influx of Mexican silver coins in payment for Chinese goods, swelled the supply of silver. One authority estimates that China's silver supply rose by some 274 million Mexican dollars in the period 1752–1800.[19] But it was after the 1760s that the silver influx was most profuse, as can be seen in the record of silver imports:[20]

Years	Silver (ounces, *liang*)
1681–1690	189,264
1691–1700	139,833
1701–1710	769,665

1711–1720	6,312,798
1721–1730	2,287,676
1731–1740	2,528,338

(Ch'ien-lung reign begins, 1736)

1741–1750	642,000
1751–1760	412,800
1761–1770	3,411,453
1771–1780	7,564,320
1781–1790	16,431,160
1791–1800	5,159,542
1801–1810	26,658,835
1811–1820	9,932,442
1821–1830	(2,282,038)
1831–1833	(9,922,712)

The decreasing availability of silver in the early Ch'ien-lung period may have made it harder to sustain living standards in the face of population growth. The marked increase beginning in the 1760s and gathering force in the 1780s probably made it possible, for a time, to realize prosperity despite intense crowding. Yet the benefits of silver trickled only slowly into local society. For the lower Yangtze, the turnabout seems to have occurred around 1780. For that crucial region, at least, qualitative evidence suggests that the celebrated eighteenth-century "prosperity" cannot have begun much earlier than that date. Our Hsiao-shan informant, Wang Hui-tsu, goes on to say, "For more than a decade before 1792, rice prices stayed high. [Yet] when one peck cost 200 copper cash, people thought it was cheap. In 1792, when one peck cost 330–340 copper cash, people still enjoyed life." How could this be explained? Wang believed that it was because the inflation *after* about 1780 was not confined to population-sensitive rice prices, but extended to all commodities: when rice prices had been high in the past, other commodities were not affected, "while today [1794], everything including fish, shrimp, and fruit, is expensive. Therefore, even small peddlers and rural laborers can make ends meet."[21] One explanation for this turnaround is an increase in the supply of money in general. With more money in everyone's hands, sellers could charge more for goods of all kinds.[22] Though the evidence is still sparse, Wang's account adds convincing local substance to inferences from silver-supply data.

More research will be needed before we can understand fully how men's awareness of their social surroundings was shaped by eight-eenth-century economic change, particularly population growth and the availability of money. We must get the periodization right: what temporal shifts made people aware of changes in their life chances? If Wang Hui-tsu's sense of the timing turns out to be right, then what we are seeing after 1780 is but a brief felicity. The real prosperity of the Prosperous Age extended from the 1780s until the mid-1810s (when a worldwide shortage of silver decreased foreign capacity to buy Chinese goods—at about the same time that opium imports created a catastrophic outflow of silver, causing the nationwide dis-tress that we have always associated with the beginning of the modern period).[23] If so, then the soulstealing crisis occurred just before the increased money supply had begun to relieve the burden of popu-lation pressure in the fourth quarter of the eighteenth century. Rice prices in the lower Yangtze were still weighing heavily on commoners' lives in an overcrowded society. In 1768, the outer world had only just begun to pay the bill for China's population boom.

Uneven Development

If the highly developed Hangchow region saw some hard times before the 1780s, what of the outlying mountainous areas? One did not have to travel far from the commercialized cores to find abject poverty, unemployment, and disorder. Two adjacent jurisdictions illustrate the contrasts that lay just outside the Soochow-Hangchow core of the lower Yangtze, some forty miles from Te-ch'ing, the origin of the soulstealing panic. Kuang-te, an independent department in Anhwei, lies about thirty miles from the western shore of Lake T'ai.[24] The neighboring district to the east, An-chi in Chekiang, which was connected by water to the Grand Canal, had a flourishing silk industry that had pushed mulberry cultivation even into its hilly districts. Yet economic development had passed Kuang-te by—save for the influx of population that was common to counties of the Yangtze highlands. In 1739 Magistrate Li asked that the Throne remit the grain-tribute tax so that he could use it to fill the local relief granaries: "There is little arable land, and because very little water is retained in [irrigation] ponds, the soil is unproductive. The cultiva-tors have almost no carts and draft animals with which to engage in commerce. The people also lack handicraft skills with which to eke out a living. To survive, they simply hope for a good harvest. But with long internal peace, the population has increased, and an abundant harvest barely furnishes one year's subsistence."[25] Transport routes were inadequate to permit timely purchase of grain from other areas, and the people would be in great difficulty if officials bought grain locally to stock the relief granaries. Just that summer, people were panicked by the threat of floods, and grain was being hoarded. No jurisdiction in the Kiangnan area had such difficulty feeding its people, Magistrate Li concluded. Elsewhere we learn that Kuang-te had ("despite repeated prohibitions") unusually high levels of female infanticide.[26]

How unusual was this chronic disaster area? Though it may have been a particularly bad case, the ecology of Kuang-te was not unique. This little Appalachia formed the northern anchor of a 180-mile chain of hilly counties running from northeast (near Lake T'ai) to southwest (at the Kiangsi border). Ironically, the vigor of Ch'ing commercial life has been symbolized for social historians by the empirewide success of merchants from Hui-chou, which lies toward the southwestern end of this region. But Hui-chou's local economy accords rather closely with the picture of Kuang-te just sketched: a hilly region with poor land, a settlement area for landless peasants crowded out of coastal regions, and a relatively uncommercialized agriculture. In Hui-chou, agricultural relations among long-settled folk rested on a system of virtual serfdom, in vivid contrast to the free-wheeling farm economy of the flatland.[27] The population of this region as a whole was swollen by a tide of immigration that continued well into the next century.[28]

The scholar Wang Shih-to, who lived as a refugee in this region during the 1850s (Chi-ch'i County, part of Hui-chou Prefecture), described the area as chronically poor, overpopulated, and short of basic commodities. Despite high rates of female infanticide, population expansion was sustained by extremely early marriage, to the extent that "a man could become a grandfather at the age of thirty."[29] The county he was describing exported tea, forest products, and (sporadically) precious metals and lead. Yet the bottom line was abject misery: "The county is everywhere mountainous, and the peasants toil upward, level by level, to plant a foot or reap an inch. If it is dry, they fear their crops will wither; if it rains, they fear they will be washed away. Though they labor ceaselessly all year, their clothing is fit only for oxen and horses, their food only for dogs and swine."[30] Though Chi-ch'i participated in the regional market (indeed, the commercialization of the core areas was what made its few exports salable), this county and those around it present a stark contrast to the world of Soochow and Hangchow. When hard times hit those metropolises, what of hinterland counties like this one?

No account of the eighteenth-century economy, then, can omit the gulf between core and periphery, between fertile river deltas and hardscrabble mountain uplands. What went along with this gradient in the economic map was an unceasing flow of people: migrants and sojourners, merchants and mountebanks, monks and pilgrims, cutpurses and beggars thronged the eighteenth-century roadways. The stream of travelers—some moved by enterprise, some by devotion, and some by desperation—had its effects on men's consciousness.[31]

Migration, Out and Down

Suspicion of soulstealing focused on wanderers: strangers, people without roots, people of obscure origins and uncertain purpose, people lacking social connections, people out of control. The victims of lynch mobs and of torture chambers were mostly wandering monks and beggars; and if we consider monks a species of beggars, then the suspected soulstealers were all beggars. Where did they come from, and why were they feared?

Population growth and ecological change. The population of China roughly doubled during the eighteenth century, from around 150 million in 1700 to around 313 million in 1794.[32] The precondition for this expansion was China's capacity to develop new ways—and new places—for people to make a living. These ways and places included New World crops, such as maize and sweet potatoes, which made the hills yield a living to immigrants. They included massive internal movement of population, particularly to Szechwan, which had been depopulated by the internal wars of the conquest period; to the highlands of the Yangtze and Han river systems; to Manchuria; to largely aboriginal Taiwan; and to lands overseas. All over China, people were moving upward as well as outward: forested hills became flourishing sweet potato and maize farms, until their soil eroded and became barely cultivable. The expansion of cultivated land area during the eighteenth century cannot be measured, but (taking the nation as a whole) is thought to have kept pace with population growth until around 1800. All this can be seen as a triumph of will and work—and an ecological disaster, as China's mountain soil gradually washed into her rivers.[33]

The commerce of the Ch'ien-lung reign can be seen as a sump for absorbing the increase of labor power. It enabled families with tiny landholdings to survive by selling the handicraft labor of their women and children. Yet there is plenty of evidence that neither commercial expansion nor out-migration could take care of everyone, and that a certain number of people were entirely forced out of the productive economy. Their solution was not migration outward, but downward: into an underclass of beggars. We have no reliable way of gauging the numbers or proportion of displaced persons in the Prosperous Age. Devices for registering population did not reach the homeless. Observers a century later saw plenty of vagrancy, of course, during the economic crises of the nineteenth century. By contrast, the eighteenth century looked like a golden age.[34] Yet, despite the disparity in numbers, I am struck by the social awareness of vagrancy even in the 1760s. The question is of particular interest because vagrants of all sorts, both clergy and lay, were objects of suspicion during the soulstealing panic.[35]

The clerical underclass. At the height of the sorcery crisis, an elderly "Taoist" *(tao-shih)* named Li Ying was arrested by Chihli authorities on suspicion of queue-clipping and eventually shipped to the summer capital at Ch'eng-te for interrogation by the Grand Council.[36] His confession:

> I'm from Ting-chou.[37] I'm fifty-six years old. My father, mother, wife and children are long dead. I've always been a hired laborer. In the thirty-first year of the Ch'ien-lung reign [1766/67] I'd been working in Fang-shan County, but I was so poor I couldn't go on, so I decided to join the clergy *(ch'u-chia,* lit. "leave the family"). At Yellow-lotus grotto I became a follower of the Taoist master Fu-yueh. I cut brushwood and carried water for him. Because the temple was too poor, Fu-yueh couldn't keep me there. There was a Buddhist monk of the Shih-t'ang Temple named Kuang-shan (also a Ting-chou man) repairing the temple. I went there and began to work for him.

Li later heard of the Taoist master Wang Lai-shui, "who always stayed in his mountain retreat." A disciple took him up to visit the master, "who was unwilling to accept me, because food was short." While descending the mountain ten days later, Li fell and broke his leg. "On the road I met a man called Han Chün-fa who helped me into the village and took care of me for several months. In the second month of this year, my leg had healed and I left to go begging. In the seventh month, I got to the area of Hsiao-ching, where His Excellency the Governor-general was passing by. I went over to have a look and then I was arrested."[38]

How extensive was the underclass of marginal clergy? The provincial judge of Szechwan pointed to "increasing numbers" of unemployed men and women who "concealed themselves in Buddhist establishments," but did not shave their heads. They were known as "hair-wearing Buddhist practitioners" *(tai-fa hsiu-hsing)*. As "neither clergy nor laity" they lived secretly in monasteries and convents and "conspired with one another in illegal activities, wasting the assets of the monasteries."[39] We can see this as mass pietism or as a spillover of persons whom the economy could not absorb. In either case, security-minded officials considered these people a threat. There was, of course, no reliable way to count them.

Most astonishing, in the light of the Throne's deep suspicions of the clergy, is how badly the government's system for registering the clergy (see Chapter 5) had decayed by the 1760s. In the view of the experienced provincial official G'aojin, an imperial relation and governor-general of the Liangkiang provinces, nobody bothered to assemble accurate information. G'aojin had personally checked the registers of some of his subordinate counties and found them wildly discrepant. Not only were aggregate numbers not reported; the licensing system, too, had broken down. According to G'aojin, only 20 or 30 percent of "clergy" now carried ordination certificates. This was because nobody had enforced the rule that monks and priests had to report every new disciple (that is, every newly tonsured novice) to the authorities. The result was alarming: large numbers of people were masquerading as monks and priests, "and the loyal and treacherous can not be distinguished." Not only were the *sangha* vows not observed; "there are even heterodox teachings and evil arts *(hsieh-shu)* being used to delude the simple people, in defiance of the laws."[40]

G'aojin's fears are quite in line with standard official stereotypes about the clergy, as reflected in the *Collected Statutes*. But may not mid-eighteenth-century conditions have lent such anxieties a particular urgency? There were now so many wanderers, wrote G'aojin, who "privately had themselves shaved" (that is, not through the orthodox tonsure ritual at monasteries or temples) and who were entered in no register, that it would constitute a major social disruption to round them all up and force them to return to lay life, as most would have no way to support themselves. G'aojin told his local subordinates to sweep unregistered clergy into the lists. But this was mere patchwork, he wrote to the Throne. Instead, he proposed reviving the practice of reporting registered clergy to the Throne at year's end, along with general population and harvest figures, thereby infusing some urgency back into the control system.[41] Here was a social environment in which more people than ever (men like the "Taoist," Li Ying) were on the roads, without livelihood. The "clergy" was evidently absorbing myriads of them into socially sanctioned (if not officially licensed) mendicant lives.

To the bureaucratic mind, wandering beggars of any sort threatened public security. People without homes and families were people out of control.[42] The old methods of registering and controlling the clergy were no longer enough, wrote Min O-yuan, provincial treasurer of Hupei, at the height of the queue-clipping crisis.[43] There was now a new threat in the form of thousands of vagrant monks and priests, some only marginally clerical, who formed a breeding ground for sedition and lawlessness. The statutory controls were only useful for settled clergy living within a jurisdiction. But now there were thousands of "roving clergy" *(yu-fang seng-tao)* who wandered beyond the law's reach. "They use the excuse of 'worshiping at famous mountains' or 'looking for masters or friends,' going northward in the evening and southward at dawn, and their tracks are impossible to trace." They lodge at temples that are known for putting up such persons, places they call "hanging your sack" *(kua-t'a)*. There, traitors, bandits, forgers, and imposters take their ease, "reclining on straw pallets and drinking the water, borrowing the shade and concealing themselves." Every year, each province is alerted to arrest several thousand wanted criminals, but many cannot be found. Most have adopted clerical dress, dropped out of sight, and moved elsewhere. That is why "in major cases of sorcery-books and sorcery-tales," there is invariably a "traitor-monk or heterodox Taoist" in the background, "deluding good subjects." Because they have no fixed abode, it is impossible to track them down.

Min's view of the clergy underclass turned on the idea that many "monks" and "priests" were not "really" clergy at all, but rogues who took clerical garb to evade the law. Although most clerics caught up in the queue-clipping panic were indeed not regularly ordained, many were in that intermediate stratum of tonsured novices, who will be discussed further in Chapter 5. In any case, they were more like beggars than criminals. Some (like Chü-ch'eng of Hsiao-shan or Li Ying of Ting-chou) were lone survivors of family tragedies. From an official point of view, however, any uncontrolled movement of persons was dangerous. Min now proposed new rules by which no cleric could be affiliated with a temple or monastery outside his own jurisdiction, nor could he travel more than thirty miles from such a place. If he did, officials could arrest and investigate him for "any criminal activity." Even if no criminality were found, he would be punished with a beating, according to that marvelous catch-all provision in the *Ch'ing Code,* "Doing inappropriate things, heavy punishment" (*pu-ying* [*wei*], *chung;* statute 386), and forced to return to lay life. Temples and monasteries were to send all such wanderers away and tender a bond to the authorities that none was being harbored. (The emperor replied, "This matter is worth Our concern.")[44]

Such warnings struck a sensitive nerve in the royal mind. Hungli's own suspicion of the Buddhist clergy (as distinct from his ostentatious patronage of Buddhism as such) was deeply ingrained. It was not just that monks and their movements were hard for the civil authorities to regulate. Hungli's attitude reflected a more general Confucian disdain for men who "willingly shaved their heads to become monks and even failed to care for their parents, wives, and children, and whose activities are accordingly suspicious," as he expressed himself on another occasion.[45] In this respect, monks were comparable to the despised eunuchs, who forsook their principal filial obligation, to have progeny, for the sake of employment.

If Min's description of a floating clerical underclass indicates more than jangled official nerves, how important a social phenomenon was it by mid-Ch'ing times? One would predict that population pressure had begun to erode the economic base of the lay family in many areas by the late 1760s. Yet we have so little data on the underclass that, beyond mere poverty, we know nothing systematic about their social backgrounds. Begging as an alternative to starving, and mendicant clergy as a variety of beggar, are certainly nothing new in the 1760s.[46] Yet fear of sorcery fed not upon numbers but upon perceptions. In the idiom of bureaucratic control, Min O-yuan was expressing anxiety about the uncontrolled movement of rootless people. Was there a popular analogue to this anxiety? If so, it may well have been expressed in the idiom of sorcery fear. Among the public, one of several things may have been happening: either fear of mendicant strangers was growing because there were more of

them passing through communities; or public feelings about mendicants were changing, regardless of how many of them there were;
or both. Even without social changes of this sort, fear of strangers
was deeply rooted in popular religion, as I shall explain in Chapter 5.

Lay beggars. Nearly all writers on "beggars" begin by listing the
various "types" of beggars (the blind, the deformed, those who sang
or juggled for the market crowds, the local beggars, and the seasonal
outsiders). Certain traits seem to have been quite conventional (oper-
atic airs sung only by beggars, for example, and the "professional
whine," common to street beggars).[47] It is now quite clear that a
substantial fraction of "clergy" by the 1760s was essentially a variety
of beggar. Clerical dress and behavior signaled a mendicant role that
was publicly familiar and indeed respected, however objectionable it
may have been to officialdom. An eighteenth-century observer points
out that wealthy people who would disdain to give even a penny to
an ordinary beggar would empty their pockets into a monk's begging
bowl in hopes of gaining *karma*-credit in the afterlife.[48] Certainly, lay
beggars bore a social stigma that clergy did not; their mere appearance (disgustingly filthy, hair matted, dressed in rags) contrasted with
the conventionally robed monks.[49] Even so, the distinction between
monks and lay beggars was not crystal-clear in the public mind. It
was a long-standing custom in Peking to call ordinary beggars *chiao-
hua-tzu*, from *mu-hua*—a term that originally referred to the reli-
giously sanctioned begging of Buddhist monks.[50] Monkhood was
perhaps the most acceptable of a number of specialized, conventional
roles for beggars. We may think of these roles as social templates,
already well established in the eighteenth century, to which increasing
numbers of people could cling as times got harder. That these templates still retained their power to shape behavior is perhaps the
essence of the eighteenth-century condition: those squeezed out by
the economic pressures of Ch'ing society could still find, in the world
of social symbols, acceptable paths to survival. A later age of social
breakdown would find such templates cracking under the pressure
of mass destitution.

To judge from undated evidence of a century or more later (presented by the folklorist Hsu K'o in his invaluable collection of Ch'ing
tales and social vignettes), beggars were well entrenched in various
ecological niches in local society. Some had customary jobs as warrant-
servers for county authorities. Some had worked out a seasonal
arrangement: beggars from northern Anhwei would collect in towns

along the Chekiang-Kiangsu border every winter (the slack season in their own villages), sustain themselves by begging until spring, then return home. These seem to have been ordinary peasants who lacked the by-employments to survive between crop seasons.[51] But how helpful is Hsu K'o's information (some of which must have been from the late nineteenth century or even later) for understanding eighteenth-century conditions? Even though economic conditions, crowding, and social breakdown were much worse a century later, contemporary perceptions of the growth of a clerical underclass should at least make us watchful for evidence of an actual increase of mendicancy in general in the mid-eighteenth century.

The discussion of outward migration in Ch'ing times has largely concerned movement of people into the relatively underpopulated borders, into interior uplands, and overseas. Because local officials had to cope with it, and because the state sometimes encouraged it, such outward migration shows up readily in state documents. The extent of downward migration—dropping out of the settled occupations into vagrancy and begging—is harder to estimate. It occasionally became part of the documentary record when beggars were disorderly: in the little Appalachia of Kuang-te, which I mentioned earlier, the Prosperous Age of mid-Ch'ien-lung times had produced, by 1767, gangs of "beggar-bandits" *(kai-fei)*, who now roamed the area, taking what they wanted by force and battling constables with clubs and brickbats. It turned out that ten of the beggars who were caught had previously been arrested on the same charges in nearby Hui-chou and Hsiu-ning but had been let off with beatings. Hungli now ordered stiffer punishments. The economic problems of Kuang-te he did not mention at all.[52]

Sorcery, Hostility, and Anxiety

Though such information is suggestive, it does not establish that China's economy by the 1760s was already squeezing large numbers of people into a growing underclass. Yet here is more evidence that perceptions matter: around the time of the sorcery scare, judicial records contain some suggestive cases of hostility toward beggars. In one case, a beggar named Huang comes to the door of householder Huang (possibly a kinsman, but not within the "five mourning grades") and demands alms. Householder Huang tells him to come back later. The hungry beggar tries to push his way in, shouting angrily. Householder Huang beats him with a wooden cudgel, causing his death. In another case, three beggars accost a group of neighbors who are sitting around eating and drinking. When given a handout, they complain loudly that it is too little and begin to smash the crockery. The neighbors attack and beat them. Two beggars flee, one is killed. The sentences for the killers in both cases were strangulation, commuted to prison (a common sentence for manslaughter).[53] If such homicidal hostility could be shown to have grown over time, it might mean either that the underclass was becoming more intrusive in community life, or that feelings of obligation toward the destitute were becoming weaker and more ambivalent.[54]

Can we explain fears of sorcery by pointing to social or economic anxieties? Such explanations have been attempted, but I am not entirely comfortable with them.[55] However clear the facts (sorcery fear, social tension), the *connection* between them is generally neither provable nor disprovable. I would love to be able to say that Chinese of the eighteenth century feared soul-loss because they felt their lives threatened by unseen ambient forces (overpopulation, perhaps, or the power of fluctuating market forces to "steal" their livelihoods). Such an assertion, however bewitching, can certainly never be proved. Yet the Prosperous Age was clearly capable of arousing some somber perceptions: if not of invisible economic threats to survival, then certainly of dangerous strangers on the move. And as the soulstealing story unfolds, we shall run into some social experiences more palpably linked to sorcery fear. Meanwhile, we must pursue somber perceptions of eighteenth-century life in the sphere of national politics.

CHAPTER 3

Threats Seen
and Unseen

The smile that the middle-aged Hungli offered his portraitist is not a warm one, nor (I think) one of satisfaction. Perhaps it is the bleak smile of recognition: that great enterprises are laid low by the pettiness of the men who serve them, that the pettiness of many will always overbalance the greatness of one, that to sow in joy is to reap in tears.

If any monarch was carefully groomed for rule, it was Hungli. As a boy, his imperial grandfather adored him, as much for his coolness and pluck as for his evident intelligence. His father, Injen (the Yung-cheng emperor), secretly named him heir-apparent as soon as he himself acceded to the throne in 1723, in order to spare the regime a vicious succession struggle like the one he had recently fought and won. Injen had confronted a grim scene when he took power: a polity demoralized by factional fighting among the entourages of rival imperial princes. His response had been to secure his personal position by stripping the Manchu aristocracy of its military powers, and to bring the fractious bureaucracy to heel through rigorous discipline. To tighten security and centralize imperial control, he introduced a confidential communication system that was managed by a new high-level advisory committee, the Grand Council. To rationalize the finance of local government and thereby reduce corruption, he replaced informal tax-surcharges with a new system of public levies. These accomplishments of Injen, stern rationalizer and masterful institution-builder, were presented to the twenty-five-year-

Hungli (1711–1799) in middle age.

old Hungli on his succession to the throne in October 1735. Compared with how his father had got it, Hungli was handed the empire on a platter.[1]

Upon his succession, Hungli named his reign-period "Ch'ien-lung." Although this is not susceptible of literal translation, an imperial edict explained that the new sovereign had received the "munificent *(lung)* aid of Heaven *(ch'ien)*" and that he would labor with "solemn dedication *(ch'ien-t'i)*" to further the purposes of his imperial father's "splendid legacy."[2] In fact, Hungli's reign saw the gradual dissipation of that legacy. This cannot fairly be laid to lack of solemn dedication, but to problems peculiar to the age.[3] Injen had faced direct challenges to his personal security, but Hungli faced subtler ones. Although he did not have to confront a contentious aristocracy, he had to wrestle daily with an official establishment that had become expert in finding quiet ways to protect and enrich itself. The age was one of surface amity between conquerors and conquered, signified by the monarch's own ostentatious sheen of Chinese culture and his patronage of arts and letters. The Manchu elite had learned to cope with Chinese elite culture, even as the Han elite had come to acquiesce in Manchu overlordship. Yet this dulling of cultural distinctions had its price, and Hungli suspected that his Manchu compatriots were now but feeble support for his imperial supremacy. This slow, quiet dissipation of Manchu hegemony was a threat impossible to ignore but hard to grasp effectively. And beneath the surface of politics sounded those great engines of historic change, commercial vitality and human fertility.

Material for Hungli's biography is so overwhelming that the job may never be done.[4] To penetrate his ghostwriters and reach the man himself, there is no escape from reading the monarch's own comments, instructions, and *obiter dicta,* jotted in vermilion ink upon reports as he read them and now preserved in the imperial archives.[5] This can of course be done only in the context of events. If the events of the soulstealing crisis contribute to such a biography, it will be by showing (wherever possible through documentation in his own hand) how Hungli reacted to certain problems that he perceived to be particularly troublesome: chief among them, sedition and assimilation.

Perceptions of Treason

After the thirteenth century, all China's ruling dynasties originated in conquest: no palace coups, no praetorian juntas, but instead large-

Hungli in the saddle. Archery from horseback was a traditional Manchu skill prized by the emperor.

scale military campaigning. All conquest regimes were, by their nature, military impositions upon the nation. For the Ch'ing, as for their Mongol forerunners of the thirteenth century, this imposition was complicated by the conquerors' alien culture. However cunningly the conquerors might frame the rhetoric of succession (a virtuous regime replacing a corrupt one was the conventional rhetoric of the Mandate of Heaven), there was always the danger that the symbolism of legitimate rule might be challenged by ugly ethnic feelings: the claim that these rulers were usurpers precisely because they were outsiders. It was such a possibility that kept Ch'ing rulers alert against sedition. But the terms in which the Throne confronted sedition evolved with the times.

By Hungli's time the full ornamentation of the universal empire seemed firmly in place. Here was no raw victor-vanquished relationship, but one in which sedition could plausibly be confronted in conventional terms: a legitimate and virtuous Confucian monarchy, worthily graced by Heaven's Mandate, confronting perverse and degenerate plotters. How far beneath the surface lay the old ethnic hostility, we can never determine. Yet to understand the events of 1768, when the crudely ethnic issue of headdress came back into prominence, we shall have to sample the atmosphere of the early conquest years, when the issue was very much alive. The macabre tonsure cases of the early Ch'ing suggest what dark surmises may have hidden behind the imperial smile.

Retrospective: The Conquest Years

While combat still echoed through the Yangtze Valley, the newly installed Manchu court was already preparing, in 1645, to forge chains between victors and vanquished. The young emperor, Fulin, was but nine years old and wholly dominated by his uncle, the regent Dorgon. Although Dorgon was a skillful cultivator of Han support, in this matter he was implacable: the sign of unconditional submission would be a simple, visible hallmark of Manchu culture, the shaved forehead in front and braided queue in back.[6]

The tonsure decree. Even before the Manchu armies had entered the Great Wall, Chinese who surrendered to them had to signify submission by adopting the Manchu headdress. Accounts of the conquest generally emphasize the shaved forehead as the indispensable sign of surrender. Dorgon's determination to enforce the Manchu tonsure on everyone was evident from the day he entered Peking (June 5, 1644). During the conquest of the South, headdress became the rallying point of a desperate Chinese resistance and certainly made the Manchu takeover many times bloodier than it would otherwise have been. Nevertheless, for the first year after the conquest of Peking, Dorgon wavered about enforcing the headdress even at court. At last, however, he issued the requirement as a formal statement through the agencies of civil government.[7]

The origin of the tonsure decree was Dorgon's exasperation at court officials' simpering objections to the Manchu headdress by appealing to the "System of Rites and Music" (the mandated ceremonials) of the defeated Ming Dynasty. Notwithstanding that Ming institutions would undergird the reconstituted imperial government after the conquest, Dorgon would brook no sneers at Manchu customs. Such talk was "highly improper . . . does *our* Dynasty not have a System of Rites and Music? If officials say that people should not respect our Rites and Music, but rather follow those of the Ming, what can be their true intentions?" When it came to the shaved forehead, Dorgon conceded that there might be some justifiable Confucian objection that because a man's body was inherited from his parents it ought not be violated. "But instead we hear this incessant 'Rites and Music' rubbish. I have hitherto loved and pitied the [Han] officialdom, allowing them to follow their own preference [in matters of dress and tonsure]. Now, however, because of this divisive talk, I can but issue a decree to all officials and commoners, ordering that they all shave their foreheads."[8]

The decree sent to the Board of Rites (the board that, among other things, set the dress code for all important ceremonies) on July 8, 1645, was nevertheless couched in Confucian terms.[9] Now that the empire had been pacified, it read, it was time to enforce the tonsure on all. Since the ruler was like a father and the subjects like his sons, and since father and sons were naturally a single entity, divergence between them was impermissible. If their way of life were not unified, they might eventually be of "different minds." Would not this (reverting to the political side of the simile) be almost as if they were "people *of different kingdoms (i-kuo chih jen)*"? This matter ought not require mention from the Throne, but rather should be perceived naturally by all. Now, within ten days of the decree's promulgation in Peking (or within ten days of the proclamation's reaching a province), all must conform. Disobedience would be "equivalent to a rebel's defying the Mandate [of Heaven] *(ni-ming)*." Officials who memorialized on behalf of those seeking "to retain the Ming institutions and not follow those of this Dynasty" would be put to death without mercy. On the matter of "clothing and caps," a less coercive and more leisurely approach would govern; but in the end conformity was expected in these matters as well.

Surely such language was meant to resonate with the conventional legal phrases that dealt with treason. The *Ch'ing Code (Ta-Ch'ing lü-li)* handles treason in the statute "The Ten Abominations *(shih-o)*," the third paragraph of which is titled "conspiracy to revolt *(mou-p'an)*." The sole clarification of this broadly gauged rubric is "This refers to betraying one's own kingdom *(pen-kuo)* and secretly adhering to another kingdom *(t'o-kuo)*." The penalties for "conspiracy to revolt" are listed in the Punishments section of the *Code:* decapitation for the conspirators, with no distinction between leader and followers. Their wives and children are to be given as slaves to meritorious officials, their parents and grandparents to be. banished to Turkestan.[10] It is especially striking that the tonsure decree itself does not appear as a statute or substatute in the *Ch'ing Code,* nor in any edition of the *Collected Statutes (Ta-Ch'ing hui-tien).* Perhaps the monarchs of the new regime, however implacable in enforcing it, wanted the decree to remain *outside* the body of formal written law: either to be enforced without reference to the *Code* or the *Collected Statutes,* or decorously hidden beneath the *Code's* general statutes on treason (the greater part of which had been inherited from previous dynasties and bore a thick patina of legitimacy).

The years of the Ch'ing conquest saw stirring examples of local resistance centered symbolically on the tonsure decree. Loyalty to the defunct Ming political order was less powerful a rallying cry to local communities than was the preservation of cultural self-respect implied in resisting the shaved forehead. The famous cases of local resistance in the Yangtze Valley exhibited the strong connection, in the public mind, between hairstyle and self-respect.[11] We can appreciate the importance of this cultural sticking point to the invaders as well: it channeled the application of force toward the most obdurate centers of resistance. In this respect, the tonsure decree was a shrewd move: better to flush resistance into the open and destroy it quickly than to nourish a sullen passivity toward the new regime.

But what are we to make of the continued ferreting out of individual cases of defiance in the conquered provinces? The zeal and ruthlessness with which the conquerors persecuted local hair-growers suggests that even the slightest deviation from the tonsure decree might prove a nucleus for popular resistance. And enforcement might serve as a measure of official zeal in the service of the new order. The following cases, in which deviance of isolated individuals was discovered by accident, indicate not only the minuteness of the conquerors' attention to conformity among ordinary subjects but also their determination to bend local officials to the service of the new regime. The incidents evoke the harsh and bloody mood that attended the tonsure decree in the early Ch'ing. Can this keen Manchu sensitivity to tonsure violations have died out completely by 1768? As for the general populace, must we lean on "racial memory" to imagine that the threat of family extirpation may occasionally have been mentioned by fathers to sons when it was time to visit the barber?

The scholar's cap. It was early March in 1647, three years after the Manchu conquerors had swept into North China and occupied Peking.[12] Late winter in the far northwest was dry and bitterly cold. Chang Shang, Han bannerman and governor of Kansu Province, had just received orders from Peking to make an inspection tour. By March 4 he had reached the outskirts of Yung-ch'ang, a remote county just within the Great Wall. Along the sides of the dusty road to greet him knelt the entire body of students of the county school. Astride his horse, Chang noticed to his satisfaction that all were wearing Manchu-style winter caps. As he later reported, however, "I espied one man who seemed to have retained the hair on the front of his head. After I reached the county yamen, I summoned all the students for academic examination." As they gathered in the great hall, "I personally went over to the man in question and removed his cap. Indeed, his hair was totally unshaven."

Infuriated, Chang ordered local officials to investigate. They reported that the region had been repeatedly posted with warnings about the tonsure decree, on Chang's instructions, and that even this unfortunate culprit, Lü K'o-hsing, a military licentiate living in a rural area, had no excuse. Chang clapped Lü in jail and memorialized the Throne asking that he be executed, "to uphold the laws of the ruling dynasty." Replied the Throne (the stern Dorgon speaking, we may assume), "Let him be executed on the spot. But what about the local officials, the household head, the local headman, and the neighbors? There are established precedents for punishing them, too. Why

were they not followed? Let the Board of Punishments be informed."
Lü's unshaven head was hacked from his body and publicly exposed
"to warn the masses." The patriarch of Lü's household, along with
the local headman and the neighbors, were all punished with beatings, and the county magistrate was docked three months' wages.

A disturbance in the marketplace. Later that same year, in central
China, not far from Wuchang, the capital of Hupei Province, a minor
fracas occurred in the market town of Yü-chen.[13] A peasant named
Kuo Shan-hsien, who had come into town to sell chickens, had got
himself into a loud argument over some trivial matter. Tempers
flared, and local constables were summoned. Unluckily for Kuo, his
frontal hair was discovered to be nearly an inch long, and he was
placed under arrest. On his person was discovered a paper bearing
the signature of a person named Yin, the same surname as that of a
local bandit in that area, now deceased. Kuo was suspected of being
part of Yin's gang, and was taken to the county yamen. There the
paper was found to be in the hand of Kuo's own landlord, also
surnamed Yin, and to be of no significance. The acting magistrate,
Chang Wen-teng, evidently considered Kuo's hair to be a matter of
no great significance, either, and the peasant was released. But he
was then rearrested, specifically on the hair charge, by the market
tax-collector, who had him taken once again to the county yamen.
This time Acting Magistrate Chang had the man's head shaved, but
released him as before. The tax-collector, perhaps with his own career
prospects in mind, would not let the matter rest, and complained
directly to the provincial authorities. His charge was as much directed
at the lenient Chang, whom he accused of "protecting traitors," as
against peasant Kuo, the principal culprit.

The provincial judge now had Kuo arrested once more and
brought him, the tax-collector, and Acting Magistrate Chang into his
court for direct confrontation. He found that indeed there had been
undue leniency: landlord Yin and Kuo's local neighbors, as well as
Chang and Kuo, all deserved punishment. However, he opined that
there was a difference between intentionally allowing the hair to grow
(like the defiant militiamen of the doomed Yangtze cities) and neg-
ligently failing to shave in timely fashion. Kuo, he recommended,
should get off with a beating.

This moderate judgment was reversed by the governor-general. In
a concurring opinion, the governor noted that the tonsure decree
had been broadcast repeatedly. Kuo was only an ignorant rustic, but

he had managed to get himself arrested not once but twice on the same charge. Why should he not be made a warning to others? Only when the matter had been found out was he forcibly shaved: surely he had repeated his crime intentionally. As for magistrate Chang, it was inexcusable that he could not control a contumacious subject, but rather, when the man was arrested, first procrastinated and then had him forcibly shaved, so that there was no evidence of the length of his hair. The Throne accepted the sterner verdict: Kuo was to be beheaded, Chang cashiered. As it turned out, the governor reported, Kuo died in prison "of illness," thereby "incurring Heaven's punishment . . . so the Kingly Law did not fail in the slightest particular."

Those early years after the conquest were dangerous times, and not just for martyrs. The sword struck anyone who, either from laziness or from ignorance, failed to meet the symbolic requirements of the new regime. These were not militant loyalists, but isolated subjects caught largely by accident. Moreover, for every "traitor" executed, at least one bureaucrat was disciplined. The pressure was on: even in the remotest corner of the conquered lands, to tolerate political crime could mean the end of a man's career. In this way, both the Han commoners and their co-opted masters—the Han bureaucracy—were held to account. The tonsure decree was a touchstone by which the Throne tested its servants.

Hair, shame, and submission. In none of these early tonsure cases is the queue itself an object of Ch'ing enforcement. This seems to have resulted from attitudes of both the Manchus and the Chinese. Once the tonsure decree was issued, the conquest regime seems to have focused its attention on the shaved forehead precisely because the Chinese loyalists resisted it so stubbornly. The reason, apparently, was that the deeper humiliation was not *braiding* (the queue) but *shaving* (the forehead). Although we lack direct evidence, some castration imagery may have been implied, adult manhood (and elite status) having been signalized under the old regime by long, elaborately kept hair. Ironically, what to the Manchu warriors symbolized manliness, to the Chinese symbolized effeminacy. More likely, if Edmund Leach is right about the ritual meanings of hair, the Manchu tonsure was a symbol of restraint triumphant over license.[14] A more decorous explanation, acceptable to Confucians at the time, is that propriety was offended by tampering with the body bequeathed by one's parents.[15] Another possible explanation of Chinese resistance to head-shaving is its historical link to shame and punishment. A penal code of the third century B.C., for instance, lists shaving (of head-hair and beard), along with tattooing and mutilation, as humiliations to be inflicted on slaves and convicts. These shameful connotations of head-shaving may have persisted through the imperial period.[16] In the later Ch'ing period, care was taken that convicts observe the tonsure requirements. Jail wardens had to ensure that felons under deferred death sentences had their foreheads properly shaved before the autumn assizes, and that those serving sentences of internal banishment were inspected quarterly to ensure that their foreheads were shaved (no mention whatever of the queue).[17]

So Chinese horror at forehead-shaving clearly drew Manchu enforcement to this point, and the queue remained a symbolically less potent concern. *After* a man had assumed the required headdress, however, a sudden, symbolic act of defiance was not possible except by cutting off the queue (since frontal hair would take some time to grow). Certainly, forcing someone else to display symbolic defiance would be most easily accomplished by cutting off his queue.[18] And picture the state of mind of someone whose queue was clipped against his will! Thanks to another person's action, he was now vulnerable to having his whole family exterminated by the state. Such anxiety cannot be ruled out as we try to explain why men were so afraid of queue-clippers in 1768. Nevertheless, as a component of the tonsure requirement, the queue seems to have remained much less important than the shaved forehead right up to the time of the sorcery scare.[19]

Hungli Confronts Sedition

The Prosperous Age of Hungli seemed eons away from those bloody times. If queue-clipping was indeed sedition, a symbolic rejection of Manchu hegemony, it was something no official, whether in Peking or the provinces, wanted to confront openly. Were not the days of ethnic bitterness now happily displaced by a placid and harmonious universal empire? Accordingly, during the first six weeks of the soul-stealing crisis, Hungli's secret correspondence with his provincial officials broached not a word about the tonsure. Instead, the monarch stuck to the subject of sorcery, a time-honored concern of the universal empire, whoever its rulers. Yet the tonsure question would not long stay buried, and there emerged in due course the monarchy's other face: the sensitive alien regime under symbolic attack for its alienness.

The rhetoric employed by the Manchu rulers displayed both the cosmopolitanism of the universal empire and the narrow defensiveness of the ethnic minority. As a minority people ruling a great empire, the Manchu monarchy had to have it both ways: they had to express their supremacy in both a cosmopolitan mode and an ethnic mode. Both were needed to solve the regime's basic problem: how to rule the universal empire as a legitimate dynastic house, and still preserve the coherence and élan of the conquest elite. As universal rulers, their title rested, not on ethnic identity, but on generally accepted norms of virtue and culture. But to survive as a power-holding minority group, their own special qualities had to be not only defended but celebrated. Hungli believed that Manchus, because of their precious ethnic heritage, could actually rule the Middle Kingdom *better* than could the Han, and in fact were particularly qualified to translate the moral precepts of Confucianism into imperial rule. The monarchy therefore required two rhetorical arenas: one for the cosmopolitan side of the regime, the other for the ethnic. But sedition posed delicate choices, because challenges to the Manchu monarchy often made the ethnic point: the Manchus were illegitimate because they were outsiders. Consequently sedition cases did not furnish a particularly good arena in which to celebrate ethnicity.

Hungli's ruling style was an uncomfortable mix of militant ethnicity and cosmopolitan culture. He wanted to make Manchu-ness an integral component of the imperial institution. The Throne would be *both* the guardian of Manchu cultural integrity *and* the symbol of a multiracial hegemony justified by cosmopolitan Confucian rhetoric.[20] As champion of Manchu virtues, he took two tacks: to terrorize intellectuals for real or imagined ethnic slights, and to boost the ethnic consciousness of his Manchu compatriots by lecturing them about their martial tradition and superior character. Nevertheless, in cases of real plots against the regime, to mention the ethnic issue at all seemed risky and inflammatory. His behavior in two serious sedition cases of the sixteenth and seventeenth years of his reign illustrate how careful he was to keep quiet about ethnic symbolism—particularly the deadly issue of the tonsure—when he really believed the dynasty to be in danger.

The case of the Bogus Memorial. Hungli at forty, a seasoned ruler sixteen years into his reign, encountered a crisis, of complex origins, that we still do not fully understand. He had endured the death of his beloved empress, Hsiao-hsien, in the spring of 1748. That year also brought news of military disasters, in the distant campaign against the Chin-ch'uan aborigines of Szechwan, that revealed unsuspected weakness in the Ch'ing military establishment (Hungli was so infuriated that he had the two top commanders beheaded). Then, in 1751, he launched his first southern tour, a pretentious and magnificent imperial gesture in the manner of his grandfather. Grief, frustration, and grandiosity lend this juncture in his reign a peculiar air of embattlement. It was around this time that Hungli confronted his first serious sedition crisis.

The crisis comprised two ominous cases suspiciously close in their timing, one involving the literate elite and one the common people. The "Case of the Bogus Memorial" *(wei-kao an)* and the Ma Ch'ao-chu uprising were alike only in that both remained ultimately unresolved. Yet they excited such evident alarm at court that one might suppose they were occurring at a time of extreme social or political instability, rather than in the middle of the most successful and prosperous reign in Chinese history. Though there is absolutely no evidence that the cases were connected in fact, they were certainly linked in the imperial mind. Together, they shook Hungli's confidence that the "alien rule" issue had finally been put to rest. Yet in neither case did Hungli feel secure enough to mention the ethnic issue, even in his secret correspondence.

It was in August 1751 that a curious document came to the attention of a local postal-relay supervisor in Kweichow.[21] It was a copy of what purported to be a memorial to the Throne by Sun Chia-kan (1683–1753), a senior official, currently serving in Peking as president of the Board of Works. Earlier in his career, Sun had become well known to the public because of his blunt advice to Hungli's father (who characteristically rewarded him for it) and his acerbic criticisms of official misconduct. The "memorial" found in Kweichow was full of "outrageous" and "slanderous" language, according to a secret report from the governor-general, who passed the suspicious document on to Peking. It even bore an alleged (and wholly implausible) imperial endorsement at the end. During the weeks that followed, the Throne received numerous reports from widely separated parts of the empire that other copies had turned up. By the turn of the year, the search for the originator of this "Bogus Memorial" had become a nationwide dragnet. Thousands were arrested. Copies were found as alarmingly near as the Bannerman's Academy in Peking, and as far as the distant southwest borders. Persons accused of possessing or copying the document ranged from high-ranking provincial officials to merchants, clergy, gentry, and even bannermen. After many false leads, generated by coerced confessions, the governor of Kiangsi announced in January 1753 the arrest of a lowly military official, Lu Lu-sheng, on whom a Grand Council tribunal soon fastened the ultimate guilt. After Lu's execution by slow slicing, Hungli declared the case closed. Shaky evidence and a hasty execution make the "solution" of this case exceedingly doubtful. Nevertheless, the nature of the "memorial" and its widespread dissemination offer some hints about Hungli's problems with sedition.

Although at the time "even coolies in the street" knew what the Bogus Memorial contained,[22] no copy of it now survives, so thorough was the Throne in burning all that were found (the Grand Council archives appear to contain not even a file copy, so humiliating must its contents have been to Hungli). Circumstantial evidence suggests that the "memorial" aimed a harsh, personal attack at the monarch, and at officials close to him, for "five unforgivable acts and ten great transgressions." It also seems to have alluded to the ruinous financial burdens heaped upon the localities through which the monarch had just passed on his first southern tour. It may further have attacked Hungli's harsh treatment of certain high officials, particularly the Han bannerman general, Chang Kuang-ssu, one of the two commanders he had beheaded in 1749 for allegedly botching the military campaign against the Chin-ch'uan tribes. Finally, evidence from the documents of the Ma Ch'ao-chu affair, which I shall turn to next, indicates that it even impugned the legitimacy of the Manchu dynasty.[23] Certainly the white-hot fury with which Hungli sought the originators of the Bogus Memorial, the harsh punishment he inflicted upon anyone who possessed or transmitted a copy, and his effective destruction of all copies, show how badly this attack frightened the Throne—not least because of the widespread opposition it revealed among literate men. It was characteristic of Hungli that he would shortly begin to suspect a deeply laid plot against the dynasty: one that linked the Bogus Memorial to a notorious literati sedition case that dated from his father's day, and to the mysterious case of Ma Ch'ao-chu.[24]

The Ma Ch'ao-chu conspiracy. We must assume that the Bogus Memorial impugned Manchu legitimacy, because Hungli came to believe that it was connected to the avowedly anti-Manchu conspiracy of Ma Ch'ao-chu, which was unearthed in the spring of 1752.[25] The Ma affair was Hungli's first confrontation with a Ming-restorationist movement. The vindictive and bloody campaign against it was a melodramatic overture to the second quarter of Hungli's reign.

Ma Ch'ao-chu was reportedly a peasant from Ch'i-chou in Hupei, in the Yangtze Valley about forty miles downriver from the provincial capital, Wuchang. While sojourning across the border in western Anhwei, he had fallen under the influence of a monk, who (according to the government's investigation) instilled in him visions of a grand destiny. Ma began to claim connections to a remnant Ming regime inhabiting "The Kingdom of the Western Sea" *(Hsi-yang-kuo),* ruled by a "Young Lord," a scion of the Ming royal house of Chu. In the kingdom there supposedly lived descendants of the defeated southwestern warlord, Wu San-kuei, along with 36,000 armed soldiers. There too lived a certain Li K'ai-hua, a well-known folk vision of a future emperor, and a woman called "Niang-niang," the name of a popular fertility goddess. Claiming to be a general in this kingdom, Ma told his followers that magic flying machines could bring his armies from their western stronghold to central China in a few hours, and that an attack on the Yangtze Valley was imminent.[26]

All this came to light when alert officials discovered newly forged swords along with rebel proclamations in the mountains east of Lo-t'ien, about seventy-five miles northeast of Wuchang. Just outside the highly commercialized regional core, this was a poor, rugged area where settlers eked out a precarious living from slash-and-burn agriculture. Though Ma had fled, numerous followers, including some of his relatives, were captured. So many culprits jammed the provincial jail in Wuchang that the authorities hesitated to try them all at the same time, for fear of inciting public disturbances. Hungli, however, ordered them to go right ahead.[27]

Shaken by the Lo-t'ien discoveries, Hungli ordered that the local magistrate, who had earlier failed to prosecute Ma's group, be summarily executed, a rare penalty in such a case.[28] The ferocity of the manhunt for Ma himself (who was never caught, if indeed he ever really existed) resulted in the arrests of hundreds of suspects and continued for many years.[29] Emerging as it did just as the authorities were in hot pursuit of the Bogus Memorial culprits, the Ma Ch'ao-chu affair evidently convinced Hungli that the dynasty was the target of a large-scale plot.

There can be no doubt that the Lo-t'ien plotters rejected the Manchus as aliens: they violated the Ch'ing tonsure decree. According to confessions by two men who had been "enticed" into selling their land and joining the band, "When people entered the stockade [Ma's stronghold, known as the 'Heavenly Stockade' *(t'ien-t'ang sai)*], they smeared their mouths with blood [to sanctify their oath of loyalty] and swallowed paper charms. Also *they let their hair grow and didn't shave their foreheads.*"[30] Yet Hungli phrased his response with great care. However unpleasantly surprised by these threats to his Prosperous Age, he kept his reaction well within the cosmopolitan mode. The rebels were simply attacking the universal monarchy, not an alien regime. The closest he would come to acknowledging the existence of the tonsure question was to acknowledge that the rebels had "offended Our Imperial Ancestors": "Our great Ch'ing Dynasty has reigned humanely and benevolently for more than a century. It is inconceivable that there should now arise such ungrateful and immoral monsters, secretly brewing such poison. They are truly unbearable to Heaven and Earth."[31] But the governor-general's report about the tonsure violation is never mentioned, even in Hungli's secret communications to his provincial officials, to say nothing of his public edicts.

Yet the fury of his response must have given him away: those rounded up were to be "tortured with extreme severity," their lives to be preserved only so that they could confess.[32] Hungli clearly preferred to avoid mentioning the ethnic issue altogether, even in secret correspondence with the upper bureaucracy. His primary motive for secrecy seems to have been the need to avoid shaking public confidence: even though these petty rebels are "not worth consideration," he wrote, yet this group must be crushed swiftly, because "a single spark can start a prairie-fire." And the facts of the case (he means here the anti-Ch'ing symbolism) *must be kept secret.*[33] To breathe a word about the tonsure, whether in public or private, was asking for trouble.

Here we first meet what I shall call the "panic factor": an imperial belief that the credulous masses were ever on the brink of violent, panicky reactions to hints of political crisis or cosmic disorder. This belief arises again and again in the course of our story. It conditioned imperial policy to avoid, whenever possible, the public acknowledgment of either sedition or sorcery. It even affected the language of internal official documents, as if the very mention of an evil would evoke it in reality. As a general rule, it meant that extraordinary threats were to be described in conventional language. Were we to judge the public temperament from Hungli's fears about it, we would have to call it highly volatile and unstable. Such fears were very much alive during the sorcery scare of 1768. That, I believe, is why Hungli initially forbore to mention the tonsure violation, even in secret correspondence with his highest officials.

In neither the Bogus Memorial case nor the Ma Ch'ao-chu uprising could the Throne mention the ethnic issue. Hungli's initial inclination was much the same in the soulstealing crisis of 1768, despite its provocative tonsure imagery. The "ethnic mode," though vital to the survival of the conquest regime, had to be pursued in other arenas. One that soon commended itself to Hungli was the literary purge: bullying literati for alleged written slurs against Manchu origins, a device that Hungli eventually used in a major national campaign in the 1770s. However he may have shrunk from mentioning such a blatant anti-Manchu threat as tonsure violation, Hungli showed hair-trigger militancy against petty slights to Manchu honor. Wording that offered even the subtlest suggestion of an ethnic slur could cost a writer his head. By contrast to large-scale sedition cases with a potential for mass unrest, the literary purge was an arena in which the Throne could control both the pace and the scope of events. Here was a kind of "sedition" case in which ethnic pride could safely be celebrated.

Literary purges prefigured. The rhetorical usefulness of a literary purge was demonstrated only three years after the events just described. In 1755 a Han author, Hu Chung-tsao, was accused (in what even then must have seemed a far-fetched textual construction) of using expressions in his poetry to stir up ethnic hatred for Manchus. Hu was a disciple and factional booster of the late Ortai, one of the two powerful grandees inherited by Hungli from his father's administration. Hu also cultivated Ortai's nephew, Ocang, with whom he exchanged letters and poetry. Hungli's vicious attack on Hu ("does not belong in the human race") has been interpreted as an attack on factionalism.[34] What I find striking about the case, however, is how Hungli linked his attack on Hu for slandering the Manchus with an attack on Ocang for conduct unbecoming a Manchu. The two sides of the case can only be understood together: they were Hungli's recognition that sedition and assimilation were two facets of a single threat.[35]

In denouncing Ocang's literary pretentions, the outraged monarch wrote that Manchu culture "has always based itself on respecting the sovereign and revering those in authority; and on personal qualities of simplicity and sincerity, loyalty and respect. Confining its concerns to riding and shooting, it has had no place for frivolous or decadent practices." But recently, he declared, contact with Chinese culture had led many Manchus into pompous literary affectations, which had worked evil upon their characters. Originally, Manchus had not spent their time reading books, but merely understood "the great principles" of obedience and of reverence for authority. Although the followers of Confucius used literature to spread their teachings, they also placed respect for ruler and father before anything else. If one knew only literary affectation and had no sense of basic social obligations, then of what use was learning? Hungli warned that he would punish Manchus who forgot their roots, and strictly forbade them to cultivate literary relationships with Chinese.[36] Such a warning, if observed, might indeed have curbed factionalism, because such relationships were the sinews of literati cliques. Yet we cannot overlook the substantive message, which was about sedition and assimilation.

The Rot of Assimilation

Courage and vigor, honesty and simplicity: such were the self-proclaimed virtues of the Manchu conquest elite. Here was a carefully polished mirror image of the vanquished. Not only had these qualities been victorious in battle; they were ideally suited to ruling well the empire that the defeated Ming house had ruled badly. This sturdy vision was nevertheless blemished from the outset by the need to govern the empire with the help of Chinese institutions and Chinese personnel.

Even before the Manchus had crossed the Great Wall, the struggle within the Manchu nobility had led the Throne to adopt Chinese-style bureaucratic and centralizing measures. Thereafter, the need to represent the conquest regime as a legitimate successor and a worthy vessel for Heaven's Mandate required the dynasty to promote the ideology of imperial Confucianism (whereby virtue, not ethnicity, was the basis of legitimate rule), and at the same time preserve what it considered to be its special Manchu ethos. The conquerors were separate and uncorrupted, and must remain so. How could they, at the same time, weld an alien culture to their own? It was an insoluble puzzle. Add to this the need to "get on" in the Chinese world, to say nothing of enjoying it, and one can begin to grasp the Manchu problem of the eighteenth century. To Hungli sedition and assimilation were linked dangers, but assimilation was the more insidious and may indeed have generated in him the greater anxiety. For the Manchu ruling elite, the Ch'ien-lung reign (1736–1796) was a painful time of transition. The threat of assimilation was ever more apparent—but it was not yet apparent that nothing could be done about it.

The Banner Elite

By the midpoint of his reign, Hungli sat atop a minority ruling group that was already split between a tiny elite and an impoverished mass. The warrior group that had conquered China in 1644 had three ethnic components: besides the Manchus, there were the ethnic Chinese living outside the Great Wall who had submitted to the Manchus before the conquest and enrolled in the banner organization as hereditary military retainers; and those Mongols whose tribes had become allies of the Manchus. Of this band of about 347,000 able-bodied males and their families, Manchus themselves comprised only about 16 percent. By the third decade of the eighteenth century, the number of able-bodied males had nearly doubled, and Manchus comprised about 23 percent.[37] Here was a tiny minority of the empire's total population (with their families, probably less than 1 percent by the mid-eighteenth century). Though a few thousand had lucrative careers in civil or military posts, the majority were "poor, indebted, and unemployed."[38] The lands that had been set aside for them had largely fallen under the control of Chinese estate-managers. Bannermen themselves lived almost entirely within urban garrisons, where the decrees that kept them from intermarrying with the surrounding Chinese population were of diminishing effect. Military skills languished, as did other cultural hallmarks of the conquest elite, particularly the Manchu language.[39] With neither the self-esteem afforded by a firm economic base nor the bracing challenge of military threats, the rank and file had little to buttress their pride as a conquest group. For the Throne, however, Manchu pride seemed a matter of urgency. Hungli evidently thought that his leverage over the bureaucracy, to say nothing of the regime's control of the conquered Chinese population, depended on the survival of Manchu ethnic identity. In this age of assimilation, Hungli became a champion of Manchu language and values, even while an enthusiastic patron of Chinese culture.[40]

Such an enterprise would seem hopeless; yet it was required of every ruling dynasty, whether of domestic or foreign origin. Leadership, as distinct from routine bureaucratic management, distinguished the conquerors from the thousands of civil servants who managed the empire. To survive as a ruling group, the conquerors must preserve their original élan and distinction. Yet to bring the civil service into camp, these same conquerors must appear to be legitimate participants in Confucian culture. Exclusivity and assimilation were never conceivable in isolation from each other. This was Hungli's dilemma, as head of both the Manchu people and the universal Chinese empire. For him, holding these roles together was a preoccupation, from which grew the political history of his reign.

Cultural Contagion

Hungli's fears about the Manchus' degeneration were generally phrased in terms of what they were losing (martial skills, cultural treasures, personal qualities), but these losses were also expressed as scorn for a decadent Han elite, which he feared his Manchus were coming to resemble. Bannermen ought to exemplify a superior standard of courage, simplicity, and grit that could hardly be expected of any Han (not even those semi-Manchuized Han bannermen whose forebears had been brought into Manchu service before the conquest). Yet case after case showed him that the old virtues were fading.

A Manchu guard officer of distinguished lineage had figured out how to sell choice appointments to ambitious bannermen, through a cozy arrangement with clerks of the Board of War. Hungli made him an example: "How can there be such officers among us Manchus?" Even more repellent was the very idea that Manchus would seek cushy posts: "When We appoint Manchus to provincial posts, We do so partly because they retain the old unspoiled nature and integrity of the Manchu people, as well as their admirable personal talents and their skills with bow and horse. Thus may they serve as a standard for the provincial Green Standard forces [the Han constabulary]. It is certainly not just to provide them with a route for personal advancement and emoluments." No longer was there to be special clemency for Manchu rascals. Earlier in the dynasty, such men seemed worth rehabilitating; in those great times, moral standards were higher. But as the Manchu population had increased, bannermen had been gradually "steeped in wicked customs and extravagance and have even lost the honest nature" of their forebears. Such men as these sought convenience and ease and were "virtually no different from Han."[41]

An even more shocking case was that of a bannerman, seconded to a Green Standard garrison, who hanged himself rather than face prosecution for failure to quell a local riot. The monarch was furious: when Manchus were assigned to Green Standard garrisons, he declared, it was to use their riding and archery skills, as well as their courage, to "correct the vile ways of the Green Standards."[42] Because this man "was a hereditary Manchu trooper" *(Man-chou shih-p'u),* he should have led troops to suppress this local outrage, even at the cost of his life.

> Even though this would not have been comparable to death in battle, yet We would have granted special grace to his family . . . But to die like this, fearful of punishment, is just a common death . . . How can there be such contemptible men among hereditary Manchu troopers? This trend is really vile. Let it be strictly proclaimed to all Manchu military men serving with the Green Standard that they must exert themselves bravely and energetically in all matters, to reclaim the old Manchu ways and to expunge this cowardly and decadent trend.

Decline was ominously marked, thought Hungli, by the erosion of Manchu language skills. Quite apart from the statutory bilingualism at court (which required translation bureaus to render certain classes of documents into Manchu), there was a broader assumption that bannermen would be as conversant with their linguistic heritage as they were with riding and shooting. Manchu was the language that symbolized Ch'ing power in Central Asia. If Manchus in border garrisons lost their "culture and heritage," they would be "ridiculed by the Muslim and Kazakh tribes." But linguistic standards were plummeting, in the interior as in the border garrisons. A local banner commander bemoaned the grammatical and lexicographical chaos in the Manchu-language paperwork prepared in his province. Although Manchu was the "cultural root of bannermen," their written work contained "mistakes within mistakes."[43] The rot was spreading even within the Manchu homeland. Hungli fumed that officials serving in Manchuria, who were expected to memorialize mainly in Manchu, "use only Chinese . . . If the subject-matter is too complex and

Manchu cannot wholly express what they have to say, so that Chinese must be used, yet they ought to use Manchu along with it." These personnel "are actually being infected by Han customs and are losing their old Manchu ways." Though it might not serve all the demands of present-day government, Manchu was a touchstone of cultural integrity.[44]

Hungli naturally offered himself as a model and lost no opportunity to correct a faulty translation or to question a job candidate personally in Manchu. He was fastidious about Han translations of original Manchu edicts on military affairs and reprimanded the editors of the chronicle of the Zungar campaign for their overly free translations, which "lost the proper meaning" of the original Manchu. In this case, faithfulness to the Manchu texts was surely less pedantic than talismanic.[45]

Apart from its talismanic power, Manchu was useful as a confidential language in sensitive affairs of state, particularly military matters. In 1767 Hungli sent the trusted aristocrat Fulinggan (eldest son of Prince Fuheng, Hungli's brother-in-law) to investigate the conduct of his stalled campaign against the Burmese. Fulinggan sent back secret memorials in Manchu revealing that the reports of the commanders, Yang Ying-chü and Li Shih-sheng, were "all mendacious." Yang and Li were arrested and condemned to death. Here the Manchu language added an extra level of secrecy to an already confidential communication system, in a case, significantly, where Han commanders were the targets of investigation.[46]

The Kiangnan Problem

Fear and mistrust, admiration and envy: all marked the Manchu view of Kiangnan, where soulstealing originated. In that "land of rice and fish," elegance and scholarship were nourished by lush agriculture and thriving commerce. From Kiangnan came, by way of the Grand Canal, much of Peking's food supply. Hence imperial rulers had, for centuries, found themselves in dogged competition with Kiangnan elites for the region's surplus. Just as perplexing was how to achieve political control of Kiangnan's haughty scholar elite, who took more than their share of civil-service degrees and high offices. If anyone could make a Manchu feel like a loutish outsider, it was a Kiangnan literatus. To the old Kiangnan problem, this old love-hate relationship, Hungli addressed himself in his own ways.[47] Here was the cultural center of everything the Manchus considered most essentially "Han": the most luxurious, most learned, most artistically refined culture of the realm. From a straitlaced Manchu point of view, it was also the most decadent. Its threat to Manchu values (as Hungli liked to think of them) stemmed from its very attractiveness. If Manchus were to lose themselves to Chinese culture, the culture of Kiangnan would do the worst damage.

The monarch himself was both attracted and repelled by Kiangnan. Hungli had, after visiting the region, imported fragments of Kiangnan elite culture to adorn the Manchu summer capital at Ch'eng-te. But besides refinement and elegance, Kiangnan also meant decadence and assimilation. Its decadent culture ruined good officials who served there, whether bannermen or ordinary Han.[48] Luxurious and corrupt, lower Yangtze society eroded virtue as sugar erodes teeth. Liu Yung, son of Grand Councillor Liu T'ung-hsun (a good northern family, of course), submitted a scathing memorial on the subject in 1762, having just completed a term as Kiangsu educational commissioner. He described how the power of Kiangsu's rich, commercialized elites had outgrown the government's capacity to control them. "The arrogant lower gentry cause trouble and behave outrageously, but the local officials cover up for them." These officials "fear the bad elements, but also fear the lower gentry and the clerk-runners of local government." The guilty went free, and government was negligent in the extreme. So powerful were the local elite that county and prefectural bureaucrats learned the delicate art of ignoring trouble to avoid having their own fingers burnt. Hungli responded: "Liu Yung's memorial hits the nail on the head with respect to the Kiangsu administration's evil practices. The scholars and people of Kiangnan have extravagant customs. If you add to this the perversity and leniency of the authorities, the situation has grown steadily worse and is by now incorrigible."

Of all the provincial jurisdictions, Hungli continued, "Kiangnan is the most outrageously lax. And this is not merely Liu Yung's individual opinion." Yenjišan, governor-general of Liangkiang, and Ch'en Hung-mou, governor of Kiangsu, had set a bad example. These officials had served in the area longest (Yenjišan for six years, Ch'en for four). Both had "regarded lack of trouble as a blessing." And because they had abundant administrative experience, "concord with superiors, amity with subordinates" was their habitual work style. "Those whom they supervise are mostly their old subordinates," and they covered up their misdeeds. Supervision was so lax that wicked officials actually conspired to hinder the conduct of government business. Yenjišan and Ch'en could not escape personal responsibility for this mess. If such high officials could not maintain standards, who below them would fail to get the message? They must clean up their jurisdictions by impeaching the corrupt and inept bureaucrats Liu Yung had denounced. If they merely used this as a way of impeaching their enemies, "they can hardly hope to evade Our penetrating eye."[49]

Kiangnan decadence had infected even Manchu stalwarts such as Yenjišan, to say nothing of veteran Han bureaucrats like Ch'en Hung-mou. Its miasma penetrated all levels, from provincial grandees down to county magistrates. The "rule of avoidance" (hui-pi), designed to insulate the bureaucracy from local influence, could not withstand long service in the morally corrosive atmosphere of the lower Yangtze. If Kiangnan culture was a snare for Manchus, the weaker fiber of even the best Han officials was even more susceptible. Laxity, cronyism, reluctance to face problems for fear of trouble, cautiousness and indecisiveness: all led bureaucrats to lie and dither when communicating with the Throne. These were the Kiangnan "accumulated bad practices" (chi-hsi) that menaced the integrity of government. We shall discover more about them as we examine the behavior of the bureaucracy in 1768 under the lash of the Throne's antisorcery campaign.

Hungli's fears of Kiangnan linked Manchu assimilation to a conventional concern of monarchs: the general decline of bureaucratic effectiveness. His rhetoric, by mid-reign, seemed to reflect his direst presentiment: assimilated Manchus and corrupted Han officials descending, hand in hand, the slope of dynastic decline. For confronting such anxieties, the soulstealing crisis offered Hungli a rich context. He could define and protect Manchu cultural identity by labeling, as opprobriously as possible, men who threatened or betrayed it. He could exorcise the decadence of Kiangnan culture by finding and crushing Kiangnan's grotesque counter-elite, the master-sorcerers of the South.[50] Meanwhile, sorcery was about to break out of its Kiangnan homeland and explode upon the national scene.

CHAPTER 4

The Crime Defined

Late July, 1768: The worst of the summer's heat was already upon Peking, and at the Forbidden City preparations were under way for the annual move to the summer capital at Ch'eng-te. There, in the hills and forests of the old Manchu homeland beyond the Great Wall, was a cunningly designed park in the style and spirit of Kiangnan— the lower Yangtze region where Hungli, like his grandfather before him, delighted to tour. On 1,300 acres lay palaces of sumptuous rusticity and pleasure pavilions in the southern style, set amid serene lakes fringed with willows and artfully contoured to conceal artifice. This little touch of Kiangnan in Manchuria had been created in 1702 by the K'ang-hsi emperor, Hungli's grandfather, and was greatly expanded by Hungli himself.

Spending the hot months there was more than a relief from the unpleasant Peking summer. By coming to Ch'eng-te, the monarch could lead his Manchu elite back to their old haunts, summon them to the saddle, and marshal them on grand hunts and maneuvers in the old rugged style. Here hardihood could for a season replace refinement, and the dust of settled life be shaken, however briefly, from the feet of the conquerors. High politics were served, too: here, at the gateway to the forests and steppes, Inner Asian lords could be entertained and their dependency upon the emperor reaffirmed. Here the Inner Asian faith of Lamaist Buddhism, key to controlling Mongolia and Tibet, was lavishly patronized by Hungli. To appeal to Lamaists, he constructed magnificent temples in the Tibetan style. At

Imperial hunt near Ch'eng-te, the summer capital.

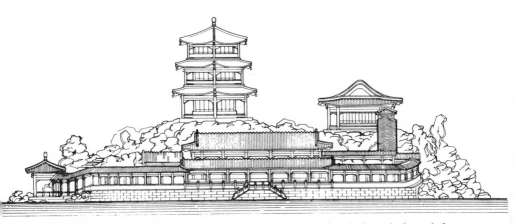

The Chin-shan temple complex, approximately 178 feet in length from left to right, at Ch'eng-te. Built in the Kiangnan style by Hungli's grandfather in imitation of a temple in Chinkiang, Kiangsu Province, that he often visited on his southern tours.

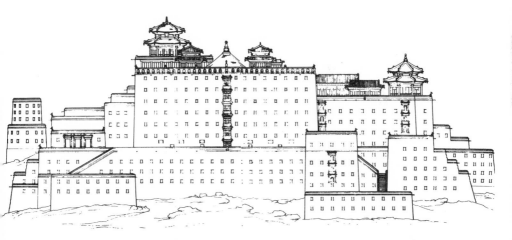

The Tibetan-style potala at Ch'eng-te, begun in 1767 and completed in 1771. Left to right, approximately 477 feet.

the time of our story, Hungli had already begun to construct the gigantic imitation of Lhasa's Potala, to serve the devotional needs of Inner Asian lords at the celebration of the imperial sixtieth birthday two years later. This curious summer capital, an amalgam of Manchu machismo, Kiangnan kitsch, and Inner Asian diplomacy, was a mere 130 miles from Peking; two days sufficed for a courier to bring a report from the committee of grand councillors left behind in Peking and return with an imperial reply. The business of the empire went on uninterrupted.

Evil from the South

Just before the court set forth for these summer pursuits, the emperor received some secret intelligence. How he found out about the situation in Shantung is carefully hidden behind the vague beginning of the July 25 court letter in which he first broached the case. The drafting of the letter was entrusted to the three senior grand councillors, Fuheng, Yenjišan, and Liu T'ung-hsun, and addressed to the provincial officials of Chekiang, Kiangsu (including the governor-general of the three-province Liangkiang region), and Shantung. "We have heard," it began, that

> in the Chekiang region it is said that, when bridges are being constructed, some persons are secretly clipping such things as people's hair and lapels for the purpose of casting spells for sinking the pilings. Now this belief has spread into Shantung. *These rumors are truly absurd.* It may be just petty thieves using the occasion to cast suspicion on others, so that they may more brazenly play their clever tricks. However, this kind of *false story* can easily *delude and incite the public.* Naturally it should be rigorously investigated and forbidden, in order to put an end to evil customs. Let it be known to the governors-general and governors in those jurisdictions that they are to order their subordinates *secretly* to undertake a thorough investigation. If this situation *really exists,* the culprits should be arrested forthwith and punished severely. Or it may be that arresting and severely punishing one or two ringleaders will serve as warning to others. Also they must proceed *as if nothing momentous were happening (pu-tung sheng-se),* conduct their investigations in a proper manner, and not permit yamen underlings to get involved and use the occasion to stir up trouble and disturb local communities.[1]

A curious document: we are left in some doubt as to what His Majesty "really" believed. Despite the "absurdity" of the rumors, he believed it possible that someone was maliciously spreading them.

Did he also believe that someone was actually attempting to practice sorcery? Whatever else he may have believed, it is evident that foremost in his mind was the panic factor. A credulous public is easy to "delude and incite." Officialdom must not only punish the rumormongers, but must do so without panicking the common people. The final curiosity about this document is its conflation of the "bridge-building" and the "queue-clipping" images of popular sorcery lore. Whoever was Hungli's source of information from the South had heard of both the masons of Te-ch'ing and the monks of Hsiao-shan. Here too are linked, for the first time in an imperial document, sorcery and the tonsure.

Information is power, but it is also security. Just as Hungli had his own sources of information from Shantung, so the governor of Shantung, Funihan, seems to have had sources at court. It is too much to accept as coincidence that the governor wrote his first report on queue-clipping July 24, just one day before Hungli approved the draft of his first court letter on the case. It was more likely a matter of preemptive reporting: covering up information was a serious matter between emperor and bureaucrat. The troublesome business of local sorcery could have been kept from Hungli's attention only at some risk of his hearing about it through the rumor network. Once Governor Funihan had heard that Hungli had such information, only speedy reporting could protect him from charges of concealment.[2] As it turned out, what Funihan had now to report went beyond the spreading of "absurd" stories: actual sorcery had been attempted.

The Shantung Cases

Funihan had been going about his master's business of ensuring the security of the realm. Having heard "in the fifth month" (mid-June to mid-July) that there were persons in the provincial capital, Tsinan, "clipping men's queues after stupefying the victims," he considered that this was a matter of "evil arts" *(hsieh-shu)* that required swift action. He immediately ordered local officials to investigate "secretly" and to set a dragnet for the culprits. Later, while in the southern Shantung city of Yen-chou inspecting troops, Funihan learned from the prefect that in two counties of his jurisdiction, Tsou and Yi, two beggars had been arrested for clipping queues. On the west, these counties bordered the Grand Canal that carried grain shipments to granaries near the capital. On the east, they lay beside the main overland route from Hangchow to Peking.³ Funihan had the criminals, along with one of their victims, brought to the Yen-chou yamen, where he interrogated them personally. The criminals, he reported, made the following confessions, which became officialdom's window upon the dark realm of sorcery. Here the identities of the master-sorcerers were first revealed, and upon these confessions was founded the government's campaign.⁴

Ts'ai T'ing-chang Learns about Soul-force

Far from his family home in Szechwan, beggar Ts'ai T'ing-chang's strange adventures had begun while he was sojourning in Peking. There he lived at the Lung-ch'ang Temple in Hsi-ssu p'ai-lou Street, where he made a meager living selling his calligraphy. While there he made the acquaintance of a monk named T'ung-yuan. Later, unable to support himself, he left Peking for the South, and in late March or early April encountered monk T'ung-yuan again, outside the Grand Canal metropolis of Yangchow. With T'ung-yuan were three other monks, his acolytes I-hsing, I-te, and I-an. T'ung-yuan related that he had learned of certain sorcerers in Jen-ho, in Chekiang Province: one Chang and one Wang, along with a monk, Wu-yuan, who knew marvelous magical arts. First you sprinkled a stupefying powder in a victim's face; while he was helpless you quickly clipped hair from the end of his queue. Then, by reciting magical incantations over the hair, you could steal his soul. By tying the soul-force-bearing hairs around paper cutouts of men and horses, you could use the enlivened creatures as agents to steal people's possessions. T'ung-yuan told beggar Ts'ai that, back in Chekiang, monk Wu-yuan had assembled a group of sixteen confederates, some monks and some laymen, each of whom regularly set out to recruit more followers and to clip queues. Evidently a large underground network was spreading in the South.

Beggar Ts'ai (his confession continued) was persuaded to join monk T'ung-yuan's gang and was taught the magical incantations. (Here was the essence of Chinese sorcery lore: a sorcerer's power lay in techniques that anyone could learn.) T'ung-yuan, along with beggar Ts'ai and acolyte I-an, now set out northward in hopes of clipping queues along the way. When they reached the town of Chung-shan-tien in Shantung's Tsou County, Ts'ai obtained some "stupefying powder" from his master. He then went to a shop where a local man, one Hao Kuo-huan, was buying steamed bread. Ts'ai sprinkled his powder in Hao's face and attempted to clip his queue with a small knife. Pursued by the outraged and insufficiently stupefied Hao, Ts'ai was arrested by a local constable. In the confusion, monk T'ung-yuan disappeared.

Chin Kuan-tzu Meets a Fortune-Teller

A native of Shantung's Chang-ch'iu County, in the metropolitan prefecture of Tsinan, beggar Chin Kuan-tzu had encountered an old acquaintance in a nearby Taoist temple: Chang Ssu-ju, a fortune-teller from the Kiangnan region. Fortune-teller Chang was accompanied by three confederates, all Shantungese. He told beggar Chin that in Su-chou, Anhwei Province (not to be confused with Soochow in Kiangsu, where the suspicious beggars had been arrested in May), in the Dark Dragon Temple in the town of Shih-chuang, there lived a monk called Yü-shih who had a magical technique for clipping queues and tying up paper cutouts with them for the purpose of robbing people. Beggar Chin was invited to join the gang. Fortune-teller Chang gave him a knife and a packet of stupefying powder and told him to travel about clipping the queues of young boys. After the band split up, beggar Chin got as far as the market town of Hsiao-chuang-chi in his native county, where he abducted a young boy, Chin Yü-tzu, and forcibly sodomized him. On July 1, he reached Yi County, where he clipped the queue of another young boy, Li Kou. Shortly afterward he was arrested by county authorities.

In his memorial to the Throne, Governor Funihan noted the ominous possibility that the two sources of evil arts, one in Chekiang and one in Anhwei, might spring from a single source: a dangerous plotter lurking somewhere in the area. And the dark suspicion occurred to him that sending gangs here and there, inciting and deluding people into becoming their confederates, might not be merely for the purpose of stealing goods. The conscientious governor was sending secret memoranda to the governors of Chekiang, Kiangsu, and Anhwei, as well as to the governor-general of the Liangkiang region. The prisoners he was sending to Tsinan to be interrogated further by the provincial judge and treasurer. Their initial confessions were forwarded to the emperor, along with the memorial reporting the arrests.[5]

Funihan was not treating the crime as simple sorcery. His suggestion that more was involved than mere robbery implied that the sorcerer's ultimate intent might be sedition, perhaps aided by public disorder. Public disorder was, in fact, one ostensible reason why the *Ch'ing Code* prohibited sorcery. It is nonetheless quite remarkable that Funihan, himself a bannerman, had nothing whatever to say about the political symbolism of the queue. Was this because the shaved forehead was considered the key symbol of the tonsure? In the light of later events, I believe this cannot have been the case; Funihan surely knew how incendiary was anything touching upon the tonsure. But it was not his place to look for trouble. The ethnic problem was best left for others to define. If even Hungli himself had not mentioned it in his private communications with provincial officials, how could a mere governor presume to do so?

The capture of beggars Ts'ai and Chin was only a beginning. Funihan's county magistrates soon reported more cases of queue-clipping in Shantung villages, all of which pointed even more plainly toward sorcerers hidden in the lower Yangtze provinces. On August 11, Funihan reported the arrest of five more queue-clippers, each of whom told of a different Kiangnan master-sorcerer. Han P'ei-hsien, a down-and-out literatus, provoked the keenest interest among his captors.[6]

Han P'ei-hsien Becomes a Sorcerer's Apprentice

Han told his captors that he was forty-one years old, the son of a provincial examination graduate of neighboring Chihli Province. Poverty had driven him to Shantung in search of work. There, in the region bordering I-chou and Ch'ing-chou departments, some sixty miles east of the provincial capital, he practiced medicine and taught school for many years. In the autumn of 1767, he heard of a monk called Ming-yuan who was said to have practiced a particularly fine tradition of medicine. Han journeyed to visit him in his Three Teachings Temple in Hai-chou, just down the coast in Kiangsu Province. Ming-yuan welcomed him, said he indeed "had plenty of techniques," and invited him to become his disciple.

"He used the blindfold method, like this," Han told his interrogators. "First he filled a bronze bowl with water, added some powdered drugs, and had me wash my face with it. Then he wrapped a white cloth to cover my eyes, whereupon I saw lofty towers, elegant rooms, . . . gold and silver treasures, all manner of high-class things."

Han was captivated. A few days later, monk Ming-yuan told him he wanted to obtain "ten-thousand queues in order to capture ten-thousand souls and build a ten-thousand-soul bridge *(wan-hun-ch'iao)*." He showed Han how to stupefy victims by sprinkling powder on them. All that was needed was enough queue-ends, two or three inches long. The hairs would be tied to figures of men and horses cut from "five-color paper," which would be brought to life "by filling seven large earthen jars with them, reciting incantations over them for seven times seven days, then daubing them with the blood of living persons." The life-sized legions could then be sent forth to rob people of their possessions. By late November 1767, Han had been sent forth with one of Ming-yuan's acolytes, monk Fa-k'ung. Each had been given 500 cash and a packet of stupefying powder, and each was to recruit several others to help clip queues. They were to meet monk Ming-yuan back in his temple by the end of August the following year.

Han and monk Fa-k'ung set out northward toward Shantung, but dared not clip along the route for fear of arrest. Nothing accomplished, the two separated upon reaching I-shui County, about a hundred miles into Shantung. Han himself journeyed northwest as far as Po-shan, where he settled down to resume the practice of medicine, his magical mission seemingly shelved. On June 4, 1768, he encountered monk Fa-k'ung at the temple of a local Taoist. Fa-k'ung pressed him about the queue-clipping mission, which Han now promised to fulfill. On June 7, "I clipped the queue of a fourteen- or fifteen-year-old boy south of the county seat of Lai-wu." Six days later he did the same to a boy who was delivering food to fieldworkers. On June 16 he delivered the queue-ends to Fa-k'ung at the prefectural town of T'ai-an, at the foot of sacred Mount T'ai. On July 19, he encountered "a fourteen- or fifteen-year-old boy" standing under an acacia tree. "I sprinkled drugs on him, and he passed out." Just as Han had secreted the boy's severed queue-end in his traveling bag, villagers seized him and hauled him into the county yamen.

Li Shao-shun Is Enslaved by a Sorcerer

A poor hired laborer, Li was forty-three years old when he was sent by his master to deliver 150 ounces of silver to a grain merchant in the prefectural town of Tung-ch'ang in payment of a debt for soy-beans. Li did as ordered and spent the night in town. On the way home next day, he met a man carrying a sack, who asked him his name and native place. Suddenly the stranger turned and sprinkled some powder in Li's face, whereupon the laborer felt "kind of dizzy" *(hu-hu t'u-t'u)* and could only stumble along after his captor. When his head began to clear, he realized he had been "stupefied" and begged for mercy. The stranger now ordered Li to "make obeisance to him as master" and made him swear an oath begging Heaven to strike him with a thunderbolt if he reneged. He then clapped Li in the small of his back, which cleared his head. The sorcerer "said that his powers were mighty, and that if I ran away or told anyone he would 'hook my soul' *(kou-hun)* and take my life." He then gave Li a small knife to secrete in his right hand, and a pinch of yellow powder from his sack. "I was to go up to a young man who had passed us on the road, sprinkle some powder on him from behind, and cut his queue." The victim realized nothing, and Li was able to carry out his orders.

As captor and captive rested beneath a tree, the sorcerer revealed that he was named Liu, from Pien-ch'iao in Kiangnan, but did not supply his given name. (Li could only refer to him as "Baldy Liu.") The sorcerer had learned his "techniques" in Kiangnan, and there were four or five men in his band. He himself had worked as a "roadside doctor" and recounted clipping several queues along the way. "When I asked what the queues were for, he told me to mind my own business and just follow along to help him clip. Later it would bring me benefits *(hao-ch'u)*." Soon the pair met two of Liu's confed-erates on the road, and the four sat down in a sorghum field to rest during the heat of the day. Liu shortly ordered Li into a nearby village to clip queues from people taking their noonday naps. Li entered the village but lost his nerve. As he turned to leave, a villager challenged him, but Li cast the yellow powder in his face and the man fell to the ground. Li threw down his knife and fled; quickly, however, he was caught, whereupon he told the story of his enslave-ment. The villagers were led to Baldy Liu (the confederates had fled), who resisted with his knife but was overcome. Li and Liu were dragged to the village temple, guarded by a crowd during the night, and early the next day were trussed up and taken away in a cart to the Ch'ang-ch'ing county seat. Along the way they were given no water, and Liu died of the heat before they reached their destination that afternoon. At his interrogation, Li pleaded that he was not a sorcerer but had been forced to "accept Liu as a master" in order to save his own life.

In addition to reporting the apprehension of Han P'ei-hsien and Li Shao-shun, Governor Funihan also revealed in his August 11 memorial that his local officials had captured three other queue-clippers, each of whom he now reported to the Throne, enclosing their confessions. A mendicant Taoist priest, Chang Ch'eng-hsien, was promised 300 cash per queue by another local Taoist, who taught him how to hold stupefying powder "in the creases of his finger joints and blow it into a man's face." A beggar named Chang Yü was offered a smoke by "a man sitting under an acacia tree," was stupe-fied, and awoke to find the man "chanting spells" over him, after which he was unable to resist his orders. A starving beggar called Cripple Hu was enlisted by "a monk" to clip queues for 100 cash each. Governor Funihan pointed out that, with the exception of Han P'ei-hsien, all these criminals were poor folk, coerced or paid to join the sorcerer's gang. Only Han had been to the lower Yangtze area, where these hateful practices were spawned. All signs pointed to an extra-provincial gang recruiting local people to do its work.

Indeed the record now offered a number of leads. The culprits arrested in Shantung had all been recruited by sorcerers, most of them from the South. The three sorcerers identified by name (not counting "Baldy Liu," who had died in the hands of his captors) all had special access to the world of shadow, being either Buddhist monks or (in the case of Chang Ssu-ju) a professional fortune-teller. Two of the recruiters (monk T'ung-yuan and fortune-teller Chang) had themselves been recruited by master-sorcerers lurking in the South: monks Wu-yuan (in Chekiang) and Yü-shih (in northern Anhwei). The Shantung recruits were mostly laymen who had learned enough to use the potent "stupefying powder" to clip queues, but none had been admitted to their masters' inner secrets. Obviously the regime could not stop with the arrest of these petty criminals, but had to root out the source of the evil by hunting down the master-sorcerers themselves. Interrogation of the Shantung criminals had yielded fairly exact addresses for two of them (monks Wu-yuan and Yü-shih). Fortune-teller Chang was only known to be from Kiangnan. Monk T'ung-yuan had last been seen near Yangchow, north of the

Yangtze on the Grand Canal. The hierarchy of plotters was now revealed in three tiers:

Queue-clipper	Intermediate Master	Grand Master
Ts'ai T'ing-chang	T'ung-yuan	Wu-yuan
Chin Kuan-tzu	Chang Ssu-ju	Yü-shih
Han P'ei-hsien	Ming-yuan	?

On July 29 Hungli dispatched urgent court letters to all province chiefs, announcing the Shantung arrests and demanding that the master-sorcerers be tracked down. He now considered that the sorcery uncovered in Shantung was a menace to the empire as a whole, not just to the lower Yangtze provinces. Accordingly these orders were issued to top provincial officials nationwide. How, exactly, did Hungli understand the soulstealing threat? On what basis was he mobilizing the provincial bureaucracy to confront it? These criminals, whose traces are "hidden and hard to detect," use their evil arts to "delude and ensnare good subjects *(mi-yu shan-liang)*." They constitute a "great injury to local communities." Here Hungli pictured the Throne as carrying out a mission to protect the people from supernatural harm. For such a view there existed a solid legal basis: the numerous penal sanctions against sorcery included in the *Ch'ing Code*.[7]

Sorcery in the *Ch'ing Code*

In view of its own dominating position in the empire's ritual life, it might seem odd that the state saw sorcery as a serious threat. Yet it did so, as evidenced by the penal code's stern provisions on the subject. Surely it was the central role of ritual in certifying the dynasty's mandate to rule, as well as sanctifying state authority on all levels, that made officialdom so protective of its special rights to communicate with the spirit world—and so determined to regulate how others did so. The fear of sorcery is by no means straightforwardly expressed in the *Code,* however. Sorcery is not treated as a single category, but is distributed under a number of headings and subheadings with a wide range of meanings and associations. An outline of the areas where the *Code* treats manipulation of the spirit world will locate the particular offenses we have seen in the 1768 cases:[8]

Categories under Which Sorcery Is Prohibited
in the *Ch'ing Code*

The Ten Abominations *(shih-o)*
• Crimes outside the [civilized] way *(pu-tao)*
Statutes on Ritual *(li-lü)*   [Offenses within the purview of the Board of Rites]
• Sacrifices *(chi-ssu)*
• Ceremonies *(i-chih)*
Statutes on Criminality *(hsing-lü)*   [Offenses within the purview of the Board of Punishments]
• Rebellion and Robbery *(tsei-tao)*
• Homicide *(jen-ming)*

Sorcery under the "Ten Abominations"

The "Ten Abominations" occur in the preamble to the *Code* and are duplicated later in various substantive statutes. They were a general statement of principle and not for jurists to apply directly. In this privileged position, they signal one of the culturally deepest levels of Chinese legal thought and are in fact drawn almost wholly from the *T'ang Code* of A.D. 653. Acts that we would call "sorcery" come under the "uncivilized" subheading and include: "dismembering a person to extract vitality" *(ts'ai-sheng che-ko*—cutting out ears and entrails for achieving biodynamic powers); making poison *(tsao-ku)* by magical means (as distinct from purely chemical agents, such as poisonous herbs); and inflicting "captive spirits" *(yen-mei)* upon a victim by means of incantations. All are acts or conspiracies against persons, not the state.[9] If the deepest levels of revulsion against sorcery are assumed to be reflected in this preamble, their wholly nonpolitical nature is astonishing in the light of what follows.

Sorcery under Statutes on Ritual

Under Statutes on Ritual, most of the judicial activity concerning what we would call "sorcery" is dealt with under the subcategory "Sacrifices." Here, in statute 162, are proscribed sorcerers *(shih-wu—*

wu is a term associated with shamans) and "evil arts" *(hsieh-shu)*, such as (1) "purporting to call down evil spirits" *(hsieh-shen);* (2) writing charms or reciting incantations to spiritually charge water for ritual use *(chou-shui);* (3) practicing spirit-writing (a kind of prognostication); (4) wantonly using the designation Maitreya (the Buddha-messiah), White Lotus Society (a general term for messianic popular-Buddhist sects), and all "techniques based on deviant ways and perverse principles" *(tso-tao i-tuan chih shu);* or (5) possessing diagrams or images, burning incense and gathering followers, meeting at night and dispersing by day, and falsely claiming to be practicing benevolence in order to delude people.[10] Grouped with offenses against the proper conduct of imperial sacrifices, the statute clearly is aimed at communication, through sacrificial offerings, with spirits outside the imperial cult and the pantheon of imperially sanctioned deities.

How seriously did the framers of this statute fear such ritual offenses? Did they really fear rival channels of communication with the spirit world? Shen Chih-ch'i, an early eighteenth-century commentator, suggests otherwise: the statute, he writes, "emphasizes the element of 'delusion of the people' *(huo-chung)*." Simple people, aroused by heterodox teachings, may create disturbances and "give rise to chaos."[11] He is telling us that social order and state security are really the state's main concerns. Not surprisingly, this statute was the legal peg that supported numerous substatutes aimed at sectarians: here are grouped the substatutes for the relentless prosecution, during late imperial times, of allegedly subversive popular sects, particularly after the Eight Trigrams revolt of 1813. Although the editors' choice of entries in the *Conspectus of Penal Cases* (HAHL) was based on jurisprudential interest rather than on frequency of occurrence, it is suggestive that twenty cases out of twenty-four dealt with sectarian prosecutions.[12]

Lest it be assumed, however, that this statute related exclusively to state security, note that it was used to prosecute two early nineteenth-century cases of sexual deviance involving transvestite monks: the first dressed as a female and deceived a married woman into adultery (and tried unsuccessfully to deceive another); and the second became involved in a homosexual triangle that ended in one lover's denouncing him to the authorities. Both monks were convicted of "deluding" people by means of sorcery, which suggests that the court considered the nature of the sexual lure (transvestitism) to be sufficiently unnatural as to fall under the sorcery prohibition.[13]

Sorcery prosecutions under "Sacrifices," then, convey a mixed message: the Ch'ing state viewed unauthorized traffic with spirits as a threat to public order and used the statute to attack sectarians. Nevertheless, the statute was also considered useful for remedying cases of personal injury, at least in cases where the defendant employed unnatural sexual lures. In both respects, the state's officially agnostic position about the existence or efficacy of the unauthorized communication is suggested by the prominence of the "delusion" principle in the case record: in prosecuting sorcery, the main objects of attack were said to be its social results. Nevertheless, the fact that these sectarian prosecutions were categorized under "Sacrifices" suggests that the unauthorized link to the spirit world—whether real or spurious—shaped the actual topography of this battleground.

By contrast to the "Sacrifices" heading, which emphasizes communication with spirits, "Ceremonies" emphasizes the concrete ritual behavior of men. Grouped among statutes governing official conduct at state rituals, official dress codes, and rules for court astrologers, we find a prohibition against sorcerers' *(shu-shih)* residing in official households and foretelling the future, particularly "the reigning dynasty's bad or good fortune." The official commentator states that this constitutes "meddling in affairs of state," and that it might cause "ordinary people to think upon allegiance or defection."[14] Although the *Conspectus* includes no cases under this category, a substatute of the K'ang-hsi reign forbids "people who study astronomy" (not in official employ) to foretell the future and thereby "delude" people, which indicates that it was far from a dead statute.[15] Again, the "delusion" principle protects the *Code* from appearing to place credit in the reality of the socerers' link to the spirit world.

Sorcery under Statutes on Criminality

Under the "Ceremonies" statutes, penalties against sorcerers who foretell the future are relatively light—only one hundred strokes of the heavy bamboo. Once we move into the section of the *Code* that deals with "Rebellion and Robbery," however, they bear the death penalty. Placed just after "Rebellion" and "Treason" is a statute that states, "Those who concoct books or sayings of sorcery *(yao-shu yao-yen)* involving prophecies *(ch'an-wei)* are to be jailed awaiting decapitation." A 1740 substatute effectively increases the penalty to immediate decapitation, the same as for treason.[16] The distinction, we are told, is one of intent. Though the kind of sorcerers prohibited by the "Ceremonies" statute are only swindlers, the harm they do society being incidental, those prosecuted under "Rebellion" are making predictions "with the intention of deluding people and plotting sedition." This looks like serious business, but in fact the statute seems to have been used to prosecute rather marginal cases—mostly unauthorized possession of spells for medicinal purposes or personal protection; and in those, the statute generally was applied analogically rather than directly.[17] We can only assume that the antisectarian statutes under "Sacrifices" took care of all serious sedition cases, and that this old statute (which dates from the seventh century) was largely obsolete.

Of the three statutes dealing with sorcery under "Homicide," the first two are repetitions of material in the "Ten Abominations." The first is "dismembering a person to extract vitality."[18] The horror evoked by this crime is indicated by the penalty of "death by slow slicing," the same as for killing one's parents or grandparents, and indeed the same as for rebellion (the penalty for treason is only decapitation). If the victim has only been injured rather than killed, the penalty is the same. If the crime has been set afoot but nobody has yet been injured, the penalty is merely decapitation. The official "Commentary" distinguishes this crime from mutilation after a murder, which is merely committed out of hatred for the victim. This crime, however, is done "in order to practice sorcery *(yao-shu)* for deluding people. Therefore it is treated with special gravity."

It seems odd to find the "delusion" theme displayed even in the case of so horrible a crime. Was the statute actually applied to counter the *social* effects of sorcery—that is, the use of sorcery to spread disorder in society? The only instance in the *Conspectus* suggests otherwise. It concerns a Chekiang case in which a seventy-year-old male was convicted of sucking the "vital bodily essence" *(ching-sui)* from sixteen baby girls, of whom eleven died. Apparently no actual sorcery was performed with the "essence," which is probably why the trial judge applied this statute analogically. In its emotional impact, the case seems similar to the sex crimes described earlier, even if more revolting: it was grossly unnatural, and the sorcery statutes were the remedies nearest to hand. In an impassioned edict on the case, the Chia-ch'ing emperor used the term "human demon" *(jen-yao)*, the ideographs of a term for sorcerer *(yao-jen)* reversed.[19] Here was no concern with "delusion" or social disorder, but revulsion at a crime so unnatural that only a sorcery statute could deal with its inhuman quality.[20] Related cases cited by the editors of the *Code* include "luring children" by means of spells and incantations so that their bodily essence might be extracted, or buying corpses of children to burn for medicine. In an eighteenth-century case, this statute was used to prosecute a man who murdered someone to obtain his gall bladder for concocting a cure for leprosy. Documents on the case mention no biodynamic sorcery as such, though the statute seems quite apposite otherwise.[21] The inhuman, indeed quasi-cannibalistic quality of these crimes suggests a violation of fundamental taboos. Did such violation in turn suggest a connection with the supernatural and so justify their prosecution under sorcery statutes? Although even in these cases "delusion" is brought in to debunk the efficacy of sorcery, the effect on the public was considered quite different from the mass "delusion" practiced by sectarian sorcerers on their converts and prosecuted in the "Ceremonies" category. Here, forces of darkness were unmistakably at work.

A single statute, number 289, combines the crimes of making or using magical poison from harmful insects *(tsao-hsu ku-tu)*, harming people by spells or incantations, and inflicting "captive spirits" *(yen-mei)* on others.[22] The official "Commentary" specifies such "techniques" as harming one's enemies by drawing or fabricating human images and piercing their hearts or eyes; or summoning spirits *(chao-kuei)* by carving spells on seals or burying them. However, the "Commentary" specifies that all such crimes should be prosecuted under the statute on premeditated murder. Indeed, the *Conspectus* does not offer examples of prosecutions that employ this particular sorcery statute directly.[23] The poison cases mentioned in the commentaries to the *Code* all concern ordinary chemical agents, not supernatural potions, and were in fact prosecuted under different statutes. To judge from the apparent scarcity of case material, it appears that this ancient statute on harming people by magic, which echoes the fifth of the "Ten Abominations" (crimes outside the [civilized] way), had fallen out of use by late imperial times. The kinds of sorcery it prohibits, though clearly part of folk belief, were not discerned by trial judges in the cases before them.[24]

The State and the Supernatural

The ambiguous picture of state purposes in combating sorcery mirrors the ambiguous position of the state in matters supernatural. On the one hand, the state was itself involved in communication with the spirit world through many channels. It had its own cults of Heaven, Earth, and assorted nature deities, along with the welter of popular deities it had co-opted into its religious system. Through its in-house astrologers, it was constantly involved in reading the omens of the skies. As to the reality of man's link to the spirits, it could hardly take an agnostic stance. On the other hand, to join open combat with competing cults would dignify them by admitting the reality and efficacy of their links to the spirit world. The language of the *Code,* its commentaries, and its case record leave no doubt that sorcery was practiced. Practicing it, however, could not be presented as other than futile: calling forth spirits that would not come when called, for the sake of "deluding" people into illegal combination and perhaps into revolt.

Posting the "delusion" disclaimer prominently throughout the sorcery statutes was, we can only infer, a formulaic act to deny that the state accepted the reality—or the power—of rival deities. That the state placed its antisectarian laws firmly under "Sacrifices," however, shows how flimsy this denial was in comparison with the underlying mental divisions under which human activity was perceived. Even under the "Rebellion" rubric, some of the *Code*'s most powerful strictures are directed against crimes of cognition (foretelling the future), even though they are decorously shielded by the "delusion" disclaimer.

We can, I believe, find in the "delusion" disclaimer the principal origin of the panic factor that has emerged so prominently in this account of how the Throne dealt with both sorcery and tonsure offenses. The common people were the mediating link between cosmic forces and practical politics. The withdrawal of Heaven's blessing from a failing dynastic regime was signaled by popular disturbances. Conversely, the solidity of the Mandate was signaled by public contentment and quiescence. Sorcery, in this sense, can be seen as the "black" counterpart of the imperial cult. Just as the legitimate sacrifices conveyed to the public an image of firm and worthy control, so sorcery might convey an image of instability and imminent crisis. The representation and the reality were inseparable. No point in asking whether sorcery practices were "really" loosening the dynasty's grip: the popular reaction to sorcery was what counted. Public disturbances, like astrological omens, were both signs and instruments of Heaven's displeasure. Since words, too, were signs and instruments, it is no wonder the panic factor was handled so gingerly, even in internal government communications! Here indeed was the occasion, as the commentator noted, for people to "think upon allegiance or defection."[25]

Yet the state's concern with sorcery was by no means limited by considerations of its political security. "Sorcery" was also used in a metaphorical sense to highlight crimes of particular horror, which involved some of the deepest taboos (such as cannibalism). Chinese jurists were stuck with the Nuremberg conundrum: some crimes were so inhuman that no human agency could plausibly punish them. Yet they had nevertheless to be punished. That may explain why sorcery statutes found a place in the application of the penal code to crimes considered particularly loathsome, whether or not sorcery itself could be clearly demonstrated. Certain laws, such as the sorcery clauses in the "Ten Abominations," were so hard to apply to the real world that they generated practically no case record. Their retention in the body of the *Code* itself is further evidence that imperial Chinese jurists, for all their disclaimers, believed that there was always likely to be something nasty going on out there between humans and spirits. Such unauthorized traffic with the world of shadow threatened both the security of the state and the moral foundations of society—which, in imperial rhetoric, were radically linked. Hence it is important to remember, as we consider the panic of 1768, that the Throne's campaign against sorcery cannot neatly be filed away under "political security."

What to Do about Soulstealing?

What did this elaborate legal code mean for the prosecution of soulstealing, and where did the particular offenses of 1768 fit within it? Every public officer who dealt with soulstealing, including Hungli himself, was surely aware of the extent and variety of the *Code*'s prohibitions against the "evil arts." When Hungli said that soulstealing did "great harm" to the common people, he must have assumed that it *could be* prosecuted under the law. But under exactly which law, in this welter of definitions and prohibitions, would an eighteenth-century jurist have put it? Soulstealing as such is not mentioned by the *Code*, so prosecution would have required analogic reasoning, a common recourse when a particular variant of a crime was not covered by specific legal penalties.

Communicating with "evil spirits" (statute 162) might have seemed inappropriate, because the "spirits" involved were simply the souls of the victims. A more plausible basis for prosecution would have been the statutes on practicing biodynamic sorcery by "extracting vitality" (statute 288) or on injuring people by charms or incantations (statute 289 [3]). If human hair contains vitality, as I will suggest in Chapter 5, then cutting it off and using it for magical purposes may have stirred the same revulsions as the quasi-cannibalistic perversions mentioned earlier. If the common man shared the jurist's horror at such practices, then prosecuting soulstealers under those statutes would have soothed the feelings of all concerned. Here the reader may wonder why we cannot discover how soulstealing was classified in 1768 by simply turning to the record of sentences against convicted soulstealers. A fair question indeed. The difficulty is that the soulstealing prosecution of 1768 generated *no* case record of sentences. The reasons for this odd situation will emerge as the story moves along.

We do know, at least, that Hungli had decided to launch the campaign against queue-clipping for its sorcery and not for its politics. Indeed, at first he eschewed any reference to the political significance of the Ch'ing tonsure and focused his attack on sorcery, pure and simple. This resolution is entirely in keeping with the official approach to tonsure questions in the eighteenth century: the tonsure issue lay far in the past, and no purpose was served by reviving it. On the contrary, the panic factor forbade even mentioning it as such in imperial communications. For the time being, the implied threat to Manchu legitimacy was too sensitive a matter to be whispered, even in confidential court letters.[26]

Hungli's fear of the panic factor was evident in the Ma Ch'ao-chu affair of 1752, when reports of tonsure violation were considered unmentionable. But even in the prosecution of sorcery, extreme care was needed. Take, for example, a sorcery case that occurred six years before the soulstealing crisis. In Han-shan County, Anhwei, about forty miles southwest of Nanking, a mendicant monk named Tao-sheng had been "stealing the souls of living persons by means of spells and charms."[27] Tao-sheng had reportedly attracted some followers, some of whom had been caught. Hungli found the measures taken by the local authorities to be clumsy and inflammatory. Of course the people must be protected from sorcery that employs "magic poison and curses" *(ku-tu yen-mei).* Nevertheless, the governor's heavy-handed dragnet was sure to attract public attention. "Ignorant persons who do not know the causes of things" may develop fears, leading to popular disturbances. Public panic was to be avoided by rigorous but discreet investigation.[28] But the phrases *ku-tu* and *yen-mei* are taken directly from the Ch'ing penal code and are a wholly conventional *overt* response to reports of sorcery. Why not scour the countryside for the rascals and then prosecute them openly? The reason was the potential for panic, and here prudence overrode justice. The danger posed by sorcery had both a supernatural dimension (an obligation by the state to protect the common people from criminal magic) and a political dimension (the explosive nature of public hysteria over sorcery), one leading to action and the other to caution. Six years later in Shantung, the linkage of sorcery and queue-clipping required caution all the more. Indeed, here was potential for panic that touched the Ch'ing power structure directly: all the more reason for keeping quiet about the tonsure aspect, even in secret communications with his own officials. Consequently, it was not mentioned in imperial edicts for the first six weeks of the campaign. Even the hunt for sorcerers was to be undertaken with extreme discretion.

It was as if monarch and commoner were grasping two handles of an explosive device. For the Throne, the potential for public unrest (whether over the tonsure or the sorcery threat) touched the security of the regime. The Throne could appease public fears by prosecuting sorcerers, but the ultimate effect on the public temper was unpredictable. For the people, however, the sorcery threat was immediate and personal: malevolent forces were threatening to sever the link between body and soul. The queue-clippers would give them no rest. Reports of queue outrages continued to cross official desks as sorcery spread relentlessly from its Chekiang center. In far southern Fukien, for example, one victim told his county magistrate that he had been studying in the county academy and as evening approached had fallen asleep on his bench. When shaken awake by an attendant, he found that his severed queue-end was resting nearby in an incense burner. Another victim had been walking out the city gate to buy firewood when he heard voices behind him. He turned but saw nobody. Suddenly something seemed to strike his back, and he felt "dizzy"—the end of his queue had been clipped. Yet a third had been chatting with villagers at a temple doorway when he felt a "strange wind" and fell senseless to the ground. When he regained consciousness, he discovered that half his queue was missing.[29]

CHAPTER 5

The Roots of
Sorcery Fear

On their way to join the rebellion of Wu San-kuei (1674–1681), two sorcerers *(shu-shih)* stopped to pass the night at a county town. One lay down to sleep against the western wall. The other said, "Don't sleep under that wall. It is going to collapse at 9 P.M." The other said, "Your arts are not sufficiently profound. The wall is not going to collapse toward the inside, but toward the outside." When the hour arrived, the wall collapsed toward the outside, just as predicted.[1]

In the early eighteenth century, there was a retired official in Ch'ang-shu, a connoisseur of magic tricks, who was visited by all the famous sorcerers of the day. Once there came a monk who could cause images to appear in his begging bowl; there could be seen the great ocean, with fish and dragons leaping. The monk invited the official to travel with him in the mountains. They stopped for refreshment at a temple, whereupon the monk suddenly disappeared. When the official inquired of the temple monks, they answered, "Oh, he said you were going to shave your head and remain here, never to return home." When the distressed official pleaded with them, they offered to release him if he would donate 100,000 ounces of silver for the repair of the great hall. The official had to give them a chit for the whole amount. His companion suddenly reappeared, thanked him ceremoniously, and showed him the magic begging bowl. There the official saw his whole household assembled before his own front gate. Suddenly he found himself actually standing before the gate, with no trace of the monk. When he went inside for his money sack, it was missing 100,000 taels. In their place was his chit. Some people said this was done by White Lotus magic.[2]

An eighteenth-century resident of Ch'ang-chih named Ch'en had a beautiful and talented daughter. Once a wandering Taoist beggar caught a glimpse of her and stationed himself with his begging bowl near the Ch'en gate. When the Taoist saw a blind man exiting, he asked his business. The blind man answered that he had been called in to tell the family's fortunes. The Taoist alleged that he himself had been asked to serve as an intermediary for the girl's marriage and that he needed to know her birth-signs (the year, month, day, and hour of birth). When he had the information, he departed. Some days later, the girl felt her legs grow numb and fell into a trance. Drawn mysteriously out of her house, she found herself on a deserted road with only the Taoist leading her on. He brought her into a house that seemed like her own, then drew a knife and stabbed her to the heart. She felt her soul floating out of her body and could see the Taoist daubing drops of her heart's blood upon a wooden doll while muttering incantations. She felt that she was one with the wooden doll. "Henceforth," commanded the Taoist, "you must do my bidding. Fail not!"[3]

From the curious to the hideous, these are samplings of the thousands of sorcery stories in Chinese fiction and folklore. What I call "sorcery" in such accounts is the enhancement of personal power by manipulating the spirit world, which is the general definition I shall use. "Sorcerers," in this sense, were persons who were portrayed as having several kinds of enhanced power: *cognitive* (the power to see through time and space, but mainly to foretell the future); *telekinetic* (the power to move matter through space); and *biodynamic* (the power to manipulate life-force by extracting it from living beings or instilling it into inanimate matter). These powers were commonly described as "arts" *(shu)*, which suggests that we should call them "sorcery" rather than "witchcraft," following Evans-Pritchard's distinction between powers that can be learned by anyone (sorcery) and powers innate to the practitioner (witchcraft).[4] There is no single Chinese term that embraces all the meanings of sorcery, largely because "sorcery" is not a unified Chinese concept.[5] Establishment foes of unauthorized communications with the spirit world used the general terms *hsieh-shu* or *yao-shu* (evil arts) and *tso-tao i-tuan* (deviant ways and perverse principles). Both terms appear in the language of the criminal codes. Also used were *yao-jen* (wizard or sorcerer) and *yao-shu* (books of sorcery). Common folk might use less opprobrious terms, depending on exactly what was thought to be going on. A sorcerer might be *shu-shih* (lit., an educated man who possesses magical arts). A spirit-medium might be called *wu*, a very ancient term for communicators with the world of shadow. There exists no comprehensive study of Chinese sorcery in any language.[6] I shall explore that vast subject here only from certain angles that relate to the events of 1768. These involve ideas about the human soul, about the magical animation of inanimate objects, and about how one could protect oneself against sorcery. What beliefs could give rise to a vision of soulstealers fearsome enough to drive ordinary subjects to homicide and an emperor to a disruptive national campaign?

Body and Soul

The Separability of Soul from Body

The notion that human agency can divide a person's soul from his body rests on a complex belief about the composition of the soul itself. The Chinese believed in a soul with multiple aspects.[7] A very old tradition held that in the living person dwelt the *hun*, or spiritual soul, and the *p'o*, or bodily soul. This dualism existed as early as the second century B.C., by which time it was already linked to the cosmological dualism of *yin* and *yang*, which, by joining, brought the world (including the human person) into existence. Like *yin* and *yang*, the two parts of the soul exist harmoniously in the body during life and separate at death. The *hun*-soul corresponds to the *yang* (associated with maleness, light, and activity) and the *p'o*-soul to the *yin* (femaleness, heaviness, and passivity). The *hun*-soul governs the higher faculties (mind, heart); the *p'o*-soul governs the physical senses and bodily functions.[8] For our purposes, the point to notice is that the light, volatile *hun*-soul may be separated from the *living* person with alarming ease. It normally separates during sleep. It normally returns, of course, but its absence, if prolonged, produces various kinds of pathology and abnormality, including disease, trance states, madness, or death. The Dutch sinologue J. J. M. de Groot found, in his southeast Chinese community (Amoy), that "fright, anxiety, and sleeplessness may be associated with prolonged absence of the soul from the body."[9] Soul-loss seems to have been especially important in the etiology of children's ailments. Nineteenth-century sources such as de Groot are echoed by modern fieldwork in this respect. In contemporary Taiwan, loss of soul is blamed for listlessness, fretfulness, or sickliness in children. The soul may have been driven out as the result of "fright," in which case the child may be cured by taking him back to the place where he was frightened and calling back the soul.[10]

The idea of "recalling" a soul that has been separated from its body is a very ancient one. It is associated with death ritual as well as with healing.[11] It seems to have played a part in shamanistic death rituals in south-central China by the early third century B.C. By Han times it is part of a ritual called *fu* (recall), of which pictures have been recovered from a second-century B.C. tomb (Ma-wang-tui): immediately after someone has died, a member of the family, acting as a "summoner," climbs to the eastern eave of the roof and, facing north, waves a set of the deceased's clothes, calling "O! Thou [name of deceased], come back!" Because it was assumed that the soul was *temporarily* separated from the body during sleep or unconsciousness, it might be coaxed back by such things as familiar clothing. The ritual has been taken to mean "to summon the *hun*-soul of the dead back to reunite with its *p'o*-soul" on the assumption that the *hun* is the airy component of the spirit, quick to dissipate and relatively easy to separate from the body, whereas the *p'o* departs rather slowly on its journey back to earth. This explains why the *hun*-soul is the part that has to be recalled.[12] (It is the *hun*-soul that is the target of eighteenth-century soulstealing—*chiao-hun*.)

Voluntary and Involuntary Soul-Loss

Chinese believed that the soul could be separated from the body by both voluntary and involuntary means. Communication with the dead could involve either "soul-travel" (shamanism) or "spirit possession" (mediumism). Soul-travel, in which the shaman sent her soul to the nether regions to visit the dead, was considered a hazardous practice, to judge by stories of the occasional trouble shamans had in getting their souls back.[13] Such stories reveal a nagging anxiety that the soul might not find its way back to its body, or that the body might meanwhile be thought dead and consequently destroyed (related, perhaps, to the fear of being thought dead while only asleep).[14]

Even more alarming, however, was the idea of *involuntary* soul-loss. In addition to the "fright" or other trauma[15] that might jar soul from body, a soul might actually be stolen by either human or supernatural agents. "Vengeance-seeking ghosts" or demons might be held responsible.[16] De Groot's Amoy informants told him of "a certain class of mischievous spectres, who are fond of drawing the vital spirits out of men." These demons are called *tsou-ma t'ien-cheng* (heavenly spirits riding horses), or *pan-t'ien hsiu-ts'ai* (literary graduates living halfway in the sky). A person who falls unconscious is taken to a priest (*shih-kung*, Taoist exorcist) who will practice a rite called *ch'iang ching-shen* (snatch the spirit) to recover the soul from "the invisible being" who has stolen it.[17] Soulstealing ghosts were known to lurk along roadsides at night, and many were the tales of "wretches who, having been accosted by such natural foes of man, were found dead on the roadside without the slightest wound or injury being visible: their souls had simply been snatched out of them." Roadside privies were particularly favored by such demons, because it was there that "man is so lonely and helpless."[18] As if such invisible specters were not fearsome enough, evil men were also thought capable of soulstealing. These sorcerers might write paper charms that worked on their victims by contagious magic.[19]

"Soul-calling" was employed, both as a death ritual and as a cure for childhood illness. In the case of the recently dead (whether adult or child), it expressed the survivors' unwillingness to accept the finality of death and their affection for the departed: they would cling to him and bring him back if they could. In the case of children, I have already mentioned that temporary soul-loss (perhaps caused by "fright") was blamed for various pathological symptoms. In such instances, the parents resorted to the ritual of soul-calling. The ritual was commonly called either *chao-hun* or *chiao-hun*, both meaning "to call (or summon) the *hun*-soul." Recall that *chiao-hun* is the same term as that used to describe soulstealing. Both devoted parent and malign sorcerer "called" the soul—the one to rejoin it *to* the body, the other to call it *from* the body.

Henri Doré observed late Ch'ing soul-calling rituals in Yangtze Valley communities. Here is one from Anhwei:

[T]he method employed in recalling the soul of a child is as follows: the child's name is first mentioned, then the person adds "where are you amusing yourself, come back home." Or thus "where were you frightened, return home" . . . If for instance the child's name is Ngai-hsi, little darling, the person will say: "little darling, where have you been scared, where have you been amusing yourself? Come back home." Another following behind, replies "he has returned." While they shout to burst their sides, a person within the house places the clothes of the deceased child on a broomstick, near the house or the door-way, and watches attentively whether a leaf or a blade of grass has moved in the vicinity, or whether an insect has been seen flitting by . . . any such occurrence is a sign that the soul has returned.[20]

That the ritual action of the murderous soulstealer can be described in the same phraseology as that of the loving parent reveals in it a special loathsomeness. As shown in Chapter 4, the language of the *Ch'ing Code* indicates the peculiarly perverse character of sorcery: like the Black Mass of European demonology, it upended and mocked the most common human rituals associated with orthodox social life.

The fear of soul-loss grew from general assumptions about the biodynamic power of sorcerers: their ability to cause harm by proxy, giving life to inanimate matter by stealing the vitality of the living from a distance. Because such biodynamic sorcery played a major part in the panic of 1768, it is worth discussing briefly here. The objects by which sorcerers exerted biodynamic power could be of numerous sorts, but the commonest seem to have been paper mannikins *(chih-jen)* that were brought to life by incantations. The popular stories of the "strange tales" sort are full of such paper men.

A Ming dynasty story tells of a sorcerer in Kwangtung named Li who practiced "Prior-to-Heaven Magic Calculation," a kind of prognostication. He said he could enliven "paper cutouts of men and horses, and of double-edged swords that could decapitate men." He also had a technique that could restore the dead to life. Such an accomplished magician was eventually recruited into a rebel band led by White Lotus sectarians.[21]

A Hupei literatus named Wu publicly ridiculed the powers of Chang Ch'i-shen, a highly respected local sorcerer, who was thought to be able to steal men's souls. Expecting Chang's revenge, Wu armed himself with a copy of the ancient divination manual, *The Classic of Changes (I-ching)*, and sat up that night waiting.[22] An armored demon burst into the room and attacked him, but when Wu smote it with the book it promptly collapsed upon the ground. Wu saw there only

A soul-calling ritual for a dead child.

a paper mannikin, which he inserted between the pages of the book. Next, two dark-faced goblins rushed in and were similarly disposed of. Shortly a tearful woman appeared at the door, claimed to be the wife of the sorcerer, and begged Wu to release her husband and sons, whose souls had entered the paper mannikins. There now remained at her home only three corpses, she wailed, which would not be revived once the cock had crowed. Wu scolded her, saying that she and her family had done enough damage and deserved their fate. However, out of pity he gave her back one mannikin. The next morning he learned that sorcerer Chang and his elder son had died, leaving only the younger son alive.[23]

The universal fear of paper mannikins as sorcerer's agents is surely associated with the common use of paper figures (of servants, horses, houses, tools, and other useful items) in funeral rites. De Groot relates that in Amoy, representations of human figures were used to inflict harm on one's enemies by sorcery,

> mostly very roughly made of two bamboo splinters fastened together crosswise, on one side of which is pasted some paper supposed to represent a human body. They are not larger than a hand, and those of men are distinguished from those of women by two shreds of paper, said to be boots. They are called "t'oe sin" [Mandarin: *t'i-shen*], "substitutes or surrogates of a person," and may be had, for a cash or so a piece in every shop where paper articles are made and sold for sacrifice to the dead and the gods, for they are also burnt as slaves for the dead in the other world.[24]

From mannikins used for transmittal to the shadow world for the *good* of the dead, to mannikins used as a conduit for magical *evil* toward the enemies they represent, to mannikins that may be used by others to harm oneself: evidently these connections were readily made. The use of "parts of the body and clothing" of the intended victim was another way of transmitting harm by biodynamic sorcery.[25] Biodynamic powers could also be acquired by the symbolic use of parts of human bodies: "The instrument of the sorcerer is a human soul, or some portion of it, obtained by appropriating certain parts of the body of a living person, but especially such organs as are deemed to be more especially impregnated with his mental or vital power. An image is then provided for his soul to settle in, and the latter totally subdued by the sorcerer to his will by charms and spells."[26]

Hair and the Evil Arts

As we observed in the sorcery prohibitions of the criminal code, biodynamic sorcery may have evoked both the Confucian horror of bodily mutilation and the culturally deeper horror of cannibalism. In any event, soulstealers' use of human hairs to extract soul-force and then transmit this force to paper cutouts of men and horses were magical practices well rooted in the popular mind. The same acts (extracting soul-force and using it to enhance one's power) were attributed to the masons of Te-ch'ing.

A properly trained sorcerer could use a victim's hair as a medium for extracting his soul even when the victim was a stranger—as was indeed the case with most of the soulstealing we encounter in 1768. There was no need to know such personal facts as the victim's name or his birth-signs. A Ming Dynasty novel relates the story of a certain monk who was born from an egg, and whose birth-signs down to the day and hour were therefore uncertain. An aspiring sorcerer hoped to use this "egg-monk" as the unwitting victim of a soulstealing experiment. His master assured him that, with his technique, it was not necessary to know the monk's birth-signs. "If you lack his birth-signs, you just need to get a piece of his underwear, along with some of his hair or fingernails," and recite over them the necessary spells.[27] If such items would do the trick, then perhaps even the victim's name might be dispensed with. A sorcerer of one's own community—a kinsman or neighbor—who knew one's name or birth-signs could inflict harm without the intermediacy of a personal object. This is what was attempted by peasant Shen Shih-liang (of Chapter 1), who wrote the names of his detested nephews upon paper slips for mason Wu to pound atop bridge pilings, and by the murderous Taoist of Ch'ang-chih, who enchanted his victim by discovering her birth-signs. But the outsider, the stranger-sorcerer, had to do his dirty work without such intimate knowledge. Here was the point of hair- and lapel-clipping: it placed one at the mercy of complete strangers. The notion that a sorcerer could enchant the inanimate ejecta or clothing of an unknown victim was the natural complement of a fear of strangers.

That hair has magical power is believed in many cultures. I suggested, in Chapter 3, some reasons why the Manchu tonsure may have been so stubbornly resisted by Chinese in the wake of the conquest. Here the same question arises in the context of sorcery: what was the connection among hair, power, and death? Edmund

Leach's suggestion that people subconsciously associate the hair with genitalia seems to me over-specific, given the range of ethnographic evidence on the subject.[28] I prefer the more general formula that he attributes to "older anthropologists" such as Frazer, to the effect that "ritual hair symbolizes some kind of metaphysical abstraction—fertility, soul-stuff, personal power."[29] Evidence from Punjabi culture shows that hair is used as an implement in sorcery precisely because it absorbs and stores fertility: a barren woman may clip hair from the head of a first-born child to cause him to be reborn in her own womb. The long, matted hair of a holy man *(sadhu)* is particularly prized because it has stored up so much fertility power (from the prolonged sexual abstinence of its wearer).[30] The power of hair to absorb and store spiritual power is certainly visible in Chinese evidence. In Cantonese funerals, hair seems to be an absorber of fertility-laden spiritual essences: married daughters and daughters-in-law of the deceased "are expected to rub their unbound hair against the coffin just prior to its removal from the village." James L. Watson believes that this intentional absorption of death pollution is thought to enhance fertility and lineage continuity, almost *as if* the soul of the deceased were reentering the lineage through the women's hair.[31] The soulstealing affair continually calls attention to the importance of hair in the lives of monks, and not only in the tonsure ceremony where they lose it. One reason monks were so often found carrying hair was that tonsure-masters commonly kept some hair of their disciples (those they had shaven and whose monastic education they were responsible for). But apparently not only intergenerational ties were served by this retention of hair. Monks were known to exchange such hair with one another along the road in order to "link destinies" *(chieh-yuan)*, perhaps to broaden the variety (and hence the potency?) of soul-force one was carrying and thereby reinforce one's links to the whole *sangha* or body of monks.[32]

Sorcery Prophylaxis

The soulstealing crisis of 1768 was marked by the frantic efforts of ordinary people to counter the baleful effects of sorcery, whether by lynching suspected sorcerers or by employing magical remedies. Magic could quash magic, as shown by the doughty Hupei literatus who smote demons with *The Classic of Changes*. Indeed, premodern China (and today's China to an extent we do not know) was an arena in which supernatural harm and supernatural remedies were arrayed in grim and deadly battle. Mankind was, in de Groot's words, "engaged every day in a restless defensive and offensive war" against malevolent spirits.[33] In this war there were, of course, professionals: the ritual specialists who conducted exorcisms and funerals and prescribed the geomantic alignment of buildings. The foot soldiers, however, were laymen. They relied upon a vast written and unwritten armory of spells, charms, and behavioral formulae for warding off evil.[34]

The use of charms and amulets to "ward off evil" *(pi-hsieh)* was universal. Much of this protective activity was directed at vengeful ghosts *(kuei)*, which proceeded from the *yang* aspect of the soul: spirits of the dead that had not been ritually cared for. In the same manner, there were remedies against magical evil inflicted by sorcery. Because the masons of Te-ch'ing were objects of a common popular suspicion of builders, let me illustrate charm remedies by referring to builders' hexes. According to the missionary folklorist N. B. Dennys, writing from Canton: "There is a well-known legend amongst the Cantonese of a builder having a grudge against a woman whose kitchen he was called upon to repair . . . The repairs were duly completed, but somehow or other the woman could never visit the kitchen without feeling ill. Convinced that witchcraft was at the bottom of it, she had the wall pulled down, and sure enough there was discovered in a hollow left for the purpose 'a clay figure in a posture of sickness.' "[35]

Why did people associate builders with sorcery? The Chinese believe that the ritual condition of buildings influences the worldly fortunes of their inhabitants. It is only natural, then, that builders had special responsibilities for practicing "good" magic when putting up structures. The timing, layout, and ritual order of construction were deemed essential to keeping evil influences out of the completed building. Of course, anyone capable of "good" magic is also capable of "bad." A carpentry manual popular in Ch'ing times, the *Lu-pan-ching*, accordingly contains not only rules for proper ritual construction but also baleful charms for builders to hide atop rafters or under floors. Quite evenhandedly, it also includes charms to be used *against* such evil builders.[36] Here are some examples of carpenters' baleful magic:

> A drawing of a broken tile inscribed with "Ice melts" [the rest of the expression is "tiles scatter"—implying collapse or dissolution]. Appended is a charm: "A piece of broken tile, a jagged edge, hidden in joint of roof-beam, husband die and wife remarry, sons move away,

servants flee, none will care for the estate." (To be hidden in a joint of the main roof-beam.)

A drawing of an ox-bone. The charm: "In center of room hide ox-bone, life-long toil, life's end death but no coffin, sons and grandsons will shoulder heavy burdens." (Bury under center of room.)

A drawing of a knife among coils of hair. The charm: "A sword worn in the hair. Sons and grandsons will leave and become monks. Having sons who found no families, perpetual misery. Widow and widower, orphaned and childless, do not forgive each other." (Bury under threshold.)

But the reader is also offered powerful magic for defending the household against builder-sorcerers:

When building a house, various kinds of carpenters, masons, and plasterers will plot to poison, curse, and harm the owner. On the day when the roof-beam is raised, offer a sacrifice of the three types of animal, laid out on a horizontal trestle, to all the gods. Then recite the following secret charm of Master Lu Pan [patron saint of carpenters]: "Evil artisans, do you not know that poisons and curses will rebound upon yourselves, and bring no harm to the owner?" Then recite seven times: "Let the artisan [responsible for the sorcery] meet misfortune." [Then say,] "I have received the proclamation of the Supreme Ruler [the Jade Emperor] ordering that I shall suffer no harm from others, and that all will redound to my good fortune: an urgent decree." Burn copy of charm in private place, especially where no pregnant woman can see you. Mix ashes with blood of black and yellow dog, then dissolve in wine. On day main roof-beam is raised, serve to builders (three cups to boss). He who is plotting sorcery will himself receive the harm. (Copy in vermilion ink and paste atop roofbeam.)

Such visions of offensive and defensive magic display the anxieties that affected most common people all the time: premature death, ritually faulty burial, loss of children, lack of proper ritual care after death. Although these anxieties center on building-sorcery, they really reflect a view of the world in which human fortunes are generally vulnerable to supernatural vandalism. In the unending confrontation between gods *(shen)* and ghosts *(kuei)*, human life needs the protection of whatever arts *(fa* or *shu)* can be mobilized, either from ritual specialists or from laymen's lore.[37]

Suspicions of the Clergy

In the campaign against soulstealing, Buddhist monks and the occasional Taoist priest were the prime suspects from the very beginning.

凡造房屋木石泥水匠作諸色人等蠱毒魘魅發害主人上樑之日須用三牲福禮橫匾一架祭告

諸神將魯班先師祕符一道念咒云惡匠無知蠱毒魘魅自作自當主人無傷暗誦七遍本匠遭殃吾奉

太上老君勅令他作吾無妨百物化為吉祥急急律令　即將符焚於無人處不可四眼見取黃黑狗血

暗藏酒內上樑時將此酒連遞匠頭三杯餘者分飲眾匠凡有魘魅自受其殃諸事符解

此符用硃砂書符貼正樑上

1

房屋中間藏牛骨
終朝辛苦忙碌碌
老來身死沒棺材
後代兒孫壓肩內
埋屋中間

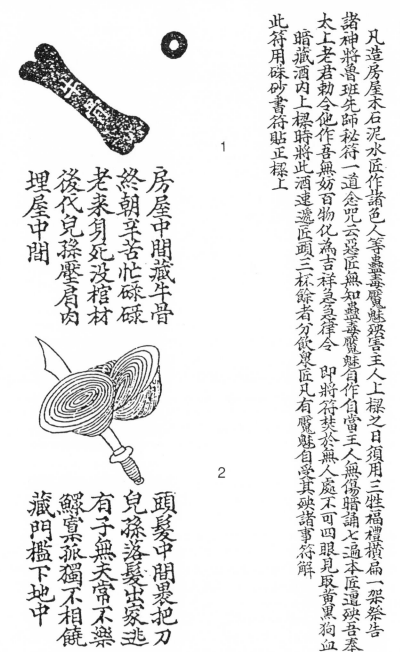

2

頭髮中間暴把刀
兒孫落髮出家逃
有子無夫常不樂
鰥寡孤獨不相饒
藏門檻下地中

Two builders' curses and an antidote: (1) the ox-bone curse;
(2) the knife-in-hair curse; (3) the householder's ritual
antidote for all such curses.

Why was Hungli so quick to believe in these monkish master-sorcerers and to turn the energies of the state against them? And why was the common man so quick to pounce on the nearest monk whenever fears of sorcery crossed his mind?

Official Treatment of the Clergy

The commoner's daily battle against evil spirits was mirrored, at the very top of society, by the concerns of the imperial state. Even as it prohibited sorcery, the state was itself constantly dealing with the spirit world. On every level of officialdom, from the imperial palace to the dustiest county yamen, agents of the state were intermediaries between man and spirits. Their role marks them, in a sense, as priests: communicating with the gods on behalf of mankind to ensure the proper ordering of worldly events, primarily good conditions for agriculture and peace for the realm. At the top, the emperor himself presided over solemn annual sacrifices to Heaven and Earth. At the bottom, the county magistrate (a little emperor in his own realm) regarded the City God (*ch'eng-huang*, a magistrate of the spirit world), as an essential coadjutor in governing.

Although the common man was barred from celebrating the imperial and bureaucratic cults, he did share some of their theology. Formal worship of Heaven was a monopoly of the monarch, but the common people were already inclined to believe in Heaven's power in human affairs. Because everyone's fate was governed by heavenly forces (the succession of the "five actions," *wu-hsing*, and the interplay of the cosmological powers of *yin* and *yang*), people easily accepted the connection of imperial Heaven-worship with human felicity. And because the fate of the individual soul after death was thought to depend on a judgment of merit by the City God, commoners considered that worship of that deity by local officials was performed on behalf of the community as a whole.[38] If the state were to sustain these popular beliefs in its own spiritual role, it had to watch carefully for potential competitors.

The state's inclusive claim to be the rightful manager of man's relations with spirits led to elaborate procedures for regulating the organized Buddhist and Taoist clergy. There was, of course, something a bit absurd about the state's rules regarding the clergy. The majority of ritual specialists were not "enrolled," in any formal sense, under organizations that could be held to account for their activities.

The priests of the popular religion, who headed an eclectic, deeply rooted system of community practices, were not even full-time clerics, in the sense that we might expect from a Western context. For the state to forbid ambiguous status, insist on clear-cut demonstration of master-disciple relationships, and require registration of all religious practioners were ludicrous presumptions in view of the actual practice of Chinese religion. Marginality (as the state would define it) was built into the social status of most ritual specialists. To fasten upon them regulations such as those I shall summarize here would have erased popular religion itself, which of course the state (in those days) would have found an impossible task. This simple fact gives discussions of "state control of religion" an unreal and fantastic aspect.[39]

Nevertheless, the attempt was made. We have to regard it as an indication of state attitudes, rather than as a "system" that actually functioned in anything like the way it was intended to. According to the rules, all temples and monasteries, along with their clergy, had to be registered and licensed. It was illegal to build a temple without formal approval of the Board of Rites. In the same spirit, the state had for centuries required Buddhist monks and Taoist priests to obtain certificates of ordination *(tu-tieh)*.[40] Why was the late imperial state so concerned to register and control ritual specialists? When the ninth-century T'ang empire confiscated vast monastic properties and returned tens of thousands of monks to lay life, the reason was partly economic: a man's withdrawal to a monastery removed him from the liabilities of taxes and labor service and so deprived the state of revenue. Yet this purpose was irrelevant in the late empires, when labor-service obligations had been commuted to money payments and assessed along with the land tax, in effect replacing corvée by paid labor. A review of the Ch'ing efforts to control the clergy suggests other purposes.

Although licensing and registration of monks and priests had been practiced by the preceding Ming Dynasty, it was not until 1674 that the Manchu throne issued its first general instructions on state governance of the clergy. In Peking, offices were established for the supervision of Buddhists and Taoists, each to be staffed by sixteen monks or priests, members apparently to be initially selected by the Board of Rites, but to be replaced by co-optation from among the capital clergy. The members of these supervisory bodies were to be reported to the Board of Civil Office *(li-pu)*.[41] A parallel system was decreed for the provinces: offices staffed by selected monks and priests were established in prefectures, departments, and counties.[42] They reported up the regular chain of bureaucratic command.

The supervisory offices were to regulate the deportment of monks, priests, and nuns, to ensure that they honored their vows by proper discipline. Beyond this, however, was the all-important licensing. Here the point was not so much to maintain the purity of the clergy themselves as to insure against unreliable laymen representing them- selves as clerics. The Throne feared that "riffraff and ruffians" would falsely assume clerical habit and claim to be invoking the spirits of (religious) patriarchs *(tsu-shih)* through divination. Such powers to communicate with spirits and foretell the future would generate "heterodox doctrines" and "wild talk" that could attract ignorant people to become their followers and form illegal sects. By heterodox doctrines and wild talk, the Throne meant not only pretensions to magical powers by sect leaders but also prognostications about the fate of the existing political order. Imperial decrees on this subject show special sensitivity to religious activities in Peking, the seat of dynastic power. Temples and monasteries in the capital were for- bidden to "establish sects and hold assemblies where men and women mix together" (a hallmark of popular religion—and further evidence, to the imperial mind, of moral degeneracy). Nor were they allowed to "erect platforms to perform operas and collect money, sacrifice to the gods, or carry them in procession."[43]

Emperor Hungli himself was particularly irritated by ambiguity of status, which led him to try to extend the regulations on the *organized* clergy (those in major monasteries or temples) to the vast majority of ritual specialists in lay communities. His first major pronouncement on the clergy concerned persons who might be called secular clergy— actually the majority of ritual specialists: those who lived permanently outside monasteries and temples, owned property, and even married. Such men played a vital role in communities by serving in funerals and exorcisms, and otherwise filling people's needs for ritual services. They were subject neither to monastic discipline nor to state control. After denouncing the decayed state of clerical morals and learning, Hungli ordered that these secular practitioners be forced either to live in monasteries or temples, or else return to lay life. Their prop- erty, save for a bare subsistence allowance, was to be confiscated and given to the poor. When it appeared that the decree was causing panic among clergy in general and provoking disorder in the prov- inces, Hungli protested that he had never meant to harm those who hewed to clerical discipline. The problem, rather, was public order. These secular personnel "steal the name of clergy but lack their discipline. They even engage in depraved and illicit activities. They are hard to investigate and control." The reason he was requiring that they obtain ordination certificates "was so that riffraff would not be able to hide in their midst and disgrace Buddhism and Taoism." The newly enthroned monarch was evidently surprised by the reaction to his harsh measures. He now recoiled from the confiscation order: "Finally, how can Our Dynasty's relief of the poor depend on the seizure of such petty properties?" The decree was rescinded. But, burdening the monarch's mind, there remained the irksome existence of a mass of ritual specialists who were not under any kind of state supervision.[44]

Hungli's view of the Buddhist clergy was colored by prudish Neo-Confucian attitudes toward sex. Of course, the clergy's own internal regulations required chastity, and the *Ch'ing Code* prescribed special penalties for monks who lured married women into adultery. Yet clerical fornication seems to have evoked from Hungli a particular loathing and vindictiveness. In 1768 a monk near Nanking was accused of having sexual relations with several married peasant women. Governor-general G'aojin noted that the Nanking area "easily harbors criminal monks *(chien-seng)*," because there were so many clerical establishments that it was hard to keep track of them all. Accordingly, G'aojin had his county officials keep alert for bad clerical behavior. Authorities near Nanking discovered that the present culprit, a "depraved monk," had been engaging in such conduct for years and had even bribed a local headman not to report it. He had also amassed considerable wealth by renting out plots of his monastery's land to tenants. "For such a depraved monk to amass wealth and flout the law at will [through sexual misconduct] is a great injury to the morals of the community," wrote G'aojin. The ordinary penalties in the *Ch'ing Code* seemed insufficient for this culprit, who should, he recommended, be sent to Ili to serve as a slave in the military colonies. Hungli replied that even such a penalty would be "too light." "Such depraved and evil monks have long injured local morals." The culprit should be "beaten to death immediately in order to make manifest Our punishments. How can he deserve anything more lenient?" G'aojin replied that he was indeed to blame for recommending too light a sentence. Not only would the criminal be beaten to death, but it would be done in the presence of all the monks of Nanking, as a warning to them all. Two-thirds of the monastery's property was to be confiscated.[45]

This bloody one-upsmanship between Hungli and his imperial in-law suggests that monk-bashing was a source of moral satisfaction for rulers who considered the clergy to be mostly hypocrites and corrupters of the community. Such expectations of clerical behavior made it plausible to connect them with other harmful and immoral activities, such as sorcery. Aggravated by officials' alarm over what they perceived to be an alarming growth of the clerical underclass, described in Chapter 2, these imperial fears of the clergy were made to order for a nationwide sorcerer-hunt. Along with beggars, the clergy, particularly those in small temples or out on the road, were among China's most vulnerable groups, with no protection forthcoming from kin or community. But why were the general public such avid participants in the persecution of 1768?

Clergy, Beggars, and the Common Man

In view of the prominent place of Buddhist monks among sorcery suspects in the 1768 scare, it is somewhat surprising that the two major eighteenth-century collections of supernatural tales (by P'u Sung-ling and Yuan Mei) picture the Buddhist clergy as relatively benign. Sorcery aplenty is attributed to Taoists, such as the homicidal Taoist beggar depicted at the beginning of this chapter. By contrast, Buddhists are attacked mainly for hypocrisy or for immorality (particularly sexual license—a theme common in European anticlericalism). The phrase "sorcerous Taoists and licentious Buddhists" *(yao-tao yin-seng)* sums up the difference.[46] We shall have to look beneath the level of elite story-writers to discover a plausible source for popular fears of monks.[47]

In a society fearful of strangers, several aspects of monks' lives seem to have placed them in harm's way. One is the long, sometimes permanent condition of being a novice: the period between taking the tonsure ("leaving the family"—*ch'u-chia*) and receiving ordination. Although being ordained required a long period of study under a master (a senior monk) and generally had to be completed in one of the elite "public monasteries," becoming a novice was relatively easy and informal. The subject pronounced his intention of renouncing lay life, had his head shaved by his tonsure-master (the "master" or *shih-fu* who would now be responsible for his training), and began to observe the "ten prohibitions" (chastity, vegetarianism, and so on). Having left his own family, he now acquired a monastic "family," in which his master served as a surrogate parent and his fellow novices as brothers. A very large proportion of monks were brought up in the monastic life from adolescence. Their training generally took place in small "hereditary" temples: those run by monastic "families" and passed down from one generation to the next. Only years later, if at all, was a monk ordained at one of the large "public" monasteries.

In the meantime the novice was part of a large intermediate stratum of the unordained, a stratum easily entered and indeed easily exited. Although classified by the state (and by society at large) as a "monk" *(seng)*, he was forbidden to reside in any of the large, elite monasteries. Such "monks" probably constituted the majority of the Buddhist clergy, and most soulstealing suspects (including two of the Hsiao-shan monks; see Chapter 1) were in fact of this group. The government's suspicions centered on such men, and it would not be surprising to find that popular fears ran along the same channels: these were men in limbo, neither of the orthodox family system nor of the certified clerical elite. This fact should lead us to question the usefulness of the designation "monk," which was used in government documents to describe virtually anyone with a robe and a shaved head, whatever his state of religious commitment or education. Many of these men, or perhaps even most of them, were not unambiguously in any of the approved categories that gave bureaucrats the reassuring idea that they had society under control.

Rootlessness was another suspicious mark of the novice. Once tonsured, he was often cast into the life of the road. The search for religious instruction, or a pilgrimage to pay respects to the grave of an "ancestor" of his monastic family, were common reasons for travel. Another, perhaps the most common, was begging: small temples commonly lacked enough land endowment to support their inhabitants, and lacking adequate donations or fees from requiem masses, begging was the only way out. Monastic begging was not universally approved (some monasteries forbade it), and attitudes toward mendicant monks were sometimes not much different from those toward beggars in general.[48] Nevertheless, eighteenth-century documents show that begging monks were everywhere to be seen.

Popular attitudes toward monks were probably conditioned by both of these situations: the ambiguous status of the novices (of the *sangha* but not really in it), and by the general ambivalence toward begging (an occupation of the rootless and shiftless, yet somehow sanctified by the holy poverty of the clergy). Toward Taoist priests, popular attitudes were probably more unreservedly fearful.

Taoist practitioners were conventionally associated with various forms of magic (alchemy, exorcism, and the search for immortality). This made them logical suspects when the "evil arts" were at issue. Although their normal community functions were such benign practices as healing-exorcism, their demonic role in fiction suggests that magical arts were considered to be turned readily to evil uses.[49] Buddhist monks, whose main community function was assisting the souls of the departed through the underworld, were not sorcerers in quite the same sense, which may explain their relative benignity in popular stories. Yet we may wonder whether, in the popular mind, the various sorts of ritual specialists were as sharply distinguished when they were strangers to the community. Wandering Buddhist monks might have seemed unpredictable and inscrutable, for example, when compared with monks based in a local temple whom everyone saw at neighborhood funerals. And it takes little imagination to perceive the menace of a "wandering Taoist." Local ritual specialists were comparatively "safe," in that their community roles were known. Indeed the neighborhood exorcist probably seemed about as threatening as the family doctor. But outsiders were another matter. To them might reasonably attach more general suspicions about people with special ritual powers.

Where commoners might fear ritual specialists for their magic, gentry scorned them for their shiftlessness. A collection of lineage homilies from Chekiang points out that every occupation has its "principle of livelihood" *(sheng-li)*, whether scholar, farmer, artisan, or merchant. "But then there are those lazy, idle drifters who wander about as Buddhist monks, Taoist priests, vagrants, or ruffians, who are registered in no native place. These people are not living according to any principle of livelihood. There is no 'principle' for living without a principle of livelihood, just stealing a living from Heaven and Earth."[50]

The taint of death pollution. An authority on Cantonese society writes that funerary priests (in this case, roughly speaking, Taoist) bear a definite social stigma "because of the nature of their work," rather like morticians in our own society. "Their neighbors . . . are never completely comfortable in their presence." The reason is the death pollution that is thought to adhere to their bodies. Even though these priests "make every effort to avoid direct contact with the corpse or with the coffin," they cannot wholly dissociate themselves from the dangerously polluting aspect of their profession.[51] Ritual specialists in the community make their living particularly at funerals, a job that puts them continually near the coffins of the newly dead. We have, as yet, no confirmation that fear of death pollution, so evident in South China, contributed to popular ambivalence toward the clergy in the rest of the country, but we cannot rule it out.

The sorcerer as outsider. The mix of reverence and fear in which commoners held ritual specialists is especially meaningful in the light of the clerical underclass of late imperial times. Wanderers with special spiritual powers were a unique sort of danger, and perhaps (given Min O-yuan's account) an increasingly visible one by the mid-eighteenth century. Studies of other cultures suggest that sorcery is often imputed to outsiders: Alan Macfarlane notes, on the basis of African and English data, that "men who wander about the country" are natural targets of sorcery accusations.[52] Sorcery, which (unlike witchcraft) involves no innate powers but merely the manipulation of magic techniques, is essentially impersonal: the evil done is more like vandalism than vendetta. The absence of community ties therefore would make wandering mendicants (whether clerical or lay) logical suspects. Though they would lack a personal motive, they would also lack social inhibitions and community responsibilities. Add to this the xenophobia of the peasant villager toward outsiders of any sort, and sorcery is quite a reasonable fear.[53]

In Chinese popular religion, the pervasive fear of aliens is expressed in the serious ritual business of propitiating "ghosts" *(kuei)*. These are conceived as unattached spirits who lack the family ties that would otherwise provide the sacrifices that would ease their distress and dispel their rancor. Dangerous social and political marginality in the *yang* or temporal world is closely associated with dangerous spiritual marginality (ghostliness) in the *yin* or shadow world.[54]

In the cases of 1768, foreignness was nearly always a detonator of soulstealing panic. It was often noticed, at first contact, as linguistic difference, by which strangers were instantly marked. Here the contrast with shamanism could not be sharper. In Cantonese communities, for example, shamans must be well-established members of the community in order to perform their job, which is to hold at bay the malevolent spirits of the discontented dead: a task that requires intimate knowledge of village social relationships.[55] It appears that "good" or "safe" ritual specialists (community priests, shamans) *must* be community members, whereas "bad" or "dangerous" ones (sorcerers) *cannot* be. If so, it is likely either that fear naturally attaches to aliens, or that sorcery accusations within the community would be so harmful to social relations that they cannot be permitted—or perhaps even conceived of. Hence it is upon the stranger that suspicion must fall.[56]

The Social Terrorism of Beggars

In one respect, mendicant clergy were more vulnerable to sorcery charges than were lay beggars. Those who make a profession of communicating with the spirit world can readily be imagined to have ways of making spirit forces serve their personal ends: the very stuff of sorcery. Nevertheless, sorcery charges were also leveled at many lay beggars during the soulstealing panic. Most often they were merely doing the legwork for evil monks (going about clipping queues for them). Fear of beggars, however, had nothing to do with mastery of ritual "techniques." Quite the opposite: it was their ritual invulnerability that made them dangerous.

Monks and beggars were the poorest and most defenseless groups in Chinese society. They were supported by no influential kinsmen, they had little or no economic reserves. Monks, as we have seen, had such important functions in community ritual that they could not be dispensed with. But how were beggars able to persist in their way of life despite public scorn and loathing? The reason seems to be that, however helpless in the respectable social world, they had the power to make the public fear them. People had two reasons to fear beggars: "contamination" and "ritual sabotage," which are in fact closely related.

Contamination. Dread of contamination enabled a beggar to make people pay to keep him at a distance. What all observers agree was a carefully cultivated (and conventional) filthy and ragged appearance—the beggars' uniform, as it were—may have excited pity, but also stirred revulsion; people shunned a beggar's touch. This practical concern to avoid diseases (such as running sores, which beggars ostentatiously displayed) was closely joined to a fear of spiritual pollution. The death of a beggar on one's premises could have "drastic cosmological implications," because his ghost would then have to be exorcised at some expense and with dubious effect.[57] The job of

A beggar makes a scene in front of an official's palanquin and is wrestled away by yamen attendants. More beggars, carrying their sleeping mats, are exiting over the bridge, at right.

pallbearers, conventionally allotted to beggars, also tainted them with death pollution, which was good to stay away from. To be "touched" for money by such people was preferable to being touched physically.

Ritual sabotage. Here we are cutting close to the core of soulstealing fear. Where was respectable society most vulnerable to attack? All the riches and connections in the world were no protection from being bullied by men who had nothing to lose. Hence it is no surprise that weddings and funerals were occasions of customary payoffs to beggars. Failure to give the beggars their due could (and sometimes did) result in gangs of ragged and filthy people barging into the festivities, their very presence embarrassing the hosts and, much worse, ruining the efficacy of the ritual. The danger was bad enough at weddings but could be ritually fatal at funerals: one nineteenth-century account tells of angry beggars actually jumping into a grave to prevent a burial from proceeding.[58] People were vulnerable to such terrorism because they felt their defenses against supernatural forces to be so tenuous, and the battle between beneficent and hostile spirits so evenly drawn. As we have seen, the nexus between body and soul was another danger point that was vulnerable to attack by malevolent forces. In this situation, social outcasts gained a peculiar power, precisely because they themselves were already so polluted or so unlucky that they seemed to care neither for social "face" nor for cosmological fortune. The mere "touch" of the queue- or lapel-clipping beggar was enough to awaken fears of lethal pollution. By extension, a beggar's anger was cause for alarm because his polluted nature was entirely compatible with magical terrorism. The beggar's *curse* at one who refused alms carried more than mere rhetorical force.

Our exploration of Chinese sorcery reveals two related structures of fear, both of which involve the fragility of a spiritual-corporeal link. The popular fear was of soul-loss: the delicacy of the bond between soul and body meant that agencies either natural or supernatural could sever it. Dreams and disease were dangers to the stability of this link, as was of course malevolent magic. The imperial fear related not to the individual but to the collectivity. The integrity and durability of Heaven's Mandate required recurrent confirmation through the imperial rites. It could be severed by natural agents (the cosmological forces visible only in nature's disasters and omens), as well as by turbulent men who wished the state ill. Such men's communication with spirits was both stoutly denied and sternly prohibited. The way imperial dignitaries scoffed at any spirit-link except their own confirmed a deeply founded anxiety about the longevity of their own mandate. For commoners, the sorcerer's magic menaced the vulnerable link between body and soul. For the imperial elite, it imperiled the tenuous link with heavenly powers. What bred such fears at both the top and the bottom of the social scale, in the third quarter of the eighteenth century, is worth considering after we have pursued the soulstealing story further. Against the soulstealing evil the Throne is now about to mount a national campaign, in the course of which the link between sorcery and politics will become plainer.

CHAPTER 6

The Campaign
in the Provinces

A nationwide prosecution of sorcery ignited a struggle between the emperor and his provincial officials, a struggle no less intense because it was well disguised. The fuel for this smouldering combat lay in the system of official accountability: failure to catch a criminal was punishable through the system of sanctions run by the Board of Civil Office in Peking. An official's supervisor was supposed to impeach him for bad performance, and failure to impeach was itself ground for impeachment by higher levels. On the exalted stratum of provincial governors-general and governors, administrative failure was taken as a breach of the monarch's personal trust.

The whole system of accountability revolved around control of information. An official could not be punished for failing to prosecute a crime, if the crime was not officially known to have been committed. This absurdly simple fact underlay the strained relations between Throne and bureaucracy in the soulstealing case. Although the Ch'ing regime lacked a professional secret service, the Throne had "eyes and ears" in the provinces. Through such a private source the Shantung cases had emerged. Through such a source Hungli discovered that provincial officials had covered up the sorcery cases of the past spring. It hardly matters whether the cover-up had resulted from official scorn of popular superstition (elite agnosticism about sorcery) or whether the tonsure offense hinted by the Soochow and Hsu-k'ou-chen affairs seemed, to provincial officials, too hot to handle. Hungli believed it happened because his officials feared awkwardness: court cases that might disrupt their comfortable routines, impeachments that might rend their patronage networks. We may forgive his suspicions: for a full two months, not a single provincial bureaucrat—whether Manchu or Han—had brought sorcery to the Throne's attention on his own initiative. Those suspicions were confirmed by the initial responses to his demands for information and action.

Hungli's Provincial Bureaucracy

How effective were Hungli's provincial prosecutors? China's civil provincial bureaucracy in 1768 was a tiny elite corps of only sixty-three men. I use "provincial bureaucracy" in a special sense: men with duties on the provincial level or higher. Such duties included (1) comprehensive responsibility for the affairs of one province (the governors) or two provinces (the governors-general);[1] (2) specialized posts on the scale of one province (the provincial treasurers and provincial judges); and (3) specialized posts of a nonterritorial nature (such as the superintendents of the Grand Canal and Yellow River). Here, surely, was the world's most exclusive club. To enter it was to join the monarch's circle of special trust and personal communication. Its members (like officials of ministerial rank in the capital) were distinguished by being allowed, indeed required, to communicate directly and confidentially with the Throne. Although it lacked the old-boy co-optation and leather-chair coziness of a "club" properly so-called (that is, its internal cohesion was weak), membership gave a man a special self-image that transcended the world of the lower bureaucracy.[2]

The Men in Charge

To prosecute this case, Hungli depended on an experienced group of middle-aged and elderly men, each with a record of service in several provinces, and who had been (at their upper ranks) serving in the provincial bureaucracy for about a decade.[3] Manchus made up a disproportionately large fraction of the group as a whole (38 percent), and an even larger fraction (58 percent) at the top levels (governors-general and governors). For the provincial bureaucracy as a whole, this was a substantial ethnic shift from the beginning of Hungli's reign: since 1736, the Manchu component had increased by 84 percent; those cultural hybrids, the Han bannermen, by 33 percent (though the number was so small as to be insignificant); and the ordinary Han had *decreased* by 51 percent. The composition of the governors-general remained almost unchanged, but there was a substantial increase in the proportion of Manchus in governor's rank (mainly at the expense of the Han bannermen), and another substantial increase of Manchus (at the expense of Han) in the post of provincial treasurer. More Manchus were working their way into provincial office by the standard route of promotion from provincial judgeships. This might be expected as Manchus became more sinicized and better at handling the affairs of the largely Han lower bureaucracy. But it also suggests a deliberate imperial policy to increase the representation of ethnic Manchus in local government.

By the standards of the eighteenth-century world, Hungli's province chiefs in 1768 ruled immense populations. In the three-province jurisdiction of the Liangkiang governor-general lived more than seventy million people, a population more than twice that of France at the time. The governor of Kiangsu, the largest province in this group and the most populous in the nation, ruled perhaps thirty million, at least triple the contemporary population of the United Kingdom. Even the smallest province involved in the soulstealing case, Shensi, contained some eight million people, which was roughly the size of Great Britain, minus Scotland.[4] Clearly the tautness of such a ship had to be far short of what we (and the Chinese) are used to in modern bureaucracies. Chiefs of such immense societies had to be left substantial discretion. Yet the vast powers of these men were kept in check by numerous institutional safeguards. Moreover, collusion among them was balked by the confidential palace memorial system, in which a man never knew what was being reported to the Throne by his colleague next door. Finally, the emperor kept his province chiefs on the move by frequent transfers.[5]

Frequent rotation meant that province chiefs could hardly be deeply knowledgable about the special problems of their jurisdictions, and that much of the work of governance devolved upon the permanent staff of clerks.[6] Each member of this highly mobile elite corps was kept busily circulating among provincial capitals, yet was bound to the imperial center by two iron cords: the personnel dossier in the Board of Civil Office that (as was the case with all officials) bore his cumulative record of promotions and demotions; and, more important, his personal tie of clientage and obligation to the monarch.

Although we are accustomed to calling provincial officials "bureaucrats," in an American political context these men would surely be

called "political appointments." Although most had followed standard tracks into the provincial bureaucracy (either from a circuit-
intendancy, which oversaw several prefectures, or from a junior vice-
presidency of one of the Six Boards), their elevation to provincial
rank immediately signaled a special relationship to the Throne, a
relationship marked by powerful rituals of loyalty and dependency.
From such favored servants, the emperor expected not just reliability,
but zeal: not merely to report accurately on local events, but to go
the extra mile to further his royal objectives. Upon these qualities,
more than upon the routine dossiers maintained by the Board of
Civil Office, hinged the special trust and favor by which their future
careers would be governed.

How did this special relationship affect the performance of a governor's job? The aspect of his job that most concerns us here is the
insidious linkage at the heart of Chinese law enforcement: a territorial official was simultaneously policeman, prosecutor, and judge.
Indeed, in every jurisdiction, the judicial power was simply an aspect
of the executive. At the county level, the magistrate was in charge of
arrests, prosecutions, and trials. Cases that carried penalties heavier
than flogging were referred upward to the governor's court, and
sentences in all capital cases were automatically reviewed by the
emperor. Because sorcery in many of its guises was classed by the
Ch'ing Code as a capital crime, soulstealing cases might be expected
to make their way to provincial courts, and ultimately to Peking. The
governor had to exhort his subordinates to scour the counties and
prefectures for sorcerers and then judge the cases of those they
caught.

As Hungli turned up the pressure to crush the "evil arts," the
governor-as-prosecutor loomed larger than the governor-as-judge.
Most provincial officials in 1768 had some legal experience, generally
obtained in the post of provincial judge through which they had
entered the provincial bureaucracy. Yet few were legal scholars or
administrators of wide reputation,[7] and I wonder whether many of
the others had judicial self-images firm enough to withstand the
political pressures inherent in their positions. Pleasing the monarch
was a central part of administering the law.

The Communication System

Making government work effectively required carefully organizing
the flow of information. From the point of view of the eighteenth-

century monarchy, this involved two problems: (1) separating routine from urgent business, so that problems could be handled at the appropriate levels and in the right order; and (2) ensuring that reports from field officials were timely and accurate. Neither problem was ever solved to Hungli's satisfaction.[8]

To deal with the first problem, Hungli had inherited from his predecessors a documentary system with a routine track and a confidential track. Ordinary matters were communicated by routine memorials *(t'i-pen)* through the Grand Secretariat, a committee of the highest ministers that oversaw the operation of the Six Boards (the ministries of the six traditional functional divisions of government). Through this channel flowed regular reports on tax receipts, criminal justice, public works, and routine personnel matters. The forms of these documents were rigidly prescribed, and irregularities were grounds for impeachment. Although today's social historian finds in these "routine" memorials the very pith of everyday Chinese life, the medium was ill suited to urgent matters that required speed and confidentiality, including such matters as sedition.

Such sensitive or high-priority information followed the confidential track: a direct, personal line of communication between every high provincial official and the Throne. Upward documents, carried either by the sender's personal servant or by military courier, reached the emperor's desk quickly and discreetly. His Majesty would normally brush his comments or instructions in vermilion ink directly on the memorial, then dispatch it back to its sender. These sealed missives we call "palace memorials" *(tsou-che),* because they were later preserved in the palace.[9]

The "palace memorial" was a personal document. Besides urgent local affairs, these documents dealt with matters growing from an official's personal relationship to the monarch.[10] The form was simpler (for example, the elaborate expression of the sender's complete official rank was omitted in favor of a simple statement of the post he held). An exchange in the confidential track exuded reciprocity: the sender was expressing loyalty and gratitude by imparting confidential intelligence to his master; the monarch, in turn, replied with a stern (but occasionally also warm) paternalism. The routine memorial was shaped by bureaucratic form, the palace memorial by interpersonal ritual. The routine memorial communicated office to office, the palace memorial man to man.

The emperor's responses to official reports, as well as initiatives taken on his own, also followed both routine and confidential channels. The routine response might be no more than pro forma approval of a rescript drafted by the Grand Secretariat, perhaps instructing that one of the Six Boards take action, or perhaps simply that the information be filed. A more portentous matter or a normative pronouncement might be communicated by an "open edict" *(ming-fa shang-yü)*, which was sent to every jurisdiction in the empire for ceremonious posting. The confidential response was nearly always, in the first instance, a "vermilion rescript" *(chu-p'i)*, an instruction or comment brushed personally by His Majesty on the sender's memorial. The memorial, bearing the royal response, was then returned to its sender, generally through the emperor's powerful privy council, the Grand Council. Sometimes a returned memorial might be adorned with vermilion in many places, as the monarch responded to particular points by writing between the lines. A more formally organized response was drawn up as a "decree" *(chih)*, which the Grand Council drafted at his instructions after having considered the original memorial, and then dispatched to the field as a "court letter" *(t'ing-chi* or *tzu-chi)*. The "open edict" was a general message to the bureaucracy as a whole; the "vermilion rescript" and "court letter" were swift, confidential, and precise action-documents designed to instruct or admonish particular officials.

For understanding the emperor's own role in the soulstealing crisis, and indeed in Chinese politics in general, the key is vermilion. Rescripts on memorials show us his instant, unmediated responses to reports from the field. And although court letters were drafted by those lofty ghostwriters, the grand councillors, the monarch always checked the final copies and often added his own remarks and editorial comments in vermilion. The amended version then went out to the field. The recipient was thus made aware of what points His Majesty considered particularly important, and the vermilion personal touch reminded him that the court letter as a whole faithfully reflected the imperial mind.

Cover-up in Kiangnan

Some Embarrassing Discoveries

The Liangkiang governor-generalship, which controlled the provinces of Kiangsu, Kiangsi, and Anhwei, was the empire's richest and most demanding provincial post. At its core was the Yangtze Delta region, which, along with part of neighboring Chekiang, was the Kiangnan spawning ground of soulstealing. In this sensitive post, Hungli was served by the eminent G'aojin, a master of river conservancy, who was sixty-two at the time of the soulstealing crisis. G'aojin was nothing if not well connected: a member of one of the upper three banners (His Majesty's own), his Han ancestors had served for generations as bondservants of the imperial household. This Manchuized Chinese was nephew of a grand secretary and first cousin of an imperial concubine (which connection had led to the emancipation of his lineage by imperial decree). Rather than follow the usual banner-insider's route to high office, G'aojin had started his public career as a lowly county magistrate at age twenty-nine and only reached his first provincial-level post fourteen years later.[11]

The governor-general had ample reason to feel secure in offering a bland response to his master's inquiry about sorcery in Liangkiang. In early August, he wrote that indeed he had heard rumors of soulstealing in Chekiang while temporarily in Soochow as acting governor the preceding spring. Local officials told him that the rumors came from the Hangchow area, and that Kiangsu itself had experienced no queue-clipping outrages. Once the rumor-spreaders were arrested and the spreading of rumors prohibited, the problem vanished. But Hungli's vermilion rejoinder showed that he believed not a word: other provinces had reported queue-clipping, so "how can Kiangnan alone have none?" The Kiangnan bureaucracy was "substandard," and its "practice of making something appear to be nothing is really hateful."[12]

The monarch now turned his ire on G'aojin's subordinate, Governor Jangboo of Kiangsu, where the Shantung confessions had revealed that several important sorcerers were hiding. An experienced Manchu official and wily bureaucratic infighter, Jangboo had risen steadily through the provincial ranks, gaining Hungli's trust for his effective prosecution of a Shansi corruption case of 1766.[13] Another corruption scandal confronted him when he moved into the governor's yamen at Soochow in the spring of 1768. This time the trouble was in the Yangchow salt administration. The most prominent official culprit, G'aoheng, was embarrassingly well connected: his first cousin was none other than Jangboo's superior, G'aojin, and his sister was the imperial concubine whose charms had won freedom for Gaojin's lineage.[14] It was just as Jangboo was prosecuting this awkward case that the hunt for soulstealers began in earnest. Governor

Jangboo quickly found himself the target of heated court letters from Peking.

The latest Shantung intelligence (confessions of beggars Ts'ai and Chin, complete with names of ringleaders) had been distributed to all high provincial officials in the east. By mid-August, however, it was apparent to Hungli that his province chiefs were not following up leads to the chief sorcerers, monks Yü-shih (Kiangsu) and Wu-yuan (Chekiang). Though numerous arrests had been made in Chihli and Shantung (Funihan had now caught five more queue-clippers), the hotbed of soulstealing in the Yangtze provinces had yielded no culprits.

To his embarrassment, Jangboo now had to admit that certain "rumors" about queue-clipping sorcery had seeped across the Chekiang border the previous spring. He had seen no need to report them, because his "investigations" turned up no evidence that anyone had actually been clipped. In early August, however, the plot thickened, as reports came in from northern Kiangsu districts near the Grand Canal. Back in the late spring, in the county of An-tung, a certain Liu Wu had clipped the queue of a man named Tsou and was now in official custody. In a P'ei-hsien market crowd, a Shantung man named Yao was reported to have "bumped" the mother of one Yang, causing the lady to feel "dizzy." And in P'i-chou, a man named Wang had hidden in some bushes, accosted the wife of Ch'iu Ta-feng and clipped a piece of cloth from her lapel. Of the last two criminals, the first had been beaten to death by the crowd, the other hounded to suicide. The surviving culprit was a wily rascal: Liu Wu had convinced county authorities that he had clipped the queue only so he could cut purses during the ensuing uproar. Governor Jangboo assured the emperor that he would interrogate him "personally." He was also rushing agents to Hai-chou to intercept the master-sorcerer Ming-yuan, who was scheduled to turn up there August 26, according to the confession of his apprentice, Han P'ei-hsien. He had also instructed local officials to be on the watch for the master-sorcerer Yü-shih, who was hiding in Su-chou across the Anhwei border, according to Chin Kuan-tzu's confession, lest he try to enter Kiangsu.[15]

Hungli snapped back that Jangboo had done "extremely improper" work: how could county officials have relied on cutpurse Liu's "slippery confession" and put such an important case on ice for several months? (Vermilion: "How could you have failed to impeach such a refractory subordinate?") And if the spring rumors had been followed up rigorously, the "little people" would not have had to lynch the culprits but would have reported them to officials, as in Shantung. The gap in quality between the administrations of Shantung and Kiangsu was all too plain. Jangboo's failure to cross the Anhwei border in pursuit of Yü-shih was further evidence of bureaucratic laxity: although in ordinary criminal cases hot pursuit across provincial boundaries might be thought excessive, how could it be so in a case like this?[16]

On an encouraging note, Jangboo cheerfully informed his master that the corruption case in the Yangchow salt administration had yielded clear evidence and would soon be solved. Not the least mollified, Hungli hectored Jangboo on priorities: salt administration is only "one of the normal affairs of local government. Moreover, once it is dealt with, there's an end to it, and it should not be unduly troublesome. But if criminals conceal themselves and carry out their evil plots, troubling the villages, the damage to people's lives will be great." Jangboo seemed to have "reversed the serious and the trivial."[17]

Although Jangboo insisted that he was pursuing all leads, the information from the Shantung confessions led up one blind alley after another. He could not find the Three Teachings Temple in Haichou, where master-sorcerer Ming-yuan was supposed to be awaiting the return of his queue-clipping acolytes. Nor could he find any monk remotely resembling Han P'ei-hsien's description of Ming-yuan. One promising lead, extracted from a vagrant arrested in Anhwei, pointed to a certain Soochow "mason" named Chu, who had hired agents to clip queues. But the tip proved worthless; no such man could be found. Finally, the fortune-teller Chang Ssu-ju, named in the confession of the Shantung beggar Chin Kuan-tzu, was supposedly to be found in a certain village near P'i-chou; but the village did not exist. To Hungli, however, the clue about the "mason" merely proved that officials were bent on a cover-up. Chekiang masons were also involved in sorcery, but rascally local officials had tried to cover up the case—to "turn something into nothing" (*hua-yu wei-wu*). Obviously Kiangsu officials were up to the same tricks. As a result, sorcery had spread into many provinces. "The administration of your two provinces is really despicable."[18]

Where was the harried governor to turn? Could something be wrong with the Shantung confessions? Jangboo wrote to Funihan asking that he reinterrogate his prisoners. The answer came back: the Shantung prisoners had been grilled again and had now changed their stories. Master-sorcerers Wu-yuan and T'ung-yuan were not "Kiangnan men" after all, but natives of Wan-p'ing County, in the western suburbs of Peking![19] At this astonishing news, Hungli issued a frantic order to sweep up all suspicious monks in the capital area, "not sticking to niceties" when names seemed not to match those in the confessions. After all, could not monks change their dharma-names at will?[20]

The following colloquy (Hungli's side is preserved as vermilion rejoinders between the lines of Jangboo's report of August 29) shows that the case was serving as a lightning rod for deeper tensions between Throne and province. Jangboo had now brought cutpurse Liu to Yangchow for interrogation. Liu confirmed that he was a homeless roving thief. A certain "Bearded Wei," proprietor of an herbal medicine shop, had commissioned him to clip three queues, for which he would get 150 cash each. Liu was soon caught in the act. Jangboo quickly sent agents to see whether Bearded Wei really existed. (Vermilion: "You are saying this because you intend to claim later that no such thing happened. Your subordinates, trying to close the case, will claim that the confession was false.")[21]

(*Jangboo*): These criminals who are caught in the provinces give out names and addresses that are later untraceable, or only give names and no addresses. This is the result of the craftiness of the criminals, who cover up clues and depose falsely by covering up the truth, hoping to delay the investigation.

(*Vermilion*): That's for sure. If you officials are like that, why be surprised if the criminals are too?

(*Jangboo, showing sincerity*): Every day these criminals are not caught . . . is a day local society is not at peace.

(*Vermilion*): That's just why We are pushing you officials. But your indecisiveness, in both high posts and low, is incorrigible. What can be done about it?

(*Jangboo*): In my humble jurisdiction, [ordinary criminals], who merely harm a particular locality, are objects of ceaseless prosecution . . . How dare I be even slightly remiss in prosecuting these vile, traitorous sorcerers?

(*Vermilion*): Highly improper. Memorialize promptly on the present situation.

The prosecution of the sorcery case had run into a problem endemic to the Ch'ing system, and indeed to any system in which field administrators are the main sources of information on field conditions. Although the palace memorial system had the potential for universal surveillance (one official privately tattling on another for personal advantage), it seems in practice not to have developed that way. The Throne presumed that the interest of the field official was always to reduce his risk of failure by underreporting the problem at hand. In this situation, the routine auditing process that checked performance against norms (as, for example, in the transmission of tax receipts) was useless: there was no norm against which to check the number of sorcerers arrested. An urgent, nonroutine prosecution like this one immediately set Throne and bureaucracy in competition for control of information and gave their relationship a keener edge of tension. But the monarch was not helpless. He now had recourse to an agent within the Kiangnan bureaucracy itself.

An Agent in Place

The post of Soochow textile commissioner *(chih-tsao)* was customarily filled by a trusted member of the Imperial Household Department *(nei-wu-fu)*. Stationed right in the middle of the politically sensitive lower Yangtze region, he could provide his master not only luxurious silks but also timely intelligence.[22] Serving now in that post was the imperial household bannerman Sacai (d. 1786), a royal relation in the collateral line and scion of a high-ranking military family.[23] He had won a provincial-level *(chü-jen)* degree through the special track in which Manchus could write examination papers in their own language. If this was anything more than affirmative action to ease bannermen into high posts, Sacai's cultural orientation must have been unusually true-blue Manchu by the standards of the day. Moreover, by the time of the sorcery crisis he had been assigned to Soochow for at least five years and could be accounted an old Kiangnan hand. There was accordingly no reason to expect anything but the best from him as imperial eyes and ears in the lower Yangtze.

Imagine, then, Hungli's annoyance when it turned out that Sacai had reported not so much as a brush stroke about the soulstealing threat. "The textile commissioner is responsible for memorializing about [important] affairs." In a teeming city like Soochow, had Sacai heard and seen nothing? In a matter of such importance, how could he remain indifferent?

Can it be that he fears the power of the governor-general and governor? Or perhaps he fears to stir resentment among local officials by unearthing hidden facts? Or is it that he regards governmental affairs to be outside his purview and matters of no concern and therefore intends to remain silent? If that is so, then perhaps the special responsibility of the commissioner to memorialize in detail has been no more than an empty name. How can he just routinely report such matters as rainfall and grain prices, thinking that piling up documents according to regulations will fulfill his responsibilities?[24]

Like G'aojin and Jangboo before him, Sacai now had to disclose the embarrassing news of the spring sorcery rumors. More embarrassing still, however, were the May events right in the Soochow area, which of course His Majesty had never heard about: the arrest of the Soochow beggars and the incident at Hsu-k'ou-chen, which I related in Chapter 1. Sacai revealed how the suspects had been released for lack of evidence, and how local officials had posted notices forbidding commoners to seize innocent people on mere suspicion of sorcery. Sacai wrote that he had not heard of local officials' following up these events with arrests, but neither had he heard of any actual victims of queue-clipping. Now he had to report on his colleagues:

When Governor-general G'aojin was in Soochow holding the Governor's seal in an acting capacity, he spoke to your slave [i.e., Sacai] about these matters. He said that the county investigations had revealed these cases to be baseless. In the fourth month [May–June], when Governor Jangboo arrived at his post, he asked whether your slave had heard any news about local affairs. Your slave informed him about this matter. He said the important thing is not to post notices [forbidding commoners to seize suspects], but rather to carry out rigorous investigations and arrests. Why he did not then memorialize Your Majesty, your slave really does not know.[25]

Hungli had caught Jangboo and G'aojin in a flagrant cover-up. Their reports had hinted of neither the Soochow nor the Hsu-k'ou-chen affairs, but merely acknowledged "rumors." Although Jangboo had not arrived at Soochow to assume his post until May 13, he was nevertheless briefed by Sacai (if Sacai is to be believed) no later than June 14, when he could very well have alerted the Throne.[26] But how could he have expected, back then, that anything would come of it? Whether failure to report these events was due to skepticism or to fear of stirring up trouble, the monarch's suspicions were now resoundingly confirmed. Both officials got scathing reprimands. "Scoundrel" local officials, who had been permitted to "turn right and wrong upside down" by forbidding commoners to seize sorcery suspects, should have been impeached by their provincial superiors. Cover-ups were common in the provinces, "reporting large matters as small, representing something as nothing." But Kiangnan was by far the worst: "G'aojin has long been habituated to fecklessness and has shown no vigor whatever. Jangboo served long in the post of Kiangsu provincial treasurer and could not avoid being imbued with bad habits. Later as governor of Shansi he was fairly vigorous, and We thought that he had repented his chronic faults. But since his transfer to the Kiangsu governorship, they evidently have re-emerged."[27]

All the criminals arrested and released in May were to be rounded up again and sent immediately to the summer capital at Ch'eng-te for interrogation. (These included the beggars of Soochow and the monks who had been nearly lynched at Hsu-k'ou-chen.) If any were allowed to escape, or if officials "coached their testimony" *(chiao-kung)*, G'aojin and Jangboo would be held personally responsible. "We shall be lenient to them no more."

Jangboo threw himself on the imperial mercy: he had "carelessly allowed subordinates" to gloss over important matters and feared that he himself had been "somewhat imbued with bad practices." He asked Hungli to have him impeached and punished by the Board of Civil Office. (Vermilion: "It is still too early to impeach you; let's see how well you can do at catching the criminals.")[28] As a practical matter, the governor could only busy himself pursuing sorcerers already implicated by others' confessions. It was only a matter of days before cutpurse Liu's master, "Bearded Wei," was arrested, and Jangboo interrogated him personally. He admitted recruiting cut-purse Liu but said that he himself had been hired by a former shop-assistant to procure the queues for him for "medicinal" uses.[29] There, for the moment, the trail went cold.

Coming Clean in Chekiang

The minor Manchu aristocrat, Yungde, had slipped perhaps too easily into the upper reaches of the provincial bureaucracy. This collateral relation of the imperial line[30] had served only a brief apprenticeship in the Board of Punishments before being posted to the premier circuit-intendancy in Chekiang, among the duties of which was coastal defense of the Hangchow region. Having served for a decade without mishap, he was elevated in 1765/66 to be provincial treasurer. His suggestions for minor administrative improvements must have pleased Hungli, for he was promoted to provincial governor, a post he assumed on April 25, 1768.[31]

The newly promoted Yungde must have been astonished and dismayed when he received a communication from Shantung governor Funihan (sent around July 24): confessions of the beggar-criminals Ts'ai and Chin had revealed the Chekiang origins of the mysterious queue-clipping cult that had now surfaced in Shantung. Yungde realized that the Throne would now have to be informed of the Chekiang "soulstealing" affair, which seemed to have been ended so neatly without disturbing His Majesty. Yungde braced himself for the inevitable imperial court letters, which indeed arrived at his Hangchow yamen on August 4 and 6, demanding information and urgent action.[32]

Yes, replied Yungde, in the early spring of this year, the rumor of soulstealing had "suddenly" arisen among the local people. He himself, then still in the subordinate post of provincial treasurer, had realized right away that sorcery was a serious felony. He had immediately "reported orally" (no documentary record, of course) to his superior, then Governor Hsiung Hsueh-p'eng. Investigation quickly turned up the stories of the Te-ch'ing and Hsiao-shan sorcery scares, which turned out to have been started by groundless rumors among credulous rustics. "That is why former Governor Hsiung did not report these affairs to Your Majesty." Once Yungde had become governor, he had "suspected that there might be criminals secretly stirring up trouble" and had warned local officials to be vigilant.

Now, Yungde continued, the confessions in the recent Shantung case had revealed hidden masters of the soulstealing cult in Chekiang. He had dispatched plainclothesmen all through the province, but no monks with the name "Wu-yuan" had turned up. All that could be found was one monk with a homophonous name (same sound, different ideographs), who could not be shown to have had any traffic with criminals. Furthermore, even in the remotest mountain monasteries, nobody could be found with the name "Chang Ssu-ju" (the fortune-teller implicated by Chin Kuan-tzu) or with other names supplied by the Shantung prisoners. All Yungde could do was to keep looking. Furthermore, he would impeach the magistrate of any county where such criminals were found to be hiding. Hungli's vermilion brush traced his contempt for such bland assurances: "I would not have expected that you would prove to be so useless."[33]

With that, the whole story had to come out. Yungde now forwarded to Peking a complete account of the interrogation of all the Chekiang criminals from last spring, including mason Wu, peasant Shen, the Hsiao-shan monks, and constable Ts'ai.[34] The monarch read it with mounting annoyance. Chekiang officials had plainly "been lenient to villains and nourished traitors." Indeed, accusations against the masons of Te-ch'ing "cannot have been entirely without cause." Punishing the *accusers* (constable Ts'ai, for instance) amounted to "turning right and wrong upside down." After this, how would commoners dare to seize malefactors, or constables dare to make arrests? As for Yungde himself, there was no use putting the blame on his predecessor. As provincial treasurer at the time, he himself was responsible for reporting directly to the Throne. If provincial treasurers merely reported financial trivia, and provincial judges merely court cases, "how would that accord with Our basic purpose in permitting you to communicate confidentially and directly with Us?" In matters so urgent, all officials were prosecutors. As for the criminals arrested and released last spring (the masons and monks): ship them in chains to the summer capital, where competent inquisitors would wring the truth from them.[35]

More Help from Shantung

Back in Kiangsu, even as Jangboo was stymied in the case of cutpurse Liu, he faced a new problem: the dragnet in neighboring Shantung, which had already caught so large and promising a batch of sorcerers, now offered fresh challenges. On September 12 Governor Funihan reported that, way back on July 3, a government runner in a county town had arrested T'ung-kao, a suspicious-looking wandering monk. The prefect of Yen-chou had just sent him a report about this case, so the criminal had actually been languishing in jail for upward of two months. The criminal had protested that he was no queue-clipper but was on his way to Chihli to visit relatives. Inquiries in Chihli had turned up nobody resembling his relatives, so he was sent to the prefectural yamen to be interrogated. He confessed that he had taken the monastic tonsure in Honan and later had become the disciple of a monk named Wu-ch'eng, who resided at the Temple of the Purple Bamboo Grove in Nanking. His new master was a sorcerer with "magical techniques of clipping queues" and enlivening paper men and horses with the soul-force drawn from clipped queue-ends. These would then become "*yin*-souls," who would serve their master by stealing people's possessions. Wu-ch'eng sent T'ung-kao forth with eight other disciples, all supplied with knives and "stupefying drugs," to clip the necessary queues where they could. T'ung-kao named two men whose queues he said he had clipped, and local authorities reported that these crimes had indeed been verified by the victims. The drugs, knife, and queues he had abandoned earlier, while on the run, so the incriminating exhibits were not available to the court. Nevertheless, his guilt was hardly in question, because his confession squared with damning circumstantial evidence.[36]

All this was by now a familiar story to the alert Governor Funihan, who immediately realized that the criminals were none other than the gang of his first culprit, beggar Ts'ai, and had changed their names to avoid detection. Yet T'ung-kao would not admit knowing fortune-teller Chang, monk Ming-yuan, or any of the other sorcerers named by previous culprits. Funihan had notified Kiangnan officials to be on the lookout for sorcerer Wu-ch'eng and his eight other disciples.[37] Kiangnan officials now had plenty of leads to pursue. Jangboo rushed his agents to Nanking to seize Wu-ch'eng; but the sorcerer had slipped away, forewarned by means unknown. Meanwhile, an even more vexing case was absorbing Jangboo's attention.

The Ill-Fortune of Chang Ssu-ju

The name of the Kiangnan fortune-teller, Chang Ssu-ju, had first emerged in the confession of Funihan's Shantung prisoner, the queue-clipper and sodomite, beggar Chin. Chin had revealed that it was fortune-teller Chang who had told him of the sorcerer-monk Yü-shih and had enlisted him in the queue-clipping gang.[38] Now the hunt for Chang was high on the agenda of officials throughout the Kiangnan region. Since Kiangnan officials began receiving communications from the Shantung governor in late July, they had been aware that the epicenter of the plot was in their jurisdiction. Through the steamy weeks of August, the names and addresses revealed in the Shantung confessions had been tracked down relentlessly. Governor-general G'aojin reported to the Throne that he had ordered the Su-chou authorities to search secretly for the Dark Dragon Temple where lurked the master-sorcerer Yü-shih.[39] Though a temple of that name was found, no monk there was called Yü-shih. (Vermilion: "What's this stuff? Can't he change his name?") Nor were there found books or paraphernalia of sorcery. Temples elsewhere with similar-sounding names were searched, also fruitlessly. The governor-general suggested that, since beggar Chin had said he had only heard of Yü-shih through fortune-teller Chang, clearly Chang was the criminal to find in order to track down this master-sorcerer.

The problem was that the elusive fortune-teller had been identified with no address, not even a county. He was "a Kiangnan man"—but the Kiangnan jurisdiction consisted of three provinces, containing perhaps seventy million people. Governor-general G'aojin now asked that the Shantung culprits be reinterrogated for more detailed information. Word came back that Chang came from a village called Wu-yueh-hu-chuang, south of the city of P'i-chou, near the Grand Canal in the northernmost part of Kiangsu, bordering on Shantung, but no such village could be found. Although the population registers contained three persons whose names sounded like Chang Ssu-ju, none fit his description. G'aojin's general alarm, based on the Shantung confessions, had produced nothing.

Quite suddenly, in the last week of August, the case broke. A report from the magistrate of Su-chou announced that a beggar called "Chang Ssu" had been arrested carrying a knife, a packet of drugs, and a severed queue. Su-chou, in northern Anhwei, was a mere eighty miles from the area where Chang had been hunted. And though "Chang Ssu" ("Chang's fourth son") was missing the last ideograph of the wanted man's name, and hence was as common a name as might be imagined, the incriminating evidence was a ray of hope to the harried Kiangnan bureaucracy.[40] G'aojin reported that he was arranging to interrogate the man personally. (Vermilion: "You should do your best to investigate this man's tracks in detail. But as soon as you use torture, he will not give you a true confession.")

Hungli was also relieved, of course, that an "important criminal" in the queue-clipping case had at last been caught. Anhwei's governor, Feng Ch'ien, had already informed him of the arrest at Su-chou, and had reported that the local prefect had already established that the prisoner was indeed the eagerly sought Chang Ssu-ju, instigator of the Shantung clipping outrages and link to the sorcerer-monk Yü-shih. Hungli again cautioned G'aojin against the use of torture; the difficulty of obtaining accurate statements was by now obvious, though he offered no suggestions on how information might otherwise be wrung from obdurate criminals. On the contrary, implicit pressure to obtain accurate confessions pervaded Hungli's court letters. Furthermore, if questioning in the field did not produce reliable results, the prisoner was to be sent under close guard to the summer court at Ch'eng-te, some seven hundred miles distant beyond the Great Wall.[41]

Although Anhwei governor Feng Ch'ien was G'aojin's subordinate, he nevertheless was responsible for sending his own memorials directly to the Throne. Accordingly, he was the official who had the privilege of breaking the Chang Ssu-ju story to Hungli. But Feng had evidently not understood the importance of his achievement: to the monarch's disgust, Feng had sent his memorial by the usual means—via a personal servant—rather than by the faster military courier service.[42] Hence it had not actually been received in the summer capital until September 6, more than a fortnight after it was dispatched. The tardy document reported that the prisoner had confessed to the following facts.

Chang, aged thirty-six, was from Chin-hsiang County, near the Grand Canal in southwestern Shantung. He and his eleven-year-old son, Ch'iu-erh, lived as itinerant beggars, pleasing the roadside crowd by singing "Lotus Petals Fall" (*lien-hua-lo*, a romantic folk-ballad conventionally sung by beggars). Father and son had reached the eastern gate of Hsu-chou on July 26, when they met a man from Hu-kuang named Chao San, "a tall Han Chinese, age about fifty." Chao asked what they did for a living, then offered them 500 cash for each queue they could clip. He explained that if the victim was touched with a certain drug, he would fall senseless and be easy clipping. Chao would not reveal what the queues would be used for, but gave Chang a small knife and a packet of the "stupefying drug" and sent him on his quest, with orders to meet later at the border of T'ung-shan. (Nothing here about the sorcerer-monk Yü-shih—the story so far was hardly different from that of Funihan's Shantung beggars.)[43]

Beggar Chang related that he and his son had reached Chao Village in Su-chou on August 12, where they began singing before the gate of the household of village headman Chao. When the ballad ended, the crowd dispersed, except for the Chao family's hired man, Fei Yung-nien. Chang approached the hired man and sprinkled him with stupefying powder so that he collapsed senseless. Chang then cut off the end of the man's queue and fled. Later when he forded a stream, his packet of drugs was drenched. After they had dried out, Chang tested them on his son and found that their efficacy had been lost. It was not long before county constables (alerted to the crime by the victim, now revived) caught up with the beggars and found the incriminating evidence of queue-end, drugs, and knife. Governor Feng reported that his subordinates were making vigorous efforts to find the mysterious Chao San, and that he personally would interrogate "Chang Ssu" to confirm that he was the fortune-teller "Chang Ssu-ju" implicated in the Shantung confession and to track down the sorcerer-monk Yü-shih who had directed the plot. Even as the Kiangnan cases seemed to be on the brink of solution, however, officials in the imperial capital were facing a threat closer to home.

Something Wicked This Way Comes

Sorcery was spreading northward. As it spread, there emerged disturbing signs that the danger was not confined to village society but might have wider implications. Early in August, the governor-general of Chihli, Fang Kuan-ch'eng, alerted the Throne that sorcery had already crept out of Shantung and into his province, the one in which Peking was located.

A Case of Prophylaxis

Protecting oneself from sorcery involved a varied counter-technology of charms, amulets, and other ritual weapons, as we saw in Chapter 5. As soulstealing rumors spread upriver from Kiangnan in June, a popular charm-jingle was heard along the Yangtze:

> Stone mason, stone monk:
> If you call, you'll harm yourself!
> First, cause the monk to die,
> Then cause the mason to perish.
> Hurry back home,
> Carry a bridge on your own head![44]

Such rubbish tried the patience of sensible officials, who feared that the spread of prophylaxis-magic would fan the flames of sorcery fear itself. Provincial officials threatened to impeach local subordinates who allowed such rumors to be repeated. But the public was not easily to be denied its self-protection. Not long after, prophylaxis of a more alarming kind surfaced nearer the imperial capital itself.

Peasant Meng Shih-hui, forty years of age, farmed in a village near the county seat of Ching-chou, in southern Chihli near the Shantung border.[45] During the hot night of July 18, he had been asleep in the back room of his hut, while his wife slept in the front room with their children. The front door stood open to catch the night air. As dawn approached, "I suddenly shivered," Meng told the authorities, "and felt stupefied. My wife called me but I didn't wake up. Then she discovered that my queue had been cut, about six inches." The alert wife had heard that if you cut off the rest of the queue and washed the head, you would escape harm. (Rumors about queue-clipping sorcerers had been drifting in from across the Shantung border since late June. Shantung folks said that to thwart such sorcery one should cut off the whole remaining part of the queue and wash the head with an infusion of artemisia, straw stalks, honeysuckle, and garlic.) So she called a barber and had the stupefied Meng shorn and treated. "By afternoon I gradually began to wake up." It was shortly discovered that the same thing had happened elsewhere in the county to Hsia Ko-pai, a twenty-nine-year-old baker and, in a nearby jurisdiction, to Wang Jan, a boy of fifteen.

The sorcery alarm quickly swept through the village rumor network to the county seat, and Magistrate Chang haled the victims to the yamen for questioning. Ultimately his findings were forwarded to the summer capital, where the alarmed emperor ordered that the victims be sent immediately to Peking for interrogation by the Grand Council. Afterward they were to be released, because one could not equate such ignorant rustics with monks, who shaved their heads and abandoned their families, an unfilial act that immediately suggested possible collusion with evildoers.[46] While the monarch and the chief grand councillor, Duke Fuheng, were summering in Ch'eng-te, business at the capital was being overseen by Grand Councillors Liu T'ung-hsun and Liu Lun. They examined the victims, found no evidence of suspicious behavior (aside from the missing queues), and recommended sending them home.

But now Hungli was not satisfied. Though the sorcery prophylaxis of such rustics was not quite the same as flouting the tonsure decree, another highly suspicious event had intervened: Magistrate Chang, at the instruction of his superior, the governor-general, had personally accompanied the victims to Peking, rather than deputing an underling. Had he been ordered to do so in order to "coach" their testimony en route, perhaps to cover up either his own negligence or something more sinister? Better have the victims sent on to the summer capital, now escorted by an official of the Board of Punishments.[47]

With that, peasant Meng and the others, under guard, set out toward the hills of Ch'eng-te to testify at the summer court. There, perhaps somewhat scrubbed up, they knelt before Grand Councillor Duke Fuheng, brother-in-law to His Majesty, who personally interrogated them about how they had lost their queues. This devoted and able servant of Hungli was the great-grandson of an illustrious military leader and grandson of one of the K'ang-hsi emperor's most trusted ministers. Fuheng had cemented his position beside the Throne by subduing the Chin-ch'uan aborigines in 1749. But his close personal relationship to Hungli was founded on more powerful feelings: the sovereign's memory of Fuheng's late sister, Hungli's beloved first empress, who had died just the previous year.[48] Only in his late forties, and twenty years a grand councillor by the time of the soulstealing crisis, Duke Fuheng was involved in drafting most of Hungli's edicts and court letters on the sorcery question.

Before the duke now groveled three men at the very opposite social pole of the Chinese world. All three stuck to their original stories: the boy, Wang Jan, was clipped while walking along the street; Hsia Ko-pai was sleeping in the outer room of his mother's house. But Meng's case was still suspicious. Since he was sleeping in the *inner* room, how could the queue-clipper have reached him unheard? Meng maintained that his wife was sleeping soundly and heard nothing. "If she had heard anything," Meng protested to the duke, "why wouldn't she have shouted right then, instead of waiting until dawn to wake me?" As for Hungli's suspicions about Magistrate Chang's "coaching," Meng and Hsia insisted that, en route to Peking, "our food along the road was all provided by His Excellency, Magistrate Chang. Aside from that, His Excellency didn't say anything to us."

Duke Fuheng was inclined to believe them. Wang Jan was a child and not to be held responsible. Peasant Meng and baker Hsia were "rustic villagers." Though they had "temporarily" cut off the rest of their queues, they now were regrowing them in normal fashion. Apparently there was nothing to link them with the "bandit gang," and they should therefore be sent home, as Liu T'ung-hsun had recommended. "Noted," Hungli wrote laconically on Fuheng's report, in effect endorsing the recommendation but reserving his inner thoughts on the case.[49] This meant that the three self-clippers could be released, but on the responsibility of his ministers. What had to be determined, in the weeks that followed, was whether this case could be treated as sorcery aimed at common folk, a crime grave enough in the *Ch'ing Code;* or whether the tonsure aspect of the case made it sedition against the ruling dynasty.

Meanwhile, Hungli was receiving alarming reports from Peking that the capital itself was being infiltrated by sorcerers who were clipping hair and clothing. Although none had yet been caught, there was increasing evidence of their presence: new victims were reported every day. Many were so powerfully affected that they fainted and collapsed on the spot. Others were completely unaware, until later, that they had been clipped. Some had their whole queues stolen, others cut off the remainder of their queues themselves as prophylaxis in the manner of peasant Meng. Never was the sorcerer seen, either by the victim or by bystanders. Among recent cases were two women: the wife of a cart-puller who had suddenly been stupefied and had her lapel clipped. Another was the sister of a soldier; her hair had been clipped while she was asleep at night next to her mother. The hair was later found abandoned in a back courtyard. Although she "did not feel very faint," she complained of "a strange feeling of romantic longing," as if the sorcerer had cast a spell upon her.[50] To protect themselves, prudent householders pasted antisorcery charms on doors and walls. A tense populace was further alarmed by rumors of "strange insects," flying in from neighboring Shansi Province, whose bite was harmful or fatal. Drawings of this insect had been posted in public places by persons unknown. And handbills were being passed among Peking residents that foretold famines, mass deaths, and ghostly visitations.[51]

Hungli immediately perceived that the Peking Gendarmerie, under bannerman Toendo, must be incompetent if such criminals could move about the city with impunity. After all, he wrote, Peking was densely populated and at night its neighborhoods were sealed by guarded barriers. What good were guards and barriers if these evil creatures were free to come and go, stupefying and clipping at will? Furthermore, he had heard through private channels that many queue-clippings were performed while the victims were in a vulnerable posture, urinating against walls in Peking's narrow back alleys. If local security forces were doing their job, how could the clippers get away with this? Toendo had a concurrent rank of provincial military commander *(t'i-tu);* what sort of job could he be doing? These matters were best handled by a combination of vigilance and restraint. Street security by the Gendarmerie was to be heightened—no excuses. At the same time, the populace had to be calmed: the authorities must seem to take no notice of rumors. They were not to question victims, nor even to insist that every clipping incident be reported. Door charms, however foolish, were to be left alone. As the homely saying had it, His Majesty reminded them, "See strange things but not take them so, strange things themselves away will go."[52]

The insect rumors, however, were another matter. These were obviously concocted by troublemakers who wanted to profit from sorcery fears. The security forces should track down and prosecute those responsible for printing and distributing the drawings.[53]

Meanwhile, the grand councillors in Peking wrote to Ch'eng-te to reassure Hungli that the queue-clippings in the capital were gradually subsiding, perhaps because of vigilant police work. Vermilion: "Just because they are hiding their tracks is no reason to close the case . . . Now Jehol [the vicinity of the summer capital] has turned up six cases. You have to prosecute with utmost urgency." Sorcery was creeping beyond the Great Wall and into the Manchu homeland.[54]

Justice in Honan

Jarred by these events close to home, and perhaps frightened by the public hysteria reported from Hupei, Hungli's advisors in the summer capital suggested a general roundup of suspicious characters in the strategic crossroads province of Honan. Hungli agreed and ordered a court letter sent to Governor Asha.[55] That ingratiating but incompetent bannerman immediately set about his task.[56] Indeed, he reported, rumors about the rise of sorcery had reached him as early as mid-July. He had "verbally ordered" his provincial judge to pass the word down to the prefectures. A few days later, three men were clipped within the prefectural city of Chang-te, north of the Yellow River near the ancient capital of An-yang. They had felt nothing at the time and had discovered the crime only later. Though it was generally believed that clipping victims would die (the three felt "dizzy" with shock and fright), none had actually succumbed. It was learned that one could avoid harm by washing the remaining hair with cinnabar and the blood of a yellow rooster (both agents would lend the red color that symbolized good fortune and shielded one from death pollution in funeral rites). Where that idea came from, Asha's agents could not discover; and no culprits were caught.[57]

Soon afterward, in nearby T'ang-yin County, a commoner named Shen was asked directions by a monk on the road. When he reached home, he discovered that his queue had been clipped. The monk, as the only stranger he had met, was the logical suspect. A crowd from Shen's village, along with county constables, gave chase and caught the culprit. They found that at the end of his carrying pole hung a dozen braided cords made of hair, each about six or seven inches long. Shen's own stolen hair was not found among them. Fearing the monk might escape, Governor Asha had him brought to his court at Kaifeng, where he personally interrogated him under torture.

The monk, whose dharma-name was Hai-yin, said that his lay surname was Jen and that he came from near the western gate of the city of Hsu-chou, some 160 miles downstream on the Yellow River. There he had taken the tonsure at the age of fifteen in the Shang-hsing Temple and studied under the monk Hsing-yuan. After his master died, he set out wandering. He denied clipping queues or practicing any other evil arts. The short lengths of hair he claimed to have obtained in previous years. This story he clung to during repeated interrogations. He pointed out that, if these lengths of hair had really been stolen, he would hardly have displayed them at the end of his carrying pole. But he was very evasive, reported the vigilant governor. It was easy to see why it would be necessary to have cords at the end of his carrying pole, but why should a monk find it necessary to make them from *human hair*? The culprit could only mumble, "I didn't steal them."

He was interrogated day after day, but still refused to reveal the truth. Very suspicious, wrote Asha: such criminal queue-clipping "must have an instigator behind it." It was necessary to apply torture to find out who. But the monk, having been interrogated many times, now seemed somewhat broken down. "If we torture him more just now, he might die, and then we would be unable to uncover any-thing." (Vermilion: "Right.") Asha had his local authorities pressing the investigation in the counties; "later we can put him to the torture again." He pointed out that clipping in Honan had been limited to Chang-te and Kaifeng, as reported. Popular fears had died down and the people were tranquil. "It is because we have not caught the main criminal, and the monk has not made a true confession, that I have not earlier memoralized Your Majesty."

Hungli shot back an urgent court letter agreeing that, in such cases, torture could defeat its own purposes. "These traitorous villains are very crafty." Though the evidence against them was obvious, they continued to resist torture, "hoping to die from the rod or the presses." Thus there would be no discovering their secrets. "The tricks of all these treacherous vermin are basically the same." Asha should press the investigation, but should "not exclusively rely on interrogation by physical torture" *(hsing-ch'iu)*. He should continue to round up suspicious characters, whether monks, priests, or laymen.[58]

Indeed Hai-yin was not bearing up well under torture, and his story became confused. Investigators failed to find a Shang-hsing Temple in Hsu-chou, or any family surnamed Jen in the west gate area. Hai-yin now said he was from Yung-ch'ang County in Honan, but was "evasive," Asha reported, about his address and temple affiliation. Yet he stubbornly maintained his innocence. "I hope to die if those cords on my carrying pole were queues." Such resistance was surely designed "to protect his confederates." Interrogation must press on, wrote the governor, but unfortunately the prisoner had "contracted a prevalent illness of the season" and suffered also from festering infections (from his torture wounds) and was eating and drinking rather little. It had become difficult to question him. A physician had been summoned, and the search for Hai-yin's secret would resume when he had recovered. Meanwhile, the roundup of suspicious characters was proceeding. There should be more criminals with whom to confront Hai-yin, but none had been arrested, and no further cases of queue-clipping had arisen. (Vermilion: "In Peking this wind has not stilled, and cases have also been reported in Jehol. How can your province alone have none? This shows that you are not attending to duty. Highly improper.")[59]

In Chihli alone, seventeen clipping cases had been reported and three suspicious monks and priests arrested. Asha's assurances that no incidents had been reported in Honan simply would not wash. "It is not consistent with what We have heard," wrote back Hungli, invoking a standard imperial technique by which the monarch implies that he has private, alternative sources of information outside the chain of command. Under this kind of bullying, Asha felt he had to make something of the Hai-yin case, even though the crafty monk would not cooperate. Despite his obstinate denials, the evidence against the wretch was plain. The trouble was that his illness grew worse daily. Medicine was of no effect, and he gasped for breath.

The governor humbly observed that "everyone loathes this kind of traitor who harms the common people." If such a villain were allowed simply to die in prison, "we shall have no way to manifest the Dynasty's laws and gladden the hearts of the people." Worse, "rumors will arise in the minds of ignorant subjects": a fearful and angry populace would interpret the disappearance of Hai-yin as an ominous lapse of state control—or perhaps a lack of commitment against sorcery? "Better to publicly execute him in order to dispel the suspicions of the crowd." This would have the added benefit of intimidating other "traitors." Your minister therefore, "without estimating the personal consequences," yesterday, "begging the Royal Order in advance *(ch'ing wang-ming),* had the criminal taken to the public square and beheaded, and the head exposed to show the crowd" (that is, hung up on a pole and left there).[60]

So Hai-yin was out of his pain, and the governor was relieved of his problem. Having a prisoner die in jail was cause for minor administrative punishment (a trifling fine for a governor), but to lose a major criminal like Hai-yin without obtaining a confession would suggest either incompetence or a cover-up (it might be suspected, for example, that he had revealed a widespread conspiracy, long undetected by provincial officials). Asha's solution rested on the wide powers granted provincial officials to execute criminals summarily, although such powers were more generally used in cases of riot or insurrection. In this case, to drag the dying monk before the market crowd and cut off his head was a powerful message about the state's commitment against sorcery—even in a case where the culprit's guilt was not supported by a confession. It was not, however, the kind of resolution Hungli was looking for. (Vermilion: "Even more futile!")

There had been so few arrests in Honan that Hungli naturally suspected Asha's subordinates of another sort of cover-up: they were withholding information from the governor in order to save themselves trouble or spare themselves prosecution for earlier neglect. The governor showed his zeal, shortly after Hai-yin's execution, by reporting sixteen cases of queue-clipping in the province. (Vermilion: "Just as We suspected!") Three suspicious-looking monks had been arrested, but against none was the evidence convincing. The campaign was at least impressing the local people with the governor's serious intent, for innkeepers and temples were now refusing shelter to wandering monks. But even such stern measures were not producing results, wrote Asha to the Throne, because these criminals were, after all, sorcerers: the reason they leave no traces "must be that they have evil arts that enable them to conceal themselves . . . the better to carry out their hateful designs." (Vermilion: "What's all this stuff? How can such a thing be? If *you* think this way, it is no wonder your subordinates do not prosecute the case conscientiously and are deceiving you!")

The governor wrote back amiably, "Just as Your Majesty pronounced in your Sage Edict, 'There must be gangs of persons with seditious plots.'" (Vermilion: "You wretched thing!") "Your humble minister is extremely stupid." (Vermilion: "Indeed you *are* extremely stupid.") Asha pointed out that "while at the triennial provincial examinations, I have been using a blue brush. But I carry with me a black brush so that I can be prepared to write memorials on this case—even while engaged in my routine duties." (Vermilion: "Use whatever you've got on you!") Anyway, fumed the monarch, in this emergency Asha should have delegated the provincial examinations to a subordinate. Asha "used to be a conscientious official" but even he had been imbued with "the disgusting habit of indecisiveness" of the provincial bureaucrat. The campaign had become such an irritant between Throne and bureaucracy that official ineptness was itself becoming one of its targets.[61]

The Plot Thickens

Throughout the month of August, Hungli (still summering amid the lakes and hills of Ch'eng-te) received a mass of contradictory news of sorcery. The spread of incidents from south to north, then from north to west, showed that the criminals were keeping several jumps ahead of his provincial officials. Though numerous suspects had been arrested, he perceived that they were all from the margins and dregs of society—monks and beggars—and all had been recruited by ringleaders unknown. By the first week of September, he was convinced that the threat was not limited to local society but might be aimed at the dynasty itself. Peasant Meng he had shown leniency by recommendation of his inquisitors. Nevertheless, commoners were getting the idea that a clipping victim could counter a sorcerer's power by severing his queue "at the root." What next?[62]

On September 7, Hungli issued a court letter to the heads of seven provinces in which at last he broached the subject of the tonsure. All the criminals caught so far, he pointed out, were obviously mere tools of master-plotters with larger aims. On the one hand, these plotters were offering vagrants and beggars cash for queues, without telling them what the queues were for. To be sure, the belief about soulstealing and bridge construction was "absurd and heterodox," which was enough to warrant rigorous prosecution. Yet who could say that the rumor about "whole-queue" prophylaxis was not started by the sorcerers themselves as a way of terrorizing people into symbolic acts hostile to Manchu overlordship? The sorcerers must know that "wearing a queue is an institution of this Dynasty, and that one who cuts off his queue is no longer a minister or servant of the Manchus." The plotters, however, are not in the northern provinces but in the South. "They are either traitor-monks or else scholars who have lost hope of advancement," and their crime is "ten times more horrible" than that of the lowly queue-clippers themselves. Although the lower Yangtze provinces are the source of this evil, upriver the inhabitants of Hunan and Hupei are "crafty and dangerous." In the past they have followed "deviant ways and perverse principles," and it is likely that the rebels *(ni-fan)* will hide among them. Let the governors of those provinces root them out.

The method of doing so, however, is different from that of prosecuting the queue-clippers themselves, which can be done by soldiers and police. This, by contrast, requires velvet-glove treatment to avoid alerting the targets. Careful but secret investigation will be needed. Hungli ended his letter with his favorite "priority" phrase, "use particular vigor and attention" *(mien-chih, shen-chih)*, an urgent note not sounded when sorcery alone was at issue. No provincial bureaucrat could doubt that the heat was on, or that the basis of the prosecution had been transformed: no longer mere sorcery, but sedition.[63]

The Quest for Salvation

Meanwhile, in the bleak uplands of Chihli, on the road to Mongolia, portentous visions were stirring among commoners as well. Whether these visions grew from fear of sorcery itself, or from the anti-Manchu implications of queue-clipping, or from anxiety about the apparent loss of dynastic control, we cannot know. But some hastened to make ready for the end of the world. They belonged to a popular Buddhist sect known as "Effortless Action" *(Wu-wei chiao)*, also named "Returning to the Origin" *(Shou-yuan)*, an expression associated with millenarian beliefs about the imminent end of the world. The sect traced its origins to the patriarch Lo Ch'ing (fl. 1509–1522). Long proscribed by imperial order, it was now revived by a man named Sun Chia-mou. This sect can be classed as the "sutra recitation" type:

congregations practicing vegetarianism and pious living, seeking salvation through the "precious scrolls" transmitted from earlier sect leaders.[64]

In Pao-an Department (now Cho-lu County), some sixty miles northwest of Peking, a sectarian convert had confessed that Sun Chia-mou had "composed rebellious sayings" in order to revive the sect. The provincial judge himself went immediately to Pao-an to investigate. Hungli was sufficiently alarmed to send secret orders that all culprits be sent directly to the summer capital for interrogation, bypassing the provincial court.[65]

The law moved fast. Only a week later, the grand councillors in Ch'eng-te were able to report on their interrogation of a band of Pao-an sectarians. The sect-master, Ts'ui Yu-fa, claimed to have inherited a five-character mantra ("Universal Felicity Nourishes Manifest Virtue"; *p'u-fu yang hsien-te*) from the Ming patriarch P'u-ming. Each sect member adopted a dharma-name that began with one of the five characters. Sun Chia-mou had joined the sect in 1750, taking the dharma-name Hsien-fu ("manifest riches"). County authorities had arrested sect-master Ts'ui in 1753 but released him on condition that he abjure the religion. Ts'ui secretly continued to practice it, however, and announced that he was "receiving instructions from the Venerable Mother of Universal Light" *(p'u-kuang lao-mu)* about the "disasters and good fortune" that would befall mankind.[66] He also concocted "golden pills and honey-liquor" and sold them as medicine. In the current year, his disciple Sun Chia-mou had written "treasonous sayings" on placards, which he planned to have distributed among sect members. Under torture, Sun confessed that these "sayings" were of two kinds: "things having to do with Ts'ui's cheating people of money" (probably soliciting contributions as offerings against calamity), and a "nine-lotus chant" *(chiu-lien-tsan)* transmitted from the patriarch P'u-ming. By the seventh month, master Ts'ui had heard of the spread of queue-clipping sorcery and "urged the people to pray for deliverance from calamity." The violence of dynastic change meant chaos and suffering for ordinary people. This was the occasion to reactivate the sect and to proselytize among the public. Authorities seized sect members distributing placards in the walled city of Pao-an, as well as persons who had collected money on Ts'ui's behalf or had kept copies of his sutras.

The inquisitors recommended harsh punishment, under the "High Treason" *(ta-ni)* statute: Ts'ui and Sun were to be executed by slow slicing. Of their principal followers, some were to be beheaded, others beaten and exiled. Since the people of that prefecture were obviously "incorrigible," the severed heads of the sect leaders were to be publicly displayed to discourage future converts. As we shall see in Chapter 9, officials who had treated Ts'ui leniently fifteen years earlier were to be found and disciplined.[67]

Hungli's ruthless destruction of the Pao-an sect followed naturally from his conclusion (September 7) that the soulstealers, by intentionally raising the issue of tonsure symbolism, had committed themselves to sedition. By that logic, the sectarian response was just what the queue-clippers had wanted. Whatever the soulstealer's strategy, it is in fact likely that the Pao-an sectarians were moved by the imminent perils that queue-clipping seemed to portend. Popular fears of dynastic change—and the natural disasters that came with it— were readily crystallized by Ts'ui and his doctrines. The panic factor was now fairly at work. Or so it must have seemed to the court at Ch'eng-te, still shaken by the spread of sorcery through the capital and provinces.

CHAPTER 7

On the Trail of the Master-Sorcerers

By early autumn, it seemed to Hungli that the spread of queue-clipping into North China was only the beginning of much more extensive trouble for the dynasty. Once aware of the political menace lurking behind the queue-clipping scare, he began to alert officials in hitherto unaffected provinces so that the movement could be contained. On September 22, he sent a court letter to the governors of Shansi and Shensi, urging preparedness. The gangs of sorcerers, he wrote, had spread from Kiangnan into Shantung, Honan, and Chihli. Peking already had "many cases," and in recent days even at the summer capital their traces had been discovered. Now that energetic measures were underway in Chihli, who could say that the criminals would not take refuge elsewhere?[1]

Sorcery Moves West

Governor Mingšan of Shensi certainly knew his way around. Though this collateral relative of the imperial house had held governor's rank only seven years, he had served at intermediate levels of provincial administration for seven years before that. He must have been credited with a just sense of proportion, for while serving as governor of subtropical Kwangtung in 1762/63, he had recommended to the Throne that local officials no longer be required to kneel in the road wearing their heavy dragon-embroidered ceremonial gowns to welcome provincial dignitaries. In Shensi, he was well acquainted with the territory: by the time of the queue-clipping crisis, his tenure as governor had so far lasted (with a year's interruption to serve in the Yangtze region) for five years.[2]

Mingšan reported on October 3 that he had heard of the Shantung cases when they first occurred and had already sent "secret orders" to county officials and military garrisons to take precautions. Rural markets were likely to "harbor traitors," so he had ordered local officials to send agents among the crowds to keep watch. On October 18, 19, and 20, three men reported that their queues had been clipped on the street by criminals unknown: two soldiers from nearby garrisons, and one schoolboy. County officials had examined the queue-ends, however, and found that they did not appear to have been clipped. Governor Mingšan himself had the complainants brought before him and found their queue-ends to be untouched.[3]

Further questioning revealed that the schoolboy, Kuo Hsing-li, aged twelve, was a student at the local academy. He had stopped on the street to watch a jugglers' troupe and made himself late for school. Rather than brave his schoolmaster's wrath, he had run home to his mother and claimed his queue-end had been clipped. Mingšan was unwilling to press charges against a twelve-year-old. The soldiers, he suspected, were either trying to find an excuse to postpone the payment of debts, or needed an excuse for being late to duty. Though he thought they "ought to be beaten," Mingšan was afraid that "the little people would not understand why, and there might be some genuine clipping-victims who would then not report the matter." The soldiers were sent back to their units to face the music.

Two other cases, however, were cause for concern. One commoner, Liu, feared that his queue had been clipped and had barber Ch'en clip off a little more as prophylaxis. Though the man was obviously "extremely stupid," his actions were "provocative and an incitement to the public." Another troublesome case was that of a seven-year-old boy, Chao Wang-pao, who was playing in the street in front of barber Wang's stall. Somehow he had heard of queue-clipping and started pestering barber Wang to cut off a little of his queue too. Barber Wang at first ignored him, then decided to humor him by cutting off just a little. The boy then became frightened and reported the incident to his mother. County deputies were sent to investigate, and barber Wang was haled into court and interrogated. Though the magistrate was satisfied that no evil was intended, the provincial judge ordered that he be brought before him and questioned under the *chia-kun.* No new revelations were forthcoming. Wang's barber stall was searched, but no "illegal articles" were discovered. Governor Mingšan then questioned the man himself and was satisfied that the deed had been done as a joke. Yet such a joke at such a time was "provocative and illegal." Barber Wang, along with imagined clipping-victim Liu and barber Ch'en, were exposed in the cangue "to show the public." In the ten days since that time, Mingšan assured his master, no further incidents had been reported. He would "redouble his supervision" of preventive police work and "dared not permit the slightest laxity." (Vermilion: "Probably just empty words. Do not fail to exert yourself. Be conscientious and watchful.")

Sorcery Afloat

As his barge made its stately way along the Grand Canal, the director-general of Grain Transport, Yang Hsi-fu, docked on September 7 at a salt inspectorate in northwest Shantung. There he encountered a case of attempted soulstealing. As the grain fleet returned empty from the North, boat-trooper Chou had come aboard the captain's boat bringing his wife, who complained that a corner of her clothing had been clipped by a beggar-woman on August 21, whereupon she felt suddenly dizzy and had to be revived by a physician. On the twenty-seventh, a tattered beggar-woman again came on board and clipped a piece of cloth from her clothes. This time the crone was caught and was found to possess scissors and a scrap of cloth that seemed to match the victim's clothing. Suspect and evidence (including the victim's cotton vest) had been turned over to Magistrate Shih of Te-chou, who undertook to dig out the truth and reported to Director-general Yang the following facts.[4]

The old woman confessed that her married name was Chang, née Wang, that she was from Wu-ch'iao County in neighboring Chihli Province, and she now lived at Yü-ch'üan Village in Ching-chou, along with her son, Yin, and his wife, also née Wang. At the age of seventy-one, she survived by begging in the streets. "One day a man named Doggie Ch'ü came up to me at the riverbank and offered me a thousand cash if I could clip the lapels of ten women." She admitted to clipping the clothing of two women, including the wife of boat-trooper Chou, at which point she was caught. "Doggie Ch'ü give me a bag of drugs. He told me that if I swallowed a pinch, the woman wouldn't see me. I still had a little left over, which I buried by the side of the road in a hole in the wall of a cartshed." Doggie Ch'ü was also from Wu-ch'iao, and the old woman implicated two other Wu-ch'iao persons and their addresses.

Off went the constables to track down the names in beggar-woman Chang's confession. Neither could be found, nor could the bag of drugs. Into court were dragged beggar-woman Chang's son, daughter-in-law, and their child, "little darkie." The son, Yin, aged fifty-one, deposed that his mother lived in the house next door belonging to Widow Han, along with another old woman named Li, her begging companion. He knew nothing of any criminal behavior by his mother. Questioned again, beggar-woman Chang now said that the addresses she had given yesterday were false, but that all the following people were part of the gang—whereupon she produced seven new names. "They worked at Po-t'ou [where she had been caught] but beat it when they heard that Your Excellency was arresting people." The bag of drugs must have been taken away "by some children."

Again, the constables could find no corroborating evidence. Beggar-woman Chang's companion, Li, also over seventy, confessed that she knew all about the lapel-clipping racket, and that she too had tried the invisibility drug. Asked who gave her the drugs, she "said whatever came into her head," according to the examining magistrate, and "her eyes had an evil look." Both women seemed dazed and confused. The magistrate ordered that remedies be administered to clear their heads, so "fire from a sacrificial censer was used to burn simulacra *(hsiang-huo shao-lei)*."[5] Then the women were given a broth made of "boiled herbs and vermilion powder, to which were added the ashes of some yellow paper bearing a vermilion seal," a concoction that seemed to revive them. Questioned separately, beggar-woman Li said that the invisibility drugs had been given them by two monks who lived in the village temple. When the two monks were questioned, they maintained that they knew nothing but "chanting scriptures and tilling the soil." Beggar-woman Chang's testimony was successfully impeached when she pointed to a local constable in a lineup and swore he was "Doggie Ch'ü."

Although the magistrate's report lent them scant credibility, Director-general Yang had little choice but to follow up on these confessions. Like all other high provincial officials, he was under heavy pressure from the Throne. Accordingly he sent the details to Governor Funihan (to whom the culprits had already been sent), as well as to officials in all the jurisdictions where members of the gang were living, according to beggar-woman Chang's testimony. Indeed, Hungli became deeply interested in the details of this case. His re-script to Yang's memorial was dark with suspicion: Behind this case "there must be persons with deep plots and far-reaching plans. You must not view the matter as merely involving the ordinary sort of rumors."

As Magistrate Shih's superior, Governor Funihan of course also received Shih's report about beggar-woman Chang and the lapel-clipping case. Because he was busy with other court cases, he had both women reinterrogated, and both now recanted. Beggar-woman Chang lamented that she had simply gone onto the grain boat to beg, when suddenly the trooper's wife began shouting that her lapel had been clipped, and she had been nabbed as a likely suspect. The new team of interrogators saw no evidence of evildoing and even suggested that the scrap of cloth might have been planted. Funihan then called the culprits up for his personal interrogation, but was told that beggar-woman Chang had just died of illness in the county jail ("a cold contracted on her journey here").[6]

However shaky the case, Funihan was stuck with the women's previous confessions and the names of their collaborators. Under imperial pressure, he could hardly let the matter rest. He assured Hungli that he had sent the names of implicated persons to the authorities in neighboring Chihli, where beggar-woman Chang said they were located. Such assiduity impressed the emperor not a bit. Why, he demanded in a court letter, had Funihan not personally compared the cloth from beggar-woman Chang's bag with that of the clipped garment? Women's clothing was particularly easy to distinguish: the darkness or lightness of the cloth and the length of the piece (Vermilion: "and the looseness or closeness of the weave") could quickly distinguish true evidence from false.[7] If the Lord of the Civilized World could direct his attention to such details, how could a dutiful official do less? Fuheng and Yenjišan, grand councillors on duty at the summer capital, were giving the case their closest attention. They noted shrewdly that the question of the "two monks" brought up in Yang Hsi-fu's original memorial had not been addressed by Funihan and drafted an additional court letter to be sent to Shantung.[8] "Since these monks are culprits in this case who ought to be rigorously investigated," how could Funihan have let them go so easily? Governor Funihan replied that although beggar-woman Chang had originally spoken of them, she had since recanted her confession. Further investigation had shown that the monks indeed had no criminal associations. As for the cloth, it clearly had been cut by sharp scissors, which beggar-woman Chang's were not; and cut along a curvy, meandering line, obviously not in a way that could be done in a hurry. Despite these "doubtful aspects," Funihan could not but forward the names of implicated persons to the summer capital.[9]

We cannot tell whether torture was used on the old women, though the law forbade the torture of females. Their confusion and shock are evident in the record, and beggar-woman Chang's death in jail suggests that neither their sex nor their advanced age had earned them much solicitude from their jailers. Their testimony, impeached as it was on many counts, had nevertheless generated new leads, which were now treated as valuable in themselves. Accordingly, seven new names were dutifully entered on the investigators' docket.

Round Up the Usual Suspects

Meanwhile, officials in Chekiang, where it all had begun, were still without a plausible master-sorcerer. But after two months of vermilion abuse from the Throne, Governor Yungde had at least found an acceptable way to run the queue-clipping campaign. He reported on October 4 that numerous suspects had been rounded up and rigorously examined. Soldiers and constables had been posted at temples and pilgrimage sites to arrest suspicious characters, and county authorities had garnered a promising batch. These feats apparently sat well with the Throne, if we can judge by the fact that the abuse ceased. A brief inspection of Yungde's police work in Chekiang reveals his formula for dealing with queue-clipping and the sorts of people it brought into the case.[10]

Yungde emerged from the examination hall on the evening of September 30 and the next day joined his provincial treasurer and judge, along with the Shao-hsing circuit-intendant, to examine the criminal Kuang-ts'an. This "wandering monk" *(yu-fang)* and fortune-teller claimed no fixed abode. He had been picked up for his suspicious looks and was found to be carrying some written material. He said that in March and April of the present year he had taken lodging with a monk, Te-ts'ao, at the Chueh-huang Temple. There he spotted a book of charms for curing sickness and persuaded Te-ts'ao to lend it to him. His obliging host also gave him twenty paper slips on which were printed charms for ridding houses of evil spirits and protecting crops from pests. Kuang-ts'an denied any criminal activities and apparently managed to convince his captors. "Nevertheless," the shrewd Yungde reported to the Throne, "the writings he was carrying are all absurd and uncanonical, which makes him liable to punishment." In accordance with His Majesty's edict that prisoners found innocent of queue-clipping might be released (citing Hungli's edict of September 14 back at him), Yungde was merely convicting Kuang-tsan and Te-ts'ao (who had also been arrested) under the substatute forbidding "possessing books of prognostication which are absurd and uncanonical and failing to destroy them," for which the penalty was to be beaten one hundred strokes.[11] Then they were to be remanded to their home county and forbidden to leave it.

Another criminal, reported Yungde, was the Taoist priest Wang Ta-ch'eng, who deposed that he was from T'ung-lu County in the west Chekiang prefecture of Yen-chou. He used to make a living as a geomancer. Because business was bad, he "assumed the habit of a Taoist priest." He copied out Taoist paper charms bearing the six ideographs meaning "Golden Seal of the Home of the Nine Elder Immortals" *(chiu-lao-hsien-tu chin-yin).*[12] He carved wooden seals, one each for the "Techniques of the Five Thunder-Spirits" to stamp on charm-slips for the protection of houses and crops, "to cheat the country people out of their money and goods." The local Taoist headman *(tao-chi)* confirmed that the charms and seals were indeed such as were customarily used by Taoist priests. Although Wang stoutly protested that he had nothing to do with queue-clipping sorcery, "We have nevertheless convicted him under the substatute that forbids 'Yin-Yang sorcerers speaking wildly of disasters or good fortune'[13] and have sentenced him to be beaten and cangued."

The criminal Ts'ao Tzu-yun, reported the assiduous governor, "says he is a beggar from Jen-ho County. This past spring he traveled as far as Soochow, where he fell ill. Because his queue was full of lice, he cut it off. By late summer it had grown back." Because the queue-clipping bandits have lately been "frightening the ignorant people into cutting off their queues entirely," the interrogators felt they had to persevere. But even under exhaustive questioning, beggar Ts'ao maintained that his actions had nothing to do with queue-clippers. "At present this criminal is critically ill; we have released him to local officials with instructions to watch him carefully."

The next criminal on Yungde's list, the monk T'ung-yuan, was a more complicated case, because his name was homophonous with one of the head sorcerers revealed in the Shantung confessions. Surnamed Ts'ao in his former lay existence, he lived as a wandering beggar. Not only was his manner suspicious ("looks stupid but is not stupid"); he also had suspicious writings tattooed on his body. On his forehead was the character *wan*, a Buddhist swastika ("he says he saw it on a Buddhist statue"). On his right arm was tattooed "Leading Me to the Western Pure Land." On the paper slips he gave out in return for alms was written, incomprehensibly, "Worshiping the Buddha in Shantung, tender—trifling." In *Shantung:* surely here was a culprit. But under questioning, the monk explained that these slips had been printed for him by a man named Chin in Chia-hsing, and that "Shantung" had been written wrongly for the homophonous *san-tung,* meaning "three winters" (southern speech lacks a retroflex, so that *shan* and *san* are indistinguishable). Similarly, the character "tender," *nen,* was homophonous in southern speech with "cold," *leng* (many Yangtze Valley dwellers cannot distinguish between an initial "l" or "n," nor do they have an "ng" ending). The monk insisted that the ideographs, correctly rendered, meant "For three winters I have worshiped the Buddha and have accounted cold but a trifle." This, he claimed, was simply to convince his donors of his will to suffer. As for his suspicious name, he claimed that the *yuan* character was the one from the expression meaning "to beg for alms" *(hua-yuan),* and was not the one meaning "origin," as was written in the confession of the Shantung queue-clipper, beggar Ts'ai, whom he had never met.

It was highly suspicious, though, that no printer named Chin could be found in Chia-hsing. The monk then said he had written the ideographs himself, but when asked to write them in court, he could not. Anyway, Yungde noted, the characters *san-tung* were of no great complexity, so why should the suspicious "Shantung" have resulted? Moreover, *leng* for "cold" was a character in common use, so why should the more complicated *nen* have been written? It was all too much to believe. In any event, this monk was clearly "not a good type" *(fei shan-lei,* a common phrase for labeling deviants). (Vermilion: "Have this man sent under close guard to Peking.")

What a cultural distance separated these ragged wanderers from their interrogators! Confronted by the everyday language of popular religion, Yungde and his silk-gowned colleagues professed to be astonished and baffled—who could guarantee that these bizarre expressions were not cryptic references to sorcery or sedition? The everyday malapropisms of the illiterates and semiliterates who were dragged into court might be a secret language, once they were objectified into real ideographs of written Chinese. Who would write *nen* for *leng* without some deeper intent?

In any event, the official system was well equipped to deal with miscellaneous deviants. The *Ch'ing Code* was full of rubrics under which almost any noncanonical popular writing could, if necessary, be classed as heterodox and illegal. Possessing such writings was a crime, even though not one as serious as writing them. Such a prohibition could be applied selectively to label marginal people of whom no more serious crime could be proven. In the last resort there was the catch-all statute 386, "doing what ought not be done" (*pu-ying wei*), which could subject the perpetrator to a severe beating.

Yungde's roundup in Chekiang apparently had got him off the hook. His detailed report was graced with no vermilion abuse. It even received the somewhat more approving rescript "noted" (*chih-tao-liao*), a tiny but significant step up from the laconic "seen" (*lan*), which Hungli inscribed even on the most boring of palace memorials. After all, Yungde had clearly exerted himself, had personally questioned a number of criminals, and had managed to pack one suspicious character off to Peking, where the Grand Council would have ways of making him talk.[14]

An Affair of the Heart

An increasingly frustrated Hungli had urged special vigilance on officials in Hunan and Hupei, where the inhabitants were "crafty and dangerous." In the past they had followed "deviant ways and perverse principles," and rebels would likely hide among them.[15] Just as he suspected, a report from Hunan reached him a month later to the effect that placards had been found in Ch'i-yang County with "uncanonical expressions" predicting imminent disasters. More promising, a thirty-year-old wandering monk named Chueh-hsing and four traveling companions had been picked up on suspicion of queue-clipping. On Chueh-hsing had been found a small bag of red silk containing a lock of hair and two Ming coins. Chueh-hsing's interrogation by local officials had revealed that a monk named Mao-yuan had showed him how to concoct a magic potion from human hair and old coins that could be used to beguile women. He protested that he had only shaved the hair from someone on request. Hunan's governor, Fang Shih-chün, ordered the suspects brought under close guard to Changsha, the provincial capital.[16]

Serving Hungli as governor-general of Hunan and Hupei was Dingcang, a veteran Manchu bureaucrat who had served in high provincial posts for two decades. An imperial collateral relation, son of a governor-general whom Hungli had particularly trusted, Dingcang was solidly in the upper crust of the Manchu elite.[17] When he received copies of the interrogation reports on the shifty monk Chueh-hsing, he realized that he had better not leave such a sensitive matter entirely to his subordinate, the Hunan governor. He decided to leave immediately for Changsha and "handle it in concert" (*hui-pan*) with Governor Fang. In keeping with the gravity of a sedition case, Dingcang and Fang, along with the provincial judge and the local circuit-intendant, examined the prisoners personally in the main hall of the provincial yamen. Back in the summer capital awaiting the results, Hungli was evidently on the edge of his seat. (Vermilion: "This time, we finally have a clue.")

But to everyone's astonishment, monk Chueh-hsing recanted his original confession, insisting that it had been extorted under torture. Now he told the following story: after being thrown out of his master's temple for unruly behavior, he had wandered about southern Hunan. At the prefectural city of Heng-yang, he stayed at an inn run by one Liu San-yuan. There he made friends with innkeeper Liu's young wife, née Ch'en, who served him food and drink. He returned to the inn often and became a close friend of the family. Innkeeper Liu's father even loaned him 1,000 cash to sustain him on the road. On one visit, he and wife Ch'en found themselves alone and had intimate relations. The affair went undetected, and the wanderer returned to pass the New Year's holiday with the family. Unhappily, this time he quarreled with innkeeper Liu, and his frightened lover told him he must leave and never return. Chueh-hsing begged her for a memento, but took to his heels without receiving any. Later, he sent his boy-servant back to the Liu inn for a pair of cotton shoes that his lover had been making for him. Wife Ch'en cut a lock of her own hair, sewed it with two old coins into a piece of red silk cut from her purse, and stuffed the present into one of the shoes. Chueh-hsing had carried the precious keepsakes ever after.

Properly suspicious, the interrogators brought all the principals into court and examined them. One problem was that the hair in the red silk bag had two strands of white in it—hardly to be expected from a woman in her late twenties. However, Ch'en was brought into court, and kneeling before the governor's bench was ordered to unbind her hair. Indeed, it matched exactly. Further, she maintained under insistent questioning that Chueh-hsing had used no potion on her, and that she had yielded to him out of affection.

The official judgment was that none of the suspects (including those who had posted the placards) had anything to do with the queue-cutting sorcerers. (With such compromising evidence in hand, how easy it would have been to convict to please the zealous monarch!) Monk Chueh-hsing, under a criminal substatute on liaisons between monks and married women, was to be beaten and then exiled for three years (his crime was aggravated by his having falsely implicated another monk for supposedly teaching him to make the magic potion—even though the false statements were uttered under torture). Wife Ch'en was sentenced to exposure in the cangue for a month but might redeem the sentence with a money payment. Innkeeper Liu was permitted to divorce or keep her, as he wished. All monk Chueh-hsing's traveling companions were released.

By October 2, the frustrated Hungli had reached his own conclusions: soulstealers were scattered everywhere, but their main gang was moving from province to province. Having come north from Kiangnan into Shantung, Chihli, and Jehol, they now were plainly moving westward into Shansi, Shensi, and the middle Yangtze area. Their traces faded in one province, only to emerge in another. Furthermore, it was now evident that the plotters were trying to incite tonsure violations by scaring the common people into cutting off their own queues. Hungli was certain of this because queue-prophylaxis had virtually stopped, now that it was officially forbidden. "This shows that the belief [in queue-prophylaxis] was *unfounded*" (that is, had no preexisting basis in popular lore), and that it therefore could only have resulted from traitors' "concocting evil doctrines to delude ignorant commoners." The culprits caught so far were all small fry. This meant that there must be others behind them, men who harbored seditious designs, who sought "to injure the Dynasty's established institutions" (that is, the tonsure decree) to provoke rebellion.[18]

Three days later he amplified these somber thoughts in an unusual court letter to all province chiefs, but with a new perspective: the plotters might be hoping to touch off a major uprising by stirring up popular anger against the bureaucracy. In response to harsh measures by local officials, "the people will surely become fearful," which may result in "touching off uprisings." The plotters would then be able to "stand on the sidelines" and yet attain their seditious purposes. Clearly the campaign could not be stopped in its tracks merely out of fear of the people's anger. But province chiefs must now use special care. Being "neither lax nor oppressive," they must ensure that the innocent are not injured while the malefactors are hunted down. Even the monks and beggars that are swept up in provincial dragnets must be treated gingerly. When a culprit is first brought to court, he must be questioned "impartially." Inquisitors must neither "seek by punishment" (that is, fish for incriminating admissions by applying torture) nor keep culprits locked up unreasonably. Of course, if there are "suspicious circumstances," then the full force of inquisition may be applied. If not, the culprits are to be released. Here Hungli appears to be reaching for a principle of "probable cause," a two-stage process in which neither torture nor lengthy imprisonment can be used in the early phases of investigation. Yet due care was not to mean relaxing the intense hunt for the main plotters, who must still be in Kiangnan. "If they are not treacherous monks, then they must be disheartened scholars. Their intentions are extremely dangerous, and their movements are extremely secretive." They must be hunted relentlessly, not only in the traditional bandit lairs around Lake T'ai, but also throughout the countryside in "secluded villages and derelict temples." How such an invasive manhunt was to be reconciled with proper concern for the innocent was a question that Hungli left to the practical sense of his provincial officials.[19]

An Obdurate Case

How difficult provincial officials found these contradictory instructions was soon to be seen in the case of master-sorcerer Ming-yuan. According to his apprentice, Han P'ei-hsien, whose confession we heard in Chapter 4, this sinister monk was supposed to be awaiting his queue-laden agents at the Three Teachings Temple in Hai-chou, but he had so far eluded the authorities. In Chekiang, Governor Yungde's agents had combed through monasteries and temples and had turned up a monk with the dharma-name Ming-yuan, who had been quickly shipped to the summer capital for questioning. But it was not until October 9 that the real Ming-yuan seemed finally to be in hand, captured in Anhwei Province, near the city of Hofei. A monk named Yü-ming, from a small local temple, who bore the "style" or second dharma-name of Ming-yuan, had been arrested for queue-clipping. Among his belongings had been found a small wooden doll, a charm written on cloth, two suspicious wooden seals, a curious sign, and a pair of scissors; but no queues.

Ming-yuan told his inquisitors that he supplemented his begging income by practicing medicine (just as Han had indicated in his confession). On July 26, he was out on the road, with his belongings loaded on a donkey, some fifty miles northwest of his home temple. At a village near Shou-chou, he stopped to drink from a well. Because there was no bucket to dip the water, he approached a house where three children were playing in the dooryard. They ignored him when he asked to borrow a bucket, so he just patted a boy on the head and walked on, still thirsty. He had gone less than a mile when he was overtaken by several villagers, who accused him of clipping the boy's queue.

> I couldn't argue them out of it. They grabbed me and searched my kit, but there was no queue. Then they took me to Liu Ming-ch'i's house and tied me up and beat me and stabbed me with an awl. They couldn't find a queue-end, but they demanded that I guarantee the father that his child wouldn't die. Because I had been beaten and stabbed, I had to draw him a charm for protection. He also wanted a written guarantee. Because I was desperate to save myself, I wrote one that said there'd been no queue-clipping.

The injured monk was let go and allowed to depart for his home temple. But government runners heard what had happened and went to investigate. Liu Ming-ch'i showed them the charms and guarantee, whereupon they alerted Ho-fei authorities, who tracked down Ming-yuan and arrested him.

In preliminary questioning, the culprit tried to explain the suspicious paraphernalia from his baggage (which, to officials, were plain evidence of "evil arts"). The two wooden seals were for "increasing the respect" of prospective donors. One read "Monk Aided by the Five Kings" *(wu wang-yeh t'i seng);*[20] the other, "Yin-kung Department Assistant Magistrate." Ming-yuan explained that his grandfather had held a post as brigade-general, which meant that the monk was falsely claiming an official title for himself. What about the suspicious wording on the sign (evidently a medical practitioner's placard for setting up by the roadside), which read, "Ming-yuan, from the Capital, by Grace of the Censorate"? This, he replied, was merely advertising to make prospective patients believe that his remedies had been used by high officials. The cloth charm was for "warding off sorcery" (*chen-hsieh*—of the sort discussed in Chapter 5). Here was just the sort of humbug one would expect to find in the kit of a traveling medicine man. To Ming-yuan's inquisitors, however, it was sinister stuff: he was "undoubtedly a major criminal," and the truth would now have to be extracted by torture.

Ming-yuan proved an obdurate case. He would say nothing under torture except that he had clipped no queues. The inquisitors, who included Governor Feng himself along with subordinate prefects and magistrates, did their best to encourage frank testimony. Whatever it was that they did, within a week it had killed him. When Hungli was told, he asked angrily if Ming-yuan had been tortured to death or somehow allowed to take his own life. Not at all, insisted Governor Feng. The prisoner had died of "a cold contracted in prison." The inquisitors had surely not tortured him to death, as examinations by the coroner and physician would attest. All they did was to have the criminal kneel on chains for three days, during which time no *chia-kun* was used on his legs, and the finger-press was applied only once. Then he was questioned nonstop by relays of officials for two more days and nights. "Whenever he closed his eyes, they shouted at him" to prevent his dozing. Fearing he might be somewhat "fatigued" by the ordeal, Feng ordered him kept in prison for a few days before interrogation was resumed. Before he could be questioned again, however, the jailers reported his death. (Vermilion: "Noted.")[21]

That was the shape of the case as it reached its final stage: a review of all the evidence by the Grand Council itself. The grand councillors had pushed the prosecution loyally for three months as instruments of the implacable Hungli. There is no documentary evidence, so far, to suggest that they had been anything but fully committed to the antisorcery campaign. Yet as they began their final task, we have to wonder what they must have thought of the record as it appeared by mid-October: confused by perjury, cluttered with trivia, and strewn with dead prisoners.

CHAPTER 8

The End of the Trail

As the chill of Manchurian autumn seeped into the summer capital, the court was preparing for its stately progress back to Peking. Duke Fuheng, however, was still vexed by soulstealing suspects who had been brought to him, and whose agonized testimony he strove to untangle. It will be recalled that Hungli had ordered the whole group of Shantung queue-clippers sent north, some to Peking and others all the way to Ch'eng-te, for interrogation by the grand councillors, once it became apparent that their confessions had led Kiangsu officials on a wild goose chase. Other criminals entrusted to the Grand Council were the singing beggar Chang Ssu and his son, and all the culprits from the spring soulstealing cases: mason Wu and the Hsiao-shan monks, along with the Soochow beggar Ch'en Han-ju and the monk Ching-chuang and his companions who had been so nearly lynched at Hsu-k'ou-chen. Some of the criminals had already arrived in the summer capital. Others remained at Peking, where they were interrogated by those grand councillors who had stayed behind at the Forbidden City. Now the empire's most powerful ministers would clear up this affair, which had so mightily troubled the court for the past three months. As they began their job, however, the inquisitors were aware of some recent unpleasantness that had clouded the already murky case.

Maledictions among the People

Sedition in the Family

Early in September a man of the lower elite (a county student, *sheng-yuan*) journeyed the six hundred miles from his Shansi home to Peking on a mission of state. He carried a sample of "seditious writings" to turn over to the Censorate, along with a report that these had been composed by his father's younger brother. Although the record does not reveal their content, these writings were hostile enough to infuriate Hungli when the Censorate duly brought them to his attention. Deputies from the Grand Council rushed to Shansi to join Governor Surde in his investigation. A delegation of silk-gowned dignitaries searched the uncle's house but found "no traces of seditious writing." Searching the homes of confederates named in the accusation proved just as futile. The uncle protested that he was unjustly accused, and even the accuser's father said he knew nothing of the charges and believed them to be groundless. The county student, Chang T'ing-jui, was now questioned. The investigators' report:

> At first his testimony was evasive, but after we had gone over it repeatedly and checked its accuracy, he bowed his head and wept bitterly. He confessed that his uncle, Chang Ju-t'iao, and his aunt had ruled like tyrants over the joint family estate. His own father and mother were weak and had suffered their oppression for many years. Student Chang had wanted to report the true situation to local officials, but feared that he would not only fail to receive a fair hearing but would, on the contrary, suffer his uncle's retribution. He brooded about it day and night, weeping and losing his desire to live. He therefore composed some seditious writings himself and went to the capital to present his accusation. All this he now regrets extremely.

The investigators could hardly believe that, for such a trifling cause as a family property dispute, student Chang would have fabricated a treason charge, or would have implicated so many people. Further, the uncle might indeed have been engaged in illegal activities, so the investigation would continue. But Hungli sensed what had happened. He noted in vermilion: "It probably is indeed a false accusation." The *Code*'s "most extreme penalties" were to be applied.[1]

A Persistent Creditor

A Chihli man, Kuan Te-lin, was accused of queue-clipping by Chang Erh, who had found a clipped queue in Kuan's possessions. The case was quickly taken out of provincial hands and brought before the grand councillors at the summer capital. Their Excellencies must have used persuasive methods on all parties, for they reported to Hungli on September 20 that the matter was not as it seemed. Kuan Te-lin was originally a Chinese bannerman from a garrison near Peking. In line with the government policy of reducing the number of Han bannermen, however, he had changed his registration to that of an ordinary subject.[2] In the process he moved to Ch'ang-p'ing, some twenty miles northwest of Peking. From Chang Erh, a villager, he rented land to farm. Later he moved back to the Peking area, where he lived in his own family cemetery and went into business as a peddler. He had loaned his former landlord, Chang Erh, the sum of 6,000 cash, and repeatedly asked that he be repaid. When landlord Chang claimed that he did not have the money, Kuan simply moved into Chang's house. He abused Chang relentlessly and even demanded his wife for sexual services. Offended and furious, Chang stormed out of the house and went over to the home of a neighbor, Liu San, to buy some warm wine. There he spied some discarded hair, recently trimmed from the head of Liu's daughter-in-law. This he took and bound into three queues. Later, when Kuan was out, he stuffed the false queues along with his wife's scissors into Kuan's sack, then hurried to the local constabulary post to accuse his creditor of queue-clipping.[3]

The monarch found this case disturbing, mainly because the evidence of queue-clipping in the provinces might now be cast into doubt. While confirming a deferred sentence of strangulation for the "despicable" Chang Erh, he cautioned his prosecutors: "Do not, because of this case of false accusation, permit your will to be swayed, or show the slightest negligence in pursuing the queue-clippers, lest the true criminals slip through the net."[4]

Although these cases were most prominent in the recent memories of the grand councillors, other curious occurrences were coming to the attention of provincial officials. In Honan, for example, "bad characters spend their fathers' money or dispose of their wives' possessions, then clip their own queues and falsely assert that someone had robbed them and clipped their queues. Sons cheat their fathers, husbands cheat their wives. There are even cases in which bad children skip school, clip their own queues, and falsely assert that someone clipped them and made them ill, as an excuse for skipping school. Such things are happening all over."⁵ The situation in Kiangsu was similar, though it was not reported to Peking until late November: "All jurisdictions have reported cases of commoners clipping the tips of their own queues and falsely accusing others, or turning in others to collect rewards."⁶ Though the full dimensions of this problem emerged only some weeks later, a certain skepticism is already discernible in Grand Council discussions of sorcery by mid-October. In this atmosphere we join the inquisitors as they reopen the cases of the most notorious of the soulstealing criminals.

Soulstealers in the Dock

Chang Ssu-ju Tells All

We left the singing beggar Chang Ssu and his eleven-year-old son in the county lockup at Su-chou, Anhwei, charged with queue-clipping at Chao Village. Acting Magistrate Liu reported that the singing beggar had admitted under torture that he had been recruited by the tall stranger, Chao San, to clip queues. Yet he was unable to make him admit that he was really the Chang Ssu-ju named by the Shantung queue-clipper, beggar Chin. A search for the tall stranger had proved fruitless. Now beggar Chang and son were bundled into criminal-transport carts and shipped to the prefectural yamen at Feng-yang, where "Chang Ssu" confessed that he was, indeed, Chang Ssu-ju. Here at last was a link to master-sorcerer Yü-shih, who had so far eluded the imperial dragnet. Governor-general G'aojin, who was then nearby in Hsu-chou managing flood control on the Yellow River, ordered the criminals brought for him to question personally. Finally, there seemed to be an end to this troublesome business.

Flanked by the local circuit-intendant and prefect, Governor-general G'aojin had beggar Chang and his son Ch'iu-erh dragged before him. But the result was not what he had expected. The criminal now recanted his entire confession and "poured out his grievances," insisting that he had been framed by village headman Chao. G'aojin decided that it was "inconvenient" to verify the story by applying torture, since the criminal's ankles already bore the marks of the *chia-*

kun and were badly swollen and infected. Village headman Chao was now brought to court, questioned sternly, and made to tell the following story.[7]

Chang Ssu and his boy had sung their song and then pleaded for food outside headman Chao's house. Two other beggars, who were hawking woven bamboo ladles, were given one piece of steamed bread between them, and beggar Chang was given half a piece. This was just enough to enrage the famished creatures, who roundly cursed their benefactor. Headman Chao warned them, "There are queue-clippers around these days. You'd better be off!" (meaning, "don't tempt me to turn you in"). Chang cursed him again, and the beggars walked away. "Then I was really angry," admitted Chao, "and I suspected they might be bad characters from outside." So he ordered his hired hands and tenants to seize them. One of beggar Chang's companions was found to be carrying a small bag of medicine, and the other a paring knife. Were these in fact the queue-clipping sorcerers everyone was talking about? "But there were no clipped queues, and they wouldn't admit it." Then the men threatened the boy with a beating and terrified him into admitting the beggars were queue-clippers. When beggar Chang and the others continued to deny it, headman Chao had them tied to trees and beaten with an iron chain. They were badly hurt, and Chao feared that if they were released they might lay charges against him. So, to fortify the evidence, he ordered hired-hand Fei, who was growing bald and wore a false queue, to donate part of it. This damning item, along with the knife and drugs, filled out the list of incriminating evidence that sorcery lore required, and the headman could confidently turn the criminals over to county authorities.

Governor-general G'aojin found witnesses to corroborate all these details. He also determined that the knife was too dull to cut hair and the drugs incapable of "stupefying" anyone. Yet both county and prefectural authorities had previously sustained the case. There was no alternative but to send the criminals to Peking to face the Shantung criminal, beggar Chin, who had been brought to the capital to have his tangled testimony combed out by the grand councillors themselves. Beggar Chin, who had named Chang Ssu-ju in the first place, would surely know him when he saw him.

The beggar and his son reached Peking on October 11, and a panel of grand councillors, led by Liu T'ung-hsun, interrogated them personally. The father, his legs infected and suppurating, was barely alive after his journey. His whole body was "yellow and swollen," and he was suffering from acute dysentery. Yet he clung to his story: that he and his son came from Wei County in southern Chihli Province (not from Kiangnan at all), and that they had taken to the road because of poverty. He denied cursing headman Chao, but corroborated all the details of the frame-up. Their Excellencies now looked down at the kneeling boy, Ch'iu-erh. "If your father really isn't Chang Ssu-ju, why did you depose that he was?" asked one.

Ch'iu-erh responded: "The prefect asked me, What's your father's name? I said, He's called Chang Ssu. The prefect said, He's obviously Chang Ssu-ju, why don't you tell the truth? Then they took the *chia-kun* and pressed it down on me and frightened me. Then he said, If you say that he is Chang Ssu-ju, I'll give you something to eat. Then he told somebody to give me a pear to eat. I was scared when I looked at the *chia-kun,* and also I didn't know what kind of person Chang Ssu-ju was, so I went ahead and said what they wanted. But my father's really called Chang Ssu, not Chang Ssu-ju."

Attendants then carried in the Shantung criminal, beggar Chin, who could not identify the prisoner. Beggar Chin now maintained that he had made the name up: there was no such person as "Chang Ssu-ju." He had known a man named "Chang Ssu" in his native county and, under pressure from his own interrogators, had simply added a "*ju*" to it. This struck the grand councillors as suspicious. Though the singing beggar denied the name Chang Ssu-ju, he could not deny the fact that he was Chang Ssu (meaning, as noted earlier, "Chang's fourth son," of whom there must have been a very large number in China). Were both these criminals simply feigning mutual nonrecognition? The questioners turned again to beggar Chang: "You used to be a regular member of Chin Kuan-tzu's gang, but now you say flatly that you do not recognize him. *What evidence have you that would make anyone believe you?*"[8] Chang Ssu repeated the same story as before.

In the light of the confused testimony, the panel dared not reach a conclusion. There was nothing but to wait for corroboration from the provinces: the trial of village headman Chao for false implication was still in progress, and the provincial judgment had to be taken into account. The supposed "Chang Ssu" in Chin Kuan-tzu's native county could also be sought. But nature would not wait. On October 25, Chang Ssu died in prison. Because of his condition, pointed out the grand councillors, doctors had been ministering to him even during his testimony. The coroner inspected the body and certified that there had been no mistreatment by jail attendants. Magistrate Liu, who had been charged with sending him to Peking in the first place, had certified that beggar Chang was already seriously ill when he was shipped off to the capital. So nobody in Peking could be held responsible. The grand councillors concluded that he was, after all, not the queue-clipper they were looking for. He was to be furnished with a coffin and buried (at state expense), and the boy Ch'iu-erh was to be escorted back to the county where he had originally been arrested.⁹

The Original Queue-Clipper's Tale

The inquisitors in Peking now went back to the beginning. By the time he was reinterrogated at Peking in mid-October, Shantung's original queue-clipper, beggar Ts'ai T'ing-chang, was already gravely ill. Though he now claimed that his original confession had been concocted under torture, the grand councillors were not so easily to be put off the track.

> *Inquisitors:* In your Shantung confession, you said you stayed in Yangchow at a hostel run by a man named Wu. Now we actually have the Yangchow hostel-keeper named Wu Lien right here in court. It's plain that you weren't lying before.
>
> *Ts'ai:* What I confessed in Shantung about being in Wu *Sheng's* hostel in Yangchow, and about splitting up with Yi-an and T'ung-yuan to go out and clip queues, was all made up as I went along. Actually, I didn't leave Peking until June fifth of this year. My kinsmen in Peking, Chu Jan and Wang Yun, have already corroborated that here in court. Obviously I was still living in Peking during late March and early April. I couldn't have gone to Shantung, much less to Yangchow. The Wu Sheng I named in my confession was made up. I don't know who this Wu *Lien* is that you've brought here to court. How could I recognize him?
>
> *Inquisitors:* Why did you lie in your Shantung confession?
>
> *Ts'ai:* "When I told the county officials that I was on my way south from Peking, they didn't believe me. *They said I must certainly have been coming north from Kiangnan.* I couldn't bear the torture, so what could I do but agree. The county officials demanded that I say I was based in Kiangnan. I couldn't bring myself to say it, but I was afraid of the torture and . . . said it was Yangchow.¹⁰

In the first Shantung case, local officials had already been convinced that sorcerers were moving northward from Kiangnan. The county bureaucracy evidently had picked up the same rumors that reached Hungli through his private channels and triggered the July 25 court letter that had begun the prosecution in the provinces. Should the grand councillors consider that this strengthened the case, or weakened it? The sorcerer's apprentice, Han P'ei-hsien, only compounded the confusion. He now insisted that all details of his Shantung confession had been invented under torture, and that there was no such person as the sorcerer-monk "Ming-yuan." The grand councillors remained puzzled, however, over the concreteness of his original testimony. Why did he know so much about the details of how sorcerers worked?[11] The case of monk T'ung-kao, soon to be interrogated in Ch'eng-te, would offer a plausible answer.

A Silly Misunderstanding

On October 25, Duke Fuheng informed the emperor about the irksome case of T'ung-kao, the monk captured in Shantung whose confession had touched off a sweep of Kiangsu monasteries and temples.[12] The dragnet had indeed turned up T'ung-kao's master, the sorcerer-monk Wu-ch'eng, and others whom T'ung-kao had named, who were now in the Board of Punishments lockup at the summer capital. Nevertheless, Wu-ch'eng, through whom Hungli had counted on getting to the bottom of the plot, disclaimed any knowledge of sorcery and insisted that he had not seen his disciple, T'ung-kao, since they had parted company two years earlier at the Temple of the Purple Bamboo Grove in Nanking. Ordinarily such a barefaced denial would hardly be worth recording, save that T'ung-kao himself now recanted. The original confession had aroused Duke Fuheng's suspicion because of its numerous absurdities. For example, "clipping a queue is an act performed when the victim is off his guard. How can the clipper have had time to ask the victim's name before committing the act?"

The scene of T'ung-kao's reinterrogation might have shaken the most resolute of prosecutors. The tattered creature who was dragged before Fuheng exhibited "suppuration of both legs from various torture wounds. His spirit was so melancholy that at the slightest scolding he cringed and begged for death." The broken monk at first persisted in his original story, but when the torture instruments were brought out he conceded that his previous confession had been an invention. Though his ancestral home was in Anhwei, he had lived since childhood in Chihli. Later he had been tonsured in Honan, then became Wu-ch'eng's disciple and moved to Nanking. In 1766, master and disciple separated, and T'ung-kao resolved to return to his old village in Chihli as a layman, so he stopped shaving his head and set out for home. He had reached Ssu-shui in Shantung, where his unfamiliar accent and half-grown hair attracted the notice of a government runner, who arrested him as a suspicious character.

The Ssu-shui magistrate was unable to get anything out of him, so the Yen-chou prefect decided to interrogate him, aided by Magistrate K'ung Ch'uan-chih of Tsou County (a descendant of Confucius in the sixty-eighth generation), who had been successful at persuading Shantung's first queue-clipper, beggar Ts'ai, to confess. Magistrate K'ung first hung T'ung-kao in chains from a tree, then had him kneel on chains spread with cinders, while pressing upon the backs of his legs with a wooden pole. Later he had his back whipped, then used the *chia-kun* to break his legs, after which T'ung-kao made up his story. The "spells" his inquisitors heard him murmuring under torture were in fact Buddhist scriptures, known to all monks. The names of his "clipping victims"? These were folk he had met along the road. His "co-conspirators" were indeed monks he had known, whose names he blurted out under torture. And the sorcery lore about stupefying powder, paper men, and paper horses? This he had heard from fellow inmates while lying in prison.[13]

Fuheng ventured that the case "seems to be a miscarriage of justice." Yet the original confession had been specific and detailed, so Magistrate K'ung must have had his reasons for subjecting the monk to repeated torture. If T'ung-kao and Wu-ch'eng were simply released, this would hardly "show due regard for the intention of the original investigator." Hungli accepted the duke's recommendation that Magistrate K'ung be temporarily detached from duty and brought to Peking for investigation, and that the two prisoners be kept, for the time being, in jail.

How could justice have so miscarried? Inquiries to Governor Funihan in Shantung revealed that the whole affair had been a silly mistake. What had happened, the governor explained much later, was that Magistrate K'ung had simply been misled by the yamen runners who had been sent to find the queue-clipping "victims" whom the agonized T'ung-kao had named. The runners had been under a five-day deadline to return with their report. They had been unable to find the "victims," whose supposed homes were some hundred miles away in another county, and feared punishment for reporting late. So they had simply said that they had found them and substantiated T'ung-kao's confession.[14]

Perils of the Road

Beggar, queue-clipper, and sodomite Chin Kuan-tzu, whose original confession had implicated "Chang Ssu-ju," was reinterrogated in detail during the third week of October. He now claimed that his original deposition had been extorted by torture, which, to judge by his crippled legs, was not implausible. Beggar Chin now told all: he and Chin Yü-tzu, the youth he was accused of sodomizing, were in fact cousins from a village near the Shantung provincial capital of Tsinan. Yü-tzu's father, Chin K'uan, had headed southward in the late autumn of the previous year to seek a living as a hired laborer and had failed to return. This past summer, a villager had told Yü-tzu he had heard that his father had struck it rich. Yü-tzu's mother sent him off to find his father, but since Yü-tzu was only seventeen, she asked his older cousin, Chin Kuan-tzu, to go along and see that he came to no harm. The two set forth toward the southern hills and on June 25 reached the home of Yü-tzu's maternal cousin Chao Ping-ju, where they borrowed some money to sustain them on the road. Their search for Yü's father proved fruitless, and eventually they ran out of money and were reduced to begging along the road. By the afternoon of June 30 they had reached a village called Li-chia-chuang in the county of Yi, near the border of Kiangsu. The village was in an uproar because someone reportedly had clipped the queue of Li Kou-erh, the young son of Li K'un, a clerk in the county office of punishments. The pair of wandering beggars sensed trouble and left the village. They had been spotted by the furious clerk Li, however, who immediately labeled them "suspicious" and set a mob after them. They found nothing incriminating in Chin Kuan-tzu's traveling sack—no knife, no drugs, no queue—but they dragged the unlucky pair back to the village and tied them up.

Each was strung up and beaten. Eventually Yü-tzu confessed to having clipped Kou-erh's queue and hidden it somewhere outside the village. Clerk Li warned him that if he failed to hand over the queue, he would hack him to death with an axe. The terrified Yü-tzu managed to bite off the end of his own queue, secrete it in his hand, and pretend to "find" it under a tree. The next morning the triumphant Li K'un turned the two wanderers over to county authorities.

Now they applied the *chia-kun* and forced Chin Kuan-tzu to say that he had thrown away his queue-clipping knife and two bags of stupefying drugs on a hillside. Runners sent out to find the evidence turned up only a small ceramic bottle. Pressed by the magistrate to find the "knife," the chief runner ordered that a knife secretly be bought. The purchased blade bore a small manufacturer's mark, so Yü-tzu was told to depose that he had noticed just such a mark on his cousin's knife. To embroider the case, Chin Kuan-tzu was put to the torture again and made to depose that he had lured his cousin out on the road both to clip queues and to commit sodomy. Yü-tzu at first denied it, but was told that unless he corroborated the story, both his legs would be crushed. It was at this point that Chin Kuan-tzu was forced to fabricate the story about his master, the fortune-teller "Chang Ssu-ju." The case thus properly prepared, the magistrate sent it up through channels.

The grand councillors now sent for witnesses: Yü-tzu's mother and wandering father, both of whom were tracked down, along with his cousins; and clerk Li and his son. Chin Kuan-tzu was able to identify everyone. However, Yü-tzu's parents denied they knew Kuan-tzu. Repeated questioning revealed that they had been threatened by the chief runner at Tsinan, to the effect that "if you admit knowing Chin Kuan-tzu when you get to Peking, you will be killed when you get back." This was enough for the grand councillors, who now reported that Chin had been framed and that the whole "Chang Ssu-ju" story was rubbish.[15] Yet the inquisitors hedged: clerk Li had not yet been confronted with Yü-tzu, nor had the yamen runners been interrogated. Furthermore, since the Grand Council interrogators had not used torture, "the results are not exhaustive or definitive." A final resolution of the case would have to wait, they wrote. What they did not write was that it waited upon a change of mind at the top.

Converting Hungli

There can be no doubt that the chief prosecutor, from first to last, was the monarch himself. This is clear from his vermilion comments, both on memorials from the field and on court letters drafted by the grand councillors. The extra push, the sharper goad, the added injunction to speed and rigor, the acerbic abuse of laggard officials:

all were his personal contributions. The role of the grand councillors must have been delicate. They may have shared his fears of sedition. Yet they also had to face the agonized prisoners, with their mangled bodies and muddled stories, who had been sent up from provincial courtrooms. When doubts began to multiply in their minds, they had a serious political problem on their hands. How could one demonstrate loyalty and ardor in such a case, with its dangerous tonsure symbolism, the unknown plots that might lie behind it, and its enormous commitment of imperial prestige, and yet fend off the scandal of miscarried justice?

One route to Hungli's attention was the issue of courtroom torture. Ch'ing law required a confession for a criminal conviction, and Hungli, like his contemporaries, considered torture an appropriate way to extract the necessary details of a confession from an obviously guilty prisoner. Language smoothed the way. Just as the concepts of "prisoner" and "criminal" were not clearly distinguished (both were called *fan*), the words for "torture" and "punishment" were both expressed by the same word *(hsing)*. There were, nevertheless, legal restraints on the use of torture. Use of unauthorized torture implements, as well as killing a prisoner by torture, were punishable, mostly by administrative discipline.[16]

Although torture, as such, presented no moral difficulties, it sometimes presented practical ones. Rightly applied, torture would elicit the right answers and lead to just judgments. Misused, however, it could produce the wrong answers, especially if an interrogator went fishing, so to speak, to see what his agonized prisoner might blurt out. This was equivalent to seeking raw material for an indictment, or what we would call "giving the third degree" to a suspect before arraignment, rather than eliciting true testimony from one formally charged with a crime. Such "seeking-by-torture" *(hsing-ch'iu)* was not forbidden by the *Code,* but neither was it considered acceptable practice. Hungli feared the disruption that could result from false confessions extorted by exploratory torture. After all, the point of interrogating the small fry was to extract the names of the masterminds. If a tortured prisoner manufactured names and addresses just to stop the pain, what had the state gained? Additional credence could be lent such faulty information by detailed circumstantial accounts in a confession, which were either concocted by a prisoner out of jailhouse scuttlebutt, as in the case of monk T'ung-kao, or suggested by an interrogator's leading questions.[17] Reliable information was what was wanted, and (in Hungli's words) "confessions obtained by the *chia-kun* and cudgel are not necessarily entirely reliable."[18] As the case began to fall apart, the falsity of all the confessions obtained under torture became increasingly plain. Once incredulity began to glimmer in the Grand Council, it was only a matter of time before it illumined the Throne.

In the highest reaches of officialdom can be traced, with some precision, the spread of doubt. When the original Shantung queue-clipper, beggar Ts'ai, was reinterrogated in mid-August (at the request of exasperated officials who found his leads useless) and changed his story, Hungli believed that the crafty queue-clippers were sending up a smoke screen to throw the prosecution off the trail or simply to end their torment. But had they originally confessed freely, or under torture? Funihan assured the Throne that no torture had been used. Yet the seeds of suspicion had been sown at court. On August 29 Hungli ordered the Shantung inquisitors to send the culprits directly to the summer capital, there to be interrogated under the watchful eyes of the grand councillors.[19]

Back in Kiangnan, the botched interrogation of the singing beggar Chang Ssu was apparent to Governor-general G'aojin by September 10 as he heard the beggar's story and examined his crippled legs. G'aojin recited the monarch's own words back to him: "It is indeed just as your Sage Edict said: as soon as you apply the *chia-kun* and the cudgel, there is a contrary effect on the case."[20] He went on to interrogate Chang Ssu's accusers and came up with the story related above. G'aojin was spared the burden of discrediting the case, for his prisoner was quickly summoned to Peking. There the grand councillors could see for themselves.

The mechanics of the court-letter system make it hard to estimate what the grand councillors, as a body or as individuals, thought about the case until their own interrogation reports began to emerge in mid-September. Liu T'ung-hsun and his colleagues in Peking wrote the summer capital on September 15 that fresh inconsistencies in the Shantung confessions were appearing daily. Kneeling before them, the original Shantung queue-clippers, beggars Chin and Ts'ai, had recanted their confessions. The inquisitors prodded them: "T'ung-yuan and Chang Ssu-ju have been arrested in Kiangnan and will arrive in Peking any day to corroborate your confessions. Then how will you evade the truth?" Because of Chin's infected legs, the finger-press was now used instead of the *chia-kun,* and the criminal obediently repeated his old confession in detail. But "as soon as the finger-press was loosened" he recanted again and blurted out the whole story of his victimization. Obviously additional witnesses would have to be summoned from Shantung. (Vermilion: "Summon them quickly.") For the time being, the panel would "wait until the prisoner's wounds had healed somewhat" before applying more torture. But meanwhile "we dare not show the slightest laxity or allow ourselves to be deceived."[21]

But the case was now badly compromised. If new evidence discredited these confessions upon which the whole case had been built, what embarrassments might be expected from the numerous provincial cases that were about to descend on Peking? And how were such embarrassments to be told to the monarch, who had invested in this case not only his personal prestige but the honor of the dynasty?

By September 21, Hungli was already reacting to the bad news. He complained that the provincial confessions were "all wild and groundless." This was either because the villains were lying, "or because the examining officials are fabricating confessions. In either case, they are not to be believed." Amid such "flickering lights and shadows," what hope is there of catching the real culprits? He rejected a suggestion that suspicious persons be held in indefinite confinement, however; skillful interrogation would identify the innocent, who must then be promptly released.[22]

The scale of the potential miscarriage of justice was becoming apparent even to the zealous monarch, and by October 5 he speculated (in an unusual letter, in the confidential channel, to all province chiefs) that the whole plot might have been conceived by traitors who sought to stir up hatred of officialdom and so incite uprisings. Yet there was no choice but to press ahead, rounding up all suspicious characters even while taking care not to oppress the innocent: a hopelessly contradictory instruction from the standpoint of the hard-pressed provincial bureaucracy.[23]

In Peking, inconsistencies continued to pile up. The confessions of Ts'ai T'ing-chang and Han P'ei-hsien were hopelessly compromised.[24] The story of how the singing beggar had been framed was duly conveyed to Hungli. Furthermore, when confronted with "Chang Ssu-ju," the original informer, beggar Chin, could not identify him. But the monarch still played the gimlet-eyed prosecutor. Surely, he wrote on October 17, these criminals would have agreed not to identify one another in court, in order to conceal their plot.

Liu T'ung-hsun was to examine the prisoners with even greater care. As soon as he "detected a hint of discrepancy between words and demeanor," he was to "seize the opportunity to press harder, so that the true thread might be discerned." Furthermore, every effort must be made to wring from monk T'ung-kao the answer to what those queue-hairs were *really* to be used for.[25] But at the summer capital, Duke Fuheng had also become a doubter. On October 17, the inconsistencies were too much for him, and he ordered Governor Jangboo to send all his prisoners from Kiangsu to Peking to have their testimonies cross-checked.[26]

An opportunity now presented itself to the grand councillors: Grand Secretary Liu T'ung-hsun was about to depart Peking for the summer capital. At sixty-eight, Liu had a distinguished record in the upper reaches of Peking politics (including twelve years on the Grand Council) and a reputation as an incorruptible official, an outspoken breaker of bad news, and an advocate of unpalatable policies. Though Hungli may sometimes have considered him meddlesome, he bore Liu an unshakable respect. He had once briefly imprisoned Liu for an unwelcome suggestion, but shortly pardoned him and continued to employ him in the highest positions, including that of chief tutor of the emperor's sons. So deeply did Hungli appreciate his tough-minded servant that upon Liu's death in 1773 he paid a personal condolence call upon his family.[27] As senior grand councillor on the scene, Liu had sweated through the Peking summer while the sovereign was at Ch'eng-te. As sorcery fear gripped the capital, he had handled the delicate job of unearthing the culprits while not raising panic among the common people. As soulstealing culprits were shipped in from provincial courtrooms, he had ample exposure to the shoddy and mendacious cases prepared by local prosecutors. His memoranda to Hungli are masterpieces of subtlety: they lay out the defects of the cases, including long quotes or paraphrases of the recantations, all carefully packaged in a dogged zealotry that refuses to accept the "crafty" and "evasive" testimony at face value. These documents, at least, could never expose Liu to charges of being soft on soulstealing. After the singing beggar recanted in Peking on October 15, it was time something was done to spare the Throne worse embarrassment. This would require concerted action in the monarch's presence.

As president of the Board of Punishments, Liu had the annual duty of journeying to Ch'eng-te to help the monarch scrutinize the reports of the autumn assizes, in which condemned prisoners' cases were reviewed. When the reviews had been presented to the Throne, Hungli would check off *(kou-tao)* those to be put to death. The routine every year was for Liu, who had remained in Peking to manage Grand Council business, to journey to the summer capital around the middle of October and accompany His Majesty back to Peking. On the leisurely southwest progress through the crisp autumn countryside, Hungli, in consultation with Liu, would brush a vermilion "check" next to each condemned name.[28] Liu left Peking on about October 18 and was in Ch'eng-te by October 21. He and Fuheng were with the monarch for the next five days.

A meeting of minds must have occurred by October 25, to judge by the tone of Duke Fuheng's subsequent interrogation reports. Gone now was the hedging about miscarriages of justice, gone the apparent reluctance to accept recantations at face value. Liu joined the procession when the court set out upon the road on October 26, while Fuheng remained in Ch'eng-te to finish interrogating the prisoners. The imperial party reached Peking on November 1, and two days later Hungli called off the soulstealing prosecution.[29]

Calling off the campaign was not a simple matter of canceling orders. The Throne had invested in it so much prestige and moral authority that a more ceremonious ending was required.[30] First, court letters were sent by Fuheng, Yenjišan, and Liu T'ung-hsun to all governors-general and governors. The queue-clipping case had "spread to various provinces" because officials in Kiangsu and Chekiang had not reported it promptly. The response to repeated imperial edicts had been maladministration by "local officials." As a result, those cases that were brought to trial "were not without incidents of extortion by torture." (This last, added to the court letter in vermilion, clearly troubled Hungli, though he certainly had known about it earlier in the campaign.) Therefore he had ordered criminals sent to Peking for reinterrogation. None turned out to be the chief criminals, and there were many instances in which innocent persons had been falsely accused. This was "all the result of local officials in Kiangsu and Chekiang letting the affair fester to the point of disaster." Any further prosecution would simply disrupt local society. This would be "inconsistent with our system of government." The prosecution was therefore to be stopped.

Curiously, however, the court letter insisted that this should not be taken by local officials as a signal to relax vigilance. Watchfulness was still the order of the day, and an official who captured a "chief criminal" would thereby be deemed to have "redeemed his faults."[31]

On the same day was promulgated an open edict that cast all the blame on provincial officials. The soulstealing menace, it began, first appeared in Kiangsu and Chekiang, then spread to Shantung and other provinces. Had provincial officials rigorously prosecuted the case "when they first heard of it," pressing their local subordinates for results, "clues could naturally have been found, and the chief criminals would have been unable to slip through the net." Instead, "right from the beginning" bureaucrats had followed their accustomed routines and failed to report the matter, "seeking to turn something into nothing," and only when pressed by the Throne itself did they begin to order prosecution.

Now, although there have been arrests in Shantung, Anhwei, Kiangsu, and Chekiang, "We feared that among them there were some whose depositions were extorted by torture." Therefore Hungli had ordered that the criminals be sent to Peking for interrogation by a tribunal drawn from the Grand Council, the Board of Punishments, and the Peking Gendarmerie. The original depositions proved unreliable, and there were indeed cases of extortion by torture. "It was apparent that in those provinces officials began by concealing the facts and followed by evading responsibility." As a result, the "principal criminals" were not caught. Nothing was done but to "send petty functionaries out in all directions to cause trouble for the villages." This was "entirely out of keeping with our system of government." Here Hungli bit the bullet: "Now, at last, it will not be necessary to continue prosecuting this case."

How are we to reconcile the ambivalence of the secret court letters and the vindictiveness of the open edict? It is plain (from the vermilion emendation) that Hungli was personally upset and embarrassed by the confessions concocted under torture. Yet the fact that he continued to insist (in the secret channel) on vigilance, and (in both channels) on the objective existence of the "chief criminals" even though not a single one had been found, suggests a face-saving compromise. Hungli's state of mind emerges most lucidly in an extraordinary vermilion rescript to a memorial from Funihan. The Shantung governor had replied to the November 3 court letter in plaintive terms. He had prosecuted the case "with dedication" and

奉　諭等信到民臺訊把匪餘力終
諭旨嚴飭查拿李等臣督飭文武實心偵緝不遺餘力終
未獲有省惡正把柔省自七月中旬以後亦不
聞後有拏到發辨之事此案行蹤詭秘我固延
訪慕嚴飭務匪跡令爷

聖主明降諭旨傳止查拿匪徒硬勾薛零武閒禁綱
　　稍覓形蹤殊滿誠如
聖訓斷致易于敗露民惟有密飭所屬隨時隨地留擒
　　心偵探設法跟尋一得正把報線迅即追蹤擒
　　　　　使少有綫得縱滿理合將接奏
諭旨欽遵緣由恭摺覆

奏伏乞
皇上睿鑒謹

Funihan's memorial of November 13, 1768, on the prosecution of soulstealing suspects (detail), with Hungli's vermilion rescript in the four columns at the far left (translated on p. 181).

had "spared no effort." Although the chief criminals had not been caught, "Shantung was then free of queue-clipping incidents after mid-August." The vermilion reads:

> Seen. Although Shantung's handling of this case did exceed the bounds of propriety, We shall not blame you. If you were held responsible for excesses after being ordered to prosecute rigorously, then how would provincial officials know, in the future, what course to follow? Nevertheless, planting evidence and seeking-by-torture are really not the Correct Way.[32]

Let such candor not tempt the governor into "negligence," warned Hungli. Yet a whiff of royal remorse was in the air, and provincial officials were exceedingly sensitive to the prevailing winds. Hungli knew that the dignity of the Throne could be maintained only by insisting on the reality of the plot and by punishing officials who had failed to prosecute with sufficient vigor. The other side of the compromise, however, was to impeach officials who had tortured false confessions out of innocent people.

Settling Accounts with the Bureaucracy

So far, there had been no concession that *the case itself* was poorly founded. On the contrary, the chief "criminals" had really existed and had eluded justice because of provincial mismanagement. Punishment was now in order: "Those governors-general and governors of Kiangsu and Chekiang, who let this case fester to the point of disaster," were to be referred to the Board of Civil Office for "rigorous discipline," in order to "rectify the bureaucratic system."[33] Here was Hungli's revenge for the cover-up. Those to be disciplined for laxity and mendacity were Governor-general G'aojin (Liangkiang), Governor Jangboo (Kiangsu), Governor Feng Ch'ien (Anhwei), Governor Hsiung Hsueh-p'eng (Chekiang), Governor Yungde (Chekiang), Governor Mingde (Yunnan, formerly Kiangsu), and Governor Surde (Shansi). A number of county-level officials were cashiered for having exonerated sorcery suspects the preceding spring. To keep the compromise in balance, a number of lower officials were impeached for manufacturing evidence through the improper use of torture on innocent prisoners. Some distinguished careers were ruined, particularly among lower officials. Prefect Shao Ta-yeh of Hsu-chou, for instance, was a renowned administrator whose flood-control work had spared his people from inundation over a tenure of seven years. In retribution for his part in botching the case of the singing beggar, he was rusticated to a remote military post, where he died a few years later.[34]

The nub of the problem, however, was Governor Funihan himself, whose memorials (and enclosed confessions) had kept the soulstealing case on the boil for three months. Day after day, the grand councillors at the summer capital and at Peking had viewed the human debris sent up from Shantung courts as they reinterrogated the soulstealing criminals. Governor Funihan had insisted all along that his own interrogations "did not rely upon torture," a statement that had greatly enhanced the credibility of the confessions.[35] What, then, asked the grand councillors, was the meaning of these gravely wounded prisoners, whose lacerated bodies still had not healed? Monk T'ung-kao, should he survive, would be maimed for life. If they had been tortured in county or prefectural courts, had not Funihan seen their condition personally when they were brought before him? Funihan was ordered to explain himself.[36]

The governor replied that, when he first saw beggars Ts'ai and Chin, it was evident that they had been tortured, but "they could still walk," and had named their masters and confederates without undergoing further ordeals. As for the crippled T'ung-kao, he had only appeared at the governor's court *after* the dispatch of the "no torture" memorial. Funihan then humbly reminded His Majesty of his own command of August 5 to "do your utmost" *(chin-fa)* to dig the truth out of the culprits. With that sort of backing, he asked, why would he have hesitated to report that "conscientious investigating officials had used torture" in pursuing the case? At this rather spunky rejoinder came the vermilion sneer: "Even more mendacious." The Board of Civil Office was ordered to recommend punishment.[37] When it came, the punishment was rather mild, considering how much trouble the governor had inflicted upon the bureaucracy, and embarrassment upon the Throne. The offense, of course, was not torturing prisoners (Hungli had already expressed a certain sympathetic understanding on that point), but lying about it to the Throne. Funihan was demoted to the post of provincial treasurer of Shansi (Vermilion: "and take away his rank while in the job") but was perhaps relieved that Hungli forbore to route the case into the criminal track, as he had for his predecessor Governor Chun-t'ai sixteen years earlier in a roughly similar context. In the light of all that had happened, Funihan had received but a slap on the wrist: an unmistakable concession of royal error.[38]

The End of the Trail

Once the monarch was firmly oriented toward calling off the prosecution, the inquisitors knew that it was all right to resolve these embarrassing cases. Exonerations followed quickly and clearly. First resolved were the cases of the monks who were nearly lynched at Hsu-k'ou-chen and the beggars of Soochow. On November 8, Fuheng confirmed the original finding of the Wu County magistrate: Ching-chuang and his companions were all "honest monks true to their calling" and should be released forthwith. Fisherman Chang, who had accosted them in the temple and pursued them into the street, was to be held responsible for the disturbance. Although they were unable to prove that this was an attempt at extortion (like that of constable Ts'ai in Hsiao-shan), the grand councillors decided that a beating was not enough for fisherman Chang. Besides being required to make restitution to the monks for their lost baggage and money, he was to be exposed in the cangue for two months "to instruct the people." The ruffians who had robbed their boat, Li San and T'ang Hua, were each to be beaten eighty strokes according to the useful statute that forbade "doing what ought not be done."[39]

Of the three original Soochow beggars, only Ch'en Han-ju was still alive (Chang Yü-ch'eng had died in jail; Ch'iu Yung-nien was reported to have died later of illness). Here, too, the original judgment by the county magistrate was upheld. The ten-year-old boy Ku Chen-nan, whose testimony had implicated the beggars in queue-clipping, had been brought to Ch'eng-te along with his father. The boy now related that "he had been ordered by the constabulary officer to identify them," but could only say that beggar Ch'en's clothing "looked like" that of the man who he thought had jerked his queue. This had not been good enough for the magistrate, nor was it now for Fuheng. Beggar Ch'en "is definitely not a queue-clipper," and should promptly be escorted back to Soochow and released. (Vermilion: "Let it be done as recommended.") The Soochow cases were closed.[40]

Mason Wu and the Hsiao-shan monks, it will be remembered, had been rearrested in early September and sent, by imperial order, on the long journey beyond the Great Wall to the summer capital. The trip took slightly over a month, and upon their arrival in early October the emperor immediately appointed an investigative team of Grand Council staff members, supervised by Duke Fuheng. All the culprits were questioned anew, including the self-confessed perjurer, constable Ts'ai, who was brought before the panel and tortured. The inquisitors asked, presumably just to make sure: Might not the Chekiang provincial authorities have concealed a real sorcery case by making him a scapegoat, "instructing a confession" to make the inquisitors believe it was all a frame-up? The doomed constable reasonably objected that he would hardly perjure himself in order to "obtain future benefits" from provincial superiors, if he would at the same time be admitting to a capital crime. The panel took his point. They sentenced him to be strangled, with execution delayed until after the autumn assizes.

On November 19 the panel confirmed the findings of the Chekiang court: the monks had been framed by constable Ts'ai, their confessions wrung from them by torture. Hair from the supposedly clipped "queues" was carefully examined and found to be of identical color and texture. Duke Fuheng narrowly observed the bearing and demeanor of Chü-ch'eng and the other monks, and found that "they exhibited no signs of sorcery or villainy." They were to be escorted home and released.[41]

It remained for the inquisitors to grill mason Wu about his role in the spring soulstealing affair in Te-ch'ing. Just as they began, there arrived from Chekiang some curious intelligence about those spring events, which cast a new light on the origins of the sorcery panic.[42]

The Temple of Mercy in the lush silk country of Te-ch'ing sheltered a small community of very poor monks. The "incense fire was dim," it was said, meaning that the temple was little frequented by pilgrims or by devotees wanting masses celebrated for the dead, and so got few donations.[43] Nearer the city, on Chien-yuan Mountain, was a prosperous temple: a Kuan-yin Hall, much favored by the local devout. Early in the spring of 1768, jealousy and privation had led the poor monks at the Temple of Mercy into uncharitable thoughts. A friend of the monks, an ingenious layman named Hsu, suggested that current popular fears about soulstealing might be turned to advantage. All the monks had to do was spread a rumor that masons were practicing sorcery in the vicinity of the prosperous temple, which would pollute the power of that establishment to bring blessings to worshipers.

The story material was ready to hand. Down at the walled city, mason Wu and his men were already at work rebuilding the watergate. As it happened, Wu had won the contract over a crew of rival masons from another county. Might not the disappointed bidders try (as masons would) to harm their competitors by sorcery? Local folk believed that death pollution could be inflicted on an enemy by "burying death-magic" in his path.[44] A slain rooster buried under a footpath would emit quite enough death pollution to do the job. All the monks had to do, suggested layman Hsu, was to spread the word that feuding masons had "buried death-magic" under paths leading to the Kuan-yin Hall. One of the monks who "knew a bit of writing" drew up the necessary posters: We have heard (he wrote) that last month a mason "buried death-magic" near Chien-yuan Mountain, and that persons passing over the spot on the way to the Kuan-yin Hall might be infected by it. Just now, when many people are going there to worship, we fear that they may come to harm. The Temple of Mercy is one of those long known as "pure gates of Buddha." It can "help one to approach good fortune and avoid calamity." Layman Hsu spread this intelligence about the county and received 500 copper cash for his trouble.

With this story on their desks, the inquisitors asked mason Wu about the reported plot by rival masons to injure them by sorcery. This looked like a plausible origin for the spring panic in the Hangchow region: another frame-up, another attempt to injure rivals by an imputation of sorcery. But mason Wu, in his down-to-earth way, offered no helpful details.

> *Mason Wu:* Last year, masons from Hai-ning named Cheng Yuan-ch'en and Mao T'ien-ch'eng came to Te-ch'ing to contract for the bridge job. They couldn't agree on a price, so they left.
> *Inquisitor:* Was there any talk of "burying death-magic"?
> *Mason Wu:* This year we haven't laid eyes on Cheng or Mao and haven't heard that they bore us any grievance.[45]

Did this incident start the panic by fanning public fears of mason-sorcerers? The grand councilors could not be sure. Yet the Temple of Mercy incident confirmed, for the skeptical among them, that "soulstealing" was a phantom conceived in ignorance and nourished in envy. Here was another case of cynical men manipulating popular fears for private ends. Mason Wu, at any rate, could not be held responsible. Along with Chü-ch'eng and the other monks, beggar Chi, and peasant Shen, he was to be escorted home and released. Here our original subjects, both victims and tormentors, drop gratefully from the historical record.

CHAPTER 9

Political Crime and
Bureaucratic Monarchy

We now have read several stories: about sorcery panic spreading among the common people; about a monarch becoming convinced that sorcery is a mask for sedition; about agnostic bureaucrats struggling to cope with demands from both sides but failing to satisfy either. These stories are layered one upon the another, several texts written on a single historical page. Beneath them lies another story, the hardest to read: how local events—including the sorcery scare—served as fuel for running the political system.[1]

Sorcery played its part in the political system as the kind of event I shall call "political crime." Political crime included sedition in all its various guises, whether religious heterodoxy, literary innuendo, or outright revolt. Because it threatened the foundations of the system itself, political crime was considered distinct from the ever-present corruption, which merely reduced the system's efficiency. But if this were the case, why were not the bureaucrats as concerned about it as the monarch? It was, after all, their system too. The answer must lie at the core of bureaucratic monarchy itself, at least as we see it in the Chinese case. Documents from the sorcery crisis suggest why political crime was a monarch's issue and not a bureaucrat's issue. The heart of the problem was the relationship between routine and arbitrary power.

Routine and Arbitrary Power in the Bureaucratic Monarchy

Study of the Chinese political system under the late empires has produced two largely distinct literatures: on the structure, personnel, and values of the administrative bureaucracy;[2] and on the development of the imperial institution, particularly the imperial communication system.[3] As a result, we now have a more sophisticated view of officialdom as a way of life; and a view of the ruler that makes him part of a political system, rather than a remote and all-powerful despot. I wonder, however, whether we have yet discovered how arbitrary power interacts with bureaucratic routine over a long period within a single system.[4] We still tend to assume that the two are inversely related: the more of one, the less of the other; as one grows, the other shrinks. The tendency of social analysis since Max Weber is in fact to show that, in the long run, autocrats yield to bureaucrats. Yet I believe that arbitrary and routine authority may not have been incompatible in the Chinese system, and may indeed have found ways to live side by side.

In his celebrated description of the Chinese polity, Max Weber actually avoids confronting the issue of how arbitrary and routine power interact. Instead, he characterizes the Chinese monarchy as incompletely centralized, and its operational norms as uncodified. The limitations of his data shielded him from a view of either arbitrary power or codified routine. The emperor himself is a shadowy figure in Weber's treatment of Chinese bureaucracy. Under the "average ruler," authority was not "centralized."[5] Weber presumably believed, however, that Chinese bureaucracy would be powerless when faced with a *non*average ruler because it lacked specialization (only modern "bureaucratic experts" can compete effectively with the "absolute monarch," whom they can dismiss as a "dilettante").[6] Although he uses the term "bureaucracy" in referring to the Chinese system, Weber actually includes that system not under "Bureaucracy," a subject heading he reserves for the specifically "modern" type, but rather under "Patriarchal and Patrimonial Domination."[7] Just as shadowy is Weber's notion of the codified routine through which the Chinese bureaucracy was disciplined and controlled. Though the "patriarchal" monarchy was able to achieve an "authoritarian and internalized bondage" of the officials by transferring them frequently and thereby keeping them from forming regional power-bases,[8] the "patriarchal character of the political association . . . was opposed to any development of formal law."[9] "Formal law," for Weber, must have included administrative codes by which the bureaucracy itself might be regulated. Although for these reasons Weber could not pose the problem sharply in the context of the Chinese state, his historical logic suggests that he saw arbitrary and routine power as incompatible. History tends to replace the former with the latter through routinization and rationalization.[10]

In his classic treatise on the evolution of the Prussian state, Hans Rosenberg distinguishes between "dynastic absolutism" and "bureaucratic absolutism." By "absolutism," Rosenberg means power essentially unchecked by constitutional limits or by compromise with influential social strata. By "dynastic," he emphasizes the dominance of the monarch himself ("a royal bully," as he describes Frederick William I) over society at large, as well as over the corps of "royal servants" recruited to carry out his orders. This system Rosenberg also characterizes as an "experiment in royal monocracy." Although he does not describe in detail the interaction between the "monocrat" and his bureaucracy, the implication is that the "hideous spirit of fearful obedience to authority" that infused Prussian society at large was a projection of the bureaucracy's own state of mind.[11] Nevertheless, Rosenberg asserts that even under the early Hohenzollerns, royal control relied upon minutely regularized procedures: the "public law" that governed the bureaucracy as well as the populace.[12] We are left uncertain about how "monocracy" or dynastic absolutism preserved its freedom of action within a system of regulations that were designed to reduce the operation of government to a finely tuned routine.

If there was a purely "arbitrary" component to this system, it was unstable and short-lived. It fell victim to "an unremitting struggle for replacing arbitrary royal powers . . . with general legal rules." Even under Frederick the Great, monocratic power was frustrated by officials who had "real power to obstruct and divert" by manipulating information and other acts of bureaucratic "sabotage." Under Frederick's weaker successors, the bureaucracy succeeded in securing itself against arbitrary sanctions by introducing life tenure and due process into the bureaucratic personnel system. The result, as Rosenberg describes post-Napoleonic Prussia, was a state ruled by career bureaucrats ("bureaucratic absolutism"); the monarch was simply the "top functionary."[13] Here arbitrary and routine power were subject to a historical process that weakened the one to the advantage of the other—a process like Weber's "routinization" and "rationalization." In Rosenberg's Prussian case, arbitrary and routine power could not long coexist.

"Bureaucratic monarchy" reads like an oxymoron. To the extent that it is "bureaucratic," what scope is left for the monarch? To the extent that it is monarchic, how can one man's autocratic power coexist with a system of universal rules? Both monarch and bureaucrat were caught in this dilemma; both were ambivalent toward formal administrative procedures. The monarch had to regulate his thousands of bureaucratic servants by written codes, to ensure that everyone stuck to the administrative procedures that underlay his own wealth and security. At the same time, he was naturally concerned to maintain his own distinctive position, his extra-bureaucratic power and autonomy. Consequently he had to struggle unceasingly to avoid becoming bureaucratized himself. Much of the normal business of government involved him in sanctioning decrees drafted for him by the Grand Secretariat, or in ratifying appointments of candidates presented to him by the Board of Civil Office. Faced by his document-drafters with a narrow range of choice, the busy monarch found himself "functioning" as a cog (albeit a bejeweled one) in a document-processing machine. How was he to break out of this trap and assert his position as master, not functionary?[14]

The bureaucratic official, for his part, was bedeviled by minute regulations on the form, timing, and routing of paperwork, fiscal and judicial deadlines, and the relations of superiors to subordinates. To break any of these regulations exposed him to impeachment, fines, transfer, or dismissal. Yet these onerous regulations at least drew certain boundaries around his responsibilities and offered him some protection from arbitrary demands by superiors and even by the monarch himself.[15]

The Monarch's Control of Bureaucrats

Rules yield predictability and standardization. They also limit the freedom of the one who applies them. In this sense they are a great leveler of status: those who apply and monitor the rules may become as entangled by them as those who are subject to them. The Ch'ing autocrats accordingly had to pick their way carefully between routine and arbitrary models of command. When rules were ineffective, the remedies included not only more rules but also procedures that rested upon arbitrary power. From early in his reign, Hungli was impatient with rules that did not work. His remedies included both tightening the screws of the routine bureaucratic machine and finding ways to inject his own arbitrary power into it. How he did this can be seen most readily in his efforts to evaluate his officials.

Surveillance of Efficiency and Conduct

At the heart of monarchic control lay the evaluation of officials: estimating their qualifications for appointment, surveying their conduct in office, and periodically evaluating their fitness for service. The history of Hungli's reign suggests how hard it is to force a bureaucracy to discipline itself. His despair at the system he inherited led him to seek alternative means of control.

The essence of the official control system was the distinction between crime and administrative failure. Criminal penalties, for corruption or worse crimes, were handled by the Board of Punishments after the culprit had been impeached and removed from office. Administrative sanctions *(ch'u-fen)* were handled by the Board of Civil Office. These penalties, which involved demotion in rank, transfer to a less desirable post, and monetary fines, covered a broad range of misdeeds, of which most were failures to meet deadlines or quotas (for solving criminal cases or collecting taxes), concealment of information, or other breaches of standard operating procedure. No official dossier was without its record of *ch'u-fen* offenses. Here are some examples of typical offenses and their penalties, drawn from the 1749 edition of the *Regulations of the Board of Civil Office, Administrative Sanctions:*

> An official who fails to report the fact of a grain-transport boat's sinking: to be reduced one grade and transferred.

> If an official supervising the collection of the land tax falls short [of the quota] by an amount less than one-tenth, he is to be blocked from promotion and fined a year's [nominal] salary. If he is short a tenth or more, he is to be reduced in rank by one grade . . . and if he is short five-tenths or more he is to be dismissed from office.

> If a local official, fearing to be disciplined for laxity in arresting criminals, under some pretext intimidates a plaintiff and forces him to avoid

using the word "robbery" and not report it as such, . . . he is to be removed from office.[16]

Although Chinese government has long included special organs to investigate and impeach officials for incompetence and wrongdoing, their history since medieval times has been one of decline. The branch of government generally called "the Censorate" (under the Ch'ing, *tu-ch'a-yuan*) historically had duties of both remonstrating with the emperor about his conduct and keeping an eye on the bureaucracy. At least as early as the seventh century A.D., "remonstrance" upward was secondary to surveillance downward. But over time even the independent surveillance function was eroded. The Manchu conquerors inherited from their Ming predecessors a Censorate that had largely lost its ability to supervise field administration. "Surveillance offices" *(an-ch'a-ssu)* in the provinces had, by the late sixteenth century, already assumed the regular judicial work of provincial government. The Manchus completed their incorporation into the provincial bureaucracy, and we now refer to these officials as "provincial judges."[17] Although there were censorial offices in the capital to check on the work of metropolitan officials, they were largely engaged in combing documents for irregularities. And although there were "provincial censors" charged with overseeing provincial administration, these men were actually stationed in Peking, which meant that the "eyes and ears" of the sovereign were considerably dimmed outside the capital. Accordingly, the job of surveillance in both capital and provinces mainly fell to line bureaucrats, each of whom was responsible for watching the conduct of his subordinates. To symbolize how administration and surveillance were melded, a provincial governor bore the brevet title of vice-president of the Censorate, to indicate his special responsibility to scrutinize the conduct of his subordinates. In effect, the bureaucracy was really watching itself.[18]

This kind of in-house bureaucratic surveillance followed two modes: *ad hoc* impeachment (for both incompetence and criminality), and periodic evaluation leading to triennial fitness reports for all officials, reports that also served as the basis for impeaching substandard officials. In both these modes, the process relied largely on the work of line bureaucrats and rather little upon the Censorate. Of 5,151 impeachment cases in the Ch'ien-lung reign, less than 8 percent were initiated by the Censorate, with the rest by line officials in Peking or the provinces.[19] Though Hungli believed that both modes worked badly, he identified the problem most clearly in the triennial fitness reports.

The Triennial Evaluations

Periodic evaluation of officials has a history as long as that of Chinese government.[20] The Manchus inherited the system from the Ming and had installed it even before the conquest.[21] By the mid-eighteenth century the basic elements of the evaluation for civil officials[22] were the Capital Investigation *(ching-ch'a)* which included all Peking officials except those of the three highest ranks, and the Grand Accounting *(ta-chi)*, which included provincial officials except for governors-general, governors, and provincial treasurers and judges.

For both the capital and provincial systems, the cumbersome procedure was that every year an official would be rated *(k'ao-ch'eng)* by his superior officer. These ratings served as raw material for the triennial evaluations. In the capital, the triennial registers would be aggregated by the heads of the Six Boards, and in the provinces by the governors. The registers (bound traditionally in imperial yellow) were then forwarded to a review commission consisting of officials from the Board of Civil Office and the Censorate, along with one Han and one Manchu grand secretary. The commission would then review the "yellow registers" and decide who should be promoted, demoted, or retained in office. The cases of men due for promotion or demotion would then be the subjects of separate memorials to the Throne from the Board of Civil Office. Men whom the Throne approved for promotion as "outstanding" *(cho-i)* still had to be recommended in separate memorials by their superiors. Strict accountability applied in these cases of promotion for merit. In the case of lower-level officials, recommendations had to note whether there were any outstanding treasury shortages or unresolved court cases that might block promotion. If any were subsequently found after promotion, the recommender himself would be punished by demotion and transfer.

The apparent rigor of this system seems less impressive when we examine the actual documents used in it. To begin with, the format was extremely stereotyped. The registers, sometimes known as "four-column books" *(ssu-chu-ts'e)*, contained, for each man, a single page with four headings: "integrity" *(ts'ao-shou)*, "executive performance" *(cheng-shih)*, "native talent" *(ts'ai-chü)*, and "physical fitness" *(nien-li)*, listed in that order. Under each heading, one of three standard ideographs would be filled in:

Standard Format for Triennial Evaluations

Category	Integrity	Executive Performance	Talent
Highest	Incorrupt	Assiduous	Exceptional
Middle	Careful	Diligent	Good
Lowest	Ordinary	Ordinary	Ordinary

Based on their ratings, officials would be grouped into three ranks. The criterion for ranking was the number of categories in which an official received better-than-average ratings. For instance, an official who received ratings of "incorrupt *(ch'ing)*," "assiduous *(ch'in)*," and "exceptional *(yu)*" in the first three categories was ranked in group one. ("Physical fitness" seems not to have played a part in the group rankings. If age or illness made the official unfit, he was impeached in a separate procedure.) Those with two above-average ratings were grouped in group two; and those with one or none comprised group three.[23] All three groups, however, were considered fit for duty. Those in group one might be recommended for promotion, which was done in separate memorials attesting to their "outstanding" *(cho-i)* qualities. Also in separate memorials, those whose general fitness was below standard were impeached *(chiu-ho)*. The provincial triennial evaluation *(ta-chi)* used substantially the same format but added, for each official, a four- or eight-ideograph evaluation *(k'ao-yü)* that offered an overall assessment of performance.

How little latitude these fitness reports permitted the evaluating officer! The scale of qualities was hardly fine enough to make careful distinctions among officials. Hardly more revealing were the four- or eight-ideograph evaluations on each man's file in the "Grand Accounting." An examination of numerous eighteenth-century yellow registers suggests that evaluators were choosing their comments from standard phrasebooks. The specificity is still crude, the result bland. Here are a few examples from a 1751 list of magistrates from Chihli ranked in the middle grade *(erh-teng)*. One is reminded of a third-grader's report card, prepared by a teacher who is struggling for something special to say about each of her charges ("participates actively in class, written work neat").

"Conduct perceptive, executive performance conscientious"
"Executive performance diligent and careful, fit for his post"
"Official conduct careful, management diligent"
"Talent perspicuous, management diligent"
"Official conduct careful, management conscientious"
"Conduct sincere, management diligent"[24]

One would expect that in the subsequent recommendations for promotion there would be more to say. Indeed the ratings are more complimentary, but the format is just as confining and stilted:

"Intelligent and clever, administration very capable"
"Perceptive and skillful, administration resolute"
"Mature and honest, administration diligent and careful"
"Bright and able, administration wholehearted"
"Talent outstanding, administration resolute"[25]

Although one finds minor differences of vocabulary among provinces (suggesting that each provincial yamen had its own handbook of such stock phrases), the impression left by these registers is of officials who were struggling to differentiate subordinates whose records seemed generally acceptable but of whom they had little or no personal knowledge.

Such stilted, conceptually cramped procedures grew naturally from bureaucratic life and reflected the mentality of the men who applied them. First, there was the need to avoid risks. Recommendation of a man who later turned out to be disappointing (or worse) could incur penalties for the recommender. Perhaps the more closely the criteria of merit hewed to a narrow, unexpressive format, the more likely were officials to risk making recommendations, on the principle that the less said, the better. Furthermore, descriptions of *acts* rather than analyses of *character* were more easily defensible, should anything go wrong. Second, the evaluations probably were adequate to describe what bureaucrats themselves considered a "good" official. In a rule-ridden environment, the best official was the one who caused the fewest problems—that is, who exemplified largely negative virtues by avoiding trouble. In any bureaucratic system, to excel can be risky.

Nor are whistle-blowers and boat-rockers appreciated. The over-zealous official trips over rules more often than does the cautious plodder. Hence prudence, circumspection, and diligence were prominent values in the routine evaluations.

Systemic Blocks to Routine Control

Hungli's Despair at the Routine System

Hungli had nothing against routine evaluations as such. On the contrary, he recognized that they "affected the fundamental institutions of state" *(ta-tien)*. The trouble was, he believed, that they were applied carelessly and dishonestly. Seven years into his reign, he complained that the Grand Accounting in the provinces was "an empty letter" and was administered "sloppily or perfunctorily." Good officials were not recommended, bad ones not impeached. Personnel evaluations hinged on affairs of the moment and said little about long-term conduct. Judgment of an incumbent official rested on whether the governor-general and governor happened to like him, and might not accord with the man's general reputation. Officials were recommended for promotion through personal favoritism, and scoundrels were shown leniency. "Only the faults of educational officials or petty functionaries are casually noted, so as to make up the necessary numbers." By such chicanery was the autocrat undone: "Our governors-general and governors are Our arms and legs, heart and backbone. If they treat such a crucial government function as mere routine, on what can We rely?"[26] Evaluation in the Capital Investigation he considered just as perfunctory.[27]

In the hands of the review commission, the triennial yellow registers got the same off-hand treatment. Hungli complained that unworthy candidates for promotion or reassignment were not screened out but were passed right through to imperial audience. "It should be possible at a glance to see [from the registers] whether a candidate is up to the job. But the Nine Chief Ministers *(chiu-ch'ing)* [that is, the review commission responsible for inspecting the registers] pass the buck to the Board of Civil Office, the Board of Civil Office passes it to the Nine Chief Ministers; and the result is that they all pass it to Us!"[28] The monarch knew that, rather than face up to the task of making personnel judgments that might arouse resentment, the bureaucracy passed the job to the one man who could always take the heat.

The routine inflation of evaluative phrases *(k'ao-yü)* was all too apparent to Hungli when a candidate for appointment received radically disparate ratings from two evaluators, or when a man he knew to be a bumbler came before him with glowing recommendations. The Yunnan governor recommended one of his circuit-intendants with a *kao-yü* of "experienced and of solid character."[29] But Hungli reviewed the man's record and found that the preceding governor had characterized him as "aged and infirm," defects that the passage of time would hardly have remedied. The new governor had, he complained,

> said nothing about his age and infirmity. And the *k'ao-yü* of all his other subordinates show only superior traits and no deficiencies. Now human talent is variously distributed. Some men are of decent character but not very able; or they are efficient administrators but insincere in their inner natures . . . but in [the new governor's] memorial, the evaluations are very general and there is absolutely no differentiation among them. It seems that in the whole province there is not a single official who can be criticized!

The *k'ao-yü* of a certain Taiwan circuit-intendant read "youthful and vigorous, of fine character, able and intelligent, apt at administration."[30] Hungli: "But We know him very well. He has a bit of cleverness, but his character is definitely not sincere, and his administrative behavior merely consists of complying with the formal requirements of his job in order to dispose of his public duty. He never had solid abilities, and his physical vigor is not that great either . . . This shows how provincial officials do not take seriously the job of evaluating personnel." Although he was aware that laziness and laxity were part of the trouble, Hungli also knew that reliable routine personnel control was hampered by certain systemic problems.

Patronage versus Discipline

The provincial governors were line administrators as well as evaluators. Hence they acted under compulsions that went with their office.[31] One of these was a powerful desire for a certain kind of personal image, which can be roughly translated as "magnanimity" *(k'uan-ta)*. The essence of a good patron, this quality warmed what might otherwise be a cold, objective bureaucratic relationship between a province chief and his subordinates. "Magnanimity" in a patron meant a concern for the human needs of his clients. Though the patron's practical payoff was loyalty, his symbolic reward was a certain personal image, one that was sullied every time he had to throw the book at a subordinate and thus treat him as a misaligned cog in a machine rather than as a human dependent. The dignity of the superior was hurt along with the career of the subordinate.

In what respect could local officials be considered dependents or clients of governors? Though the general answer is surely the paternalism that tinctured the entire Chinese bureaucracy, the specific answer lies in the governor's power to recommend his subordinates for appointment, transfer, or promotion. Except for the small number of local posts that were rated highest in administrative difficulty and were filled by recommendation of the Grand Council[32] and except for a portion of posts set aside to be filled directly by the Board of Civil Office, governors had the privilege of recommending men for particular posts within their provinces. If a governor certified that there was no suitable candidate among bureaucrats of his own jurisdiction, he could recommend someone from outside. Even in categories of appointment that the administrative code specifically placed outside their reach, governors pushed relentlessly to expand their appointive power, a power basic to personal patronage networks. Given the speed at which provincial personnel rotated from post to post, such networks could rapidly grow to national scale. Information in the *Collected Statutes* indicates that *at least* 30 percent of all posts, from circuit-intendancies down to county magistracies, were in categories that could be filled through a governor's recommendation.[33]

Quite apart from the danger of cliques and factions, however, Hungli had constantly to deal with governors' desire "to acquire a reputation for magnanimity," which made it hard for them to evaluate personnel honestly.[34] Hungli scolded G'aojin (then serving as Anhwei governor) for submitting an implausible evaluation of a previously dismissed subordinate who was now due for reassignment: "In the case of a man who has already left office, there is nothing to prevent [his superior] from skirting the truth about him in order to elicit the admiration of his subordinates. This bad practice among governors-general and governors of purchasing reputation *(ku-ming)* is wholly inappropriate."[35] Of course, Hungli considered "magnanimity" of this sort perfectly appropriate when exercised at the *top* of the system, namely by himself. Indeed, it may be a law of bureaucratic practice that every official tries to reserve this genial quality to himself (or those above him), while holding his subordinates to strict application of the rules.

Once a governor had recommended an official for a post, it was awkward for him to admit a mistake. Hence evaluations tended toward a certain consistency: no governor was likely to change his opinion of a subordinate he had recommended until the man's performance, either good or bad, was so egregious that he had no choice. Hungli complained that, if a man of modest ability had been recommended for an easy post, his superior would seldom report any outstanding accomplishments; if a promising man had been recommended for a hard post, then he would seldom report faults.[36]

Reading the Leader's Mind

Another systemic evil that stymied personnel evaluation was called "seeking to accord [with the desires of one's superiors]" *(ying-ho):* that is, currying favor by molding one's judgments to conform to what one believed the boss wanted. This produced ludicrous distortions in the routine evaluation system, as officials trimmed their standards to the winds of imperial preference. The problem was endemic to the highest officials in both capital and provinces. "When We are lenient in one or two cases in which leniency is appropriate, then all the officials scurry to be lenient. When We are strict in one or two cases that require strictness, then they all scurry to be strict." On the surface this might seem to be a case of "the grass bending before the wind"— a commendable deference to royal leadership. But in reality, Hungli warned, "it stems from self-interest and self-aggrandizement." Ignoring the "great principles," acting without proper estimation of right and wrong—were these really the right way to advance in honor and rank? When officials in the capital need correction, "We can personally admonish them." In the provinces, however, "the governors-general and governors have sole charge of their jurisdictions. If they are determined to conform themselves to whatever they think We want, without any firm views of their own, then their subordinates will flock to do the same in order to curry favor with their superiors," and national affairs will really be in parlous straits.[37]

Obstacles to Impeachment

Like any system of accountability, the personnel evaluation process included one self-defeating mechanism that nobody knew how to cope with: reporting misconduct was dangerous to the reporter, but so was failure to report it. The administrative code included a range of penalties for "failure to investigate" *(shih-ch'a)*. Failure to report a subordinate for dereliction of duty made one liable, oneself, for administrative discipline. But if one did report him, a whole range of other embarrassments might surface (including tales he might bear about his colleagues, whom one had also "failed to investigate") that might have even worse results. Hungli knew that penalties for "failure to investigate" hindered his access to information. Reporting heterodox sects, for instance, was dangerous to an official's career. "Because it arose in his jurisdiction, and hence would adversely affect his fitness report, he might consider covering it up."[38]

Here are some penalties visited upon officials who "failed to investigate," from the administrative code of the Board of Civil Office:

> In the case of an official who receives bribes in the course of duty, and whose misconduct is not reported, [when the affair finally comes to light] a prefect stationed in the same city will be charged with failure to investigate and will be demoted one grade and retained in his post. A circuit-intendant will be fined a year's [nominal] salary.[39] A prefect not in the same city but stationed within a hundred *li* will be fined one year's [nominal] salary. A circuit-intendant will be fined nine months [nominal] salary . . . When a governor-general or governor impeaches an official in a "failure to investigate" case, let him clearly state in his memorial the distance [from the scene], to serve as data for investigation. If there is a misstatement of the distance, any official through whose hands the memorial passes will be demoted two grades and transferred.[40]

In sensitive cases, willful failure to impeach could bring, not a slap on the wrist, but real terror. When one of his trusted province chiefs concealed information in an impeachment case of 1766, Hungli complained that he had been personally betrayed.[41] "Chuang Yu-kung has received Our highest favor and has been selected for choice appointments. Yet he has the nerve to strut about, flaunting his favored status . . . This case is one in which he has intentionally deceived Us!" Not only was the ingrate cashiered, but his case was switched from the track of administrative discipline to that of criminal sanctions. Chuang was arrested, haled to Peking for interrogation by the Grand Council, had all his property confiscated, and was jailed to await decapitation. Yet the point was not to destroy but to chasten. Hungli granted him amnesty some months later and appointed him acting governor of Fukien.[42]

Hungli, who well knew that bureaucratic culture made impeachment distasteful to his province chiefs, read memorials carefully and was not easily fooled. He discerned a system of mutual protection by which governors shielded the reputations of their immediate subordinates, the provincial treasurer and provincial judge, from charges of "failure to investigate." The governor's impeachment memorial would say, "just as I was writing this, the reports of the provincial treasurer and provincial judge reached my desk and were not at variance from my own inquiries." Scoffed Hungli: "This might really occur once in a thousand or a hundred cases; how could it turn up every time?" From then on, when a governor was impeaching a subordinate, he was to state whether his information came from his own inquiries or from a report, and exactly how it had been conveyed.[43] Because impeachment for irregularities in impeachment was subject to the same irregularities, could the monarch ever be confident that routine procedures would produce sound evaluations of personnel? He saw himself confronting a system in which vertical clique-formation within the provincial bureaucracy made it hard for that bureaucracy to police itself. Higher officials and their subordinates "form cliques behind the scenes" and "collude by mutually ingratiating and coercing . . . These evil ways must be rigorously stamped out."[44] They were not, however, likely to be stamped out through the routine procedures of bureaucratic control, and Hungli knew it.[45]

Nonroutine Systems of Evaluation

Confidential Reporting from the Field

Given what he saw to be the futility of routine evaluation, the monarch naturally made the most of opportunities to inject autocratic power into the system. But to do so he needed reliable, undoctored information. From the beginning of his reign, he tried to get confidential personnel evaluations from the provinces. If governors would not evaluate their subordinates honestly through the open channel for fear of stirring up resentment, perhaps reporting confidentially in palace memorials would make them feel more secure. In the first year of his reign, Hungli had so instructed them.[46] "Now, in the beginning of Our reign, We are not well acquainted with the men serving as circuit-intendants and prefects in the provinces. You [governors] may report on the worthiness and the activities of your subordinates through [confidential] palace memorials." Yet even in the confidential channel the province chiefs felt insecure. Three years later, Hungli complained that his original decree was being ignored.[47] All governors had "reported once," but not since. He pointed out that governors customarily kept their posts longer than their subordinates, so that the passage of men through various jurisdictions opened a splendid opportunity for fresh evaluations. Now all governors were to send confidential memorials *(mi-tsou)* "from time to time." Yet to enforce this demand required ceaseless struggle. In 1759 Hungli was shocked, but perhaps not surprised, to find the governor-general of Liangkiang sending in sheer boilerplate through the confidential channel: "Recently We happened to be examining a memorial from Yenjišan evaluating his subordinates. In it, Wei Che-chih still appears as Huai-an prefect, and Dingcang still appears as Hsu-chou prefect. These men held these posts more than ten years ago! How come there were no follow-up evaluations of them? This is a matter for confidential memorials, which can do no harm to one's reputation for magnanimity."[48]

Confidential reporting was also sabotaged by collusion in the field. Hungli was frustrated to find that his province chiefs were getting together to smooth out differences in their evaluations of the subordinates they had in common, which deprived him of independent views. This practice came to light when he was comparing two confidential reports on personnel: one from a governor-general and another from that official's subordinate, a governor. "The *k'ao-yü* they have entered for their subordinates are largely the same. We then went back and compared the memorials they had submitted last time, and there was absolutely no difference there, either. It was astonishing." These confidential memorials, he wrote, were vital reference material for appointments. "We keep them all in the palace to consult from time to time and We do not allow court officials to know their contents." Accordingly each provincial official "ought to report his own views. Not only is it unnecessary for officials to consolidate their views to demonstrate unanimity, it is actually better that they do not do so, so that We may refer to both in making Our judgments." If province chiefs got together to present a unified view, "what is the use of memorializing confidentially?"[49]

Hungli's goal, evidently not attained to his satisfaction, was to deroutinize the bureaucratic evaluation system by collecting secret intelligence through another channel. The trouble was that his agents, in both channels, were the same. Apparently nobody retained much confidence in the confidentiality of the palace memorial system. That system was not, as it turned out, sufficient to pry open the provincial bureaucracy's grip on personnel evaluation.

Hungli's Rejection of New Routines

One solution that did *not* commend itself to Hungli was making the recommendation process even more routinized and precise. A censor charged that promotion recommendations from governors were full of "empty words," stock phrases such as "intelligent and able, conscientious and effective," vacuous clichés with little relevance to how the official actually had performed. The censor favored concrete accounts of official performance, in the form of a list of what a man had actually done. If the appointee did not live up to his billing, his recommender would be held accountable.[50]

Not unreasonable on the face of it, Hungli responded. But what would constitute "concrete accomplishments"? Those the censor had suggested, such as "founding schools, enforcing the *pao-chia* system [in which households were registered in decimal groups and made responsible for actions of their neighbors]"—these, too, were mere "empty words." After all, if *pao-chia* were ever *really* enforced, "how come local authorities cannot promptly catch bandits and escaped criminals?" Looking deeper into the matter, the admirable principle "government by men, not by laws" could not be realized by "setting up procedures that will simply generate conventional documents." Hungli ruled out any solution that involved further routinization, particularly generating more paperwork that could serve to ritualize or formalize government. But if the monarch ruled out more effective routines, what was the answer? Apparently it was the direct injection of imperial power.

The Imperial Audience System

The Ch'ing inherited the venerable system by which all regular officials were "escorted to audience" *(tai-ling yin-chien)* before being assigned to a post (in addition to the triennial audiences that all high officials were expected to request). The "escorting" was done, for civil appointments, by the Board of Civil Office; and for military, by the Board of War. The daily accounts of audiences in the official

Court Diaries *(ch'i-chü-chu)* record throngs of officials passing through the audience chamber. Though one might suppose that such meetings were nothing but mass prostrations and perfunctory benedictions, it is astonishing to discover the detail with which the monarch interviewed each man. And he really expected the prostrate candidate to speak up.[51]

Here was the autocrat using his personal insight without the benefit of a standard phrasebook. Our evidence for this process consists of sketches, from the vermilion brush itself, of officials who came to imperial audience, written on the candidate's *vitae* (sometimes called *yin-chien-tan* or *lü-li-tan*). Hungli's father had evidently considered himself a keen judge of character.[52] From him, even a short interview evoked a shrewd character sketch, proof of the sage's capacity to judge men. Though Hungli's comments were briefer and blander, they had enormous power to propel or derail a man's career. The monarch's face-to-face impressions naturally overrode the routine judgments of the governor on the scene. Hence the career of an official with good marks from the field could be ruined by a bad audience. One hapless provincial judge brought to audience from Chekiang impressed Hungli as crude and boorish, "ignorant of proper ceremonies." When asked what he had to report about Chekiang affairs, he produced from his sleeve a poster he had prepared to overawe the commoners with graphic displays of the "five punishments." This struck Hungli as indelicate, and he fired off a query to the man's superior. The reply was that the judge had committed no administrative offenses and, although he lacked refinement, his integrity was quite sound, and he was "up to the job of Chekiang provincial judge." Hungli nevertheless had him fired the following year.[53]

Although Hungli's sixty-year reign must have produced thousands of these documents, only nineteen (from various years) have been recovered.[54] It is instructive to compare these vermilion comments with the stilted *k'ao-yü* that were generated by the routine evaluation system.

> *Li Shan:* The man seems a decent sort, can be appointed. But his capacities are really only up to the post of circuit-intendant. (1747)
> *Ch'u Yung-chung:* The man may actually make something of himself. Circuit-intendant seems about right. (1751)
> *Chou Yuan-li:* A keen and capable talent. (1758)
> *K'ung Chi-tung:* Not up to his earlier record. He seems a fellow who is looking for a life of ease. (1758)

Yao Li-te: Durable, will make something of himself. (1761)

Chao-lin: Seems to have a conscience. He can be appointed. But could he be a bit short on talent? (1761)

T'an Shan-chung: Smart, seems likely to make something of himself. He may be a bit insubstantial. (1762)

Yang Ch'ung-ying: Seems appointable. But he may be too clever by half. Conscientious. (1762)

Ma Sheng-chiao: Durable. Can appoint him. In the future, he'll make something of himself. (1762)

Shan Liang: Seems appointable. (1764)

Wu Chao-chi: A bright person. Even if We don't promote him [now], he'll still have opportunities to show his cleverness. Then We'll see. (1764)

Ti Yung-ch'ih: Seems intelligent. (1764)

Liang Chao-pang: He seems about right for this post. But he is not a great talent. (1766)

O Lu-li: Decent, conscientious. Seems durable. (1768)

Li Yuan: Appropriate, but not for a post that's too demanding. Seems all right. Appoint him. (1770)

Ku Hsueh-ch'ao: Unavoidably of the Soochow clique. Not a very great talent. (1773)

Te-er-ping-a: Can appoint him. (1780)

Chang T'ing-kuei: All right. (1781)

Shen Jung-hsu: Well, all right. (1783)

Extracted from these comments, here are the evaluative phrases:

Positive characteristics

Decent *(chung-hou)*

Has gumption, can make something of himself *(yu ch'u-hsi)*

Keen and able *(ching-kan neng-shih)*

Durable *(chieh-shih)*

Has conscience *(yu liang-hsin)*

Smart *(ming-pai)*

Intelligent *(ts'ung-ming)*

Dutiful *(pen-fen)*

Negative characteristics

Lazy *(t'u an-i)*

Short on talent *(tuan yü ts'ai)*

Insubstantial *(po)*

Not a great talent *(fei ta-ch'i)*

Hungli is, of course, making judgments on the basis of face-to-face encounters, perhaps colored by prejudices (the characteristic distrust of Kiangnan literati, for example) or previous impressions (most of these men he has met in previous audiences). He is, then, judging character (as best he can discern it—credit him with some modesty for using the word "seems," *ssu*, frequently) rather than judging performance. The list of character traits most appealing to him is headed by the phrase (common in spoken Chinese today) *yu ch'u-hsi*, which I have rendered "has gumption," or (if referring to the future) "will make something of himself." There may be an implied distinction between a man who relies on his own talents and one who clings to the patronage of others. Certainly it distinguishes the leader from the mere careerist who hews narrowly to the safe track.

Other phrases indicate that Hungli admired the virtues of solidity: "durable" *(chieh-shih)* suggests perseverence, hardiness of spirit, the kind of man who can hold his own in a troublesome post. "Decent" *(chung-hou)* and "dutiful" *(pen-fen)* are close to virtues marked in the bureaucratic evaluations. For Hungli they probably distinguish a solid character from the trickster who will exploit public office to his own advantage. The opposite of these solid virtues is "insubstantial" *(po)*, the mark of the lightweight whose surface abilities are not rooted firmly in character. Intelligence *(ming-pai, ts'ung-ming)* is a virtue of which just the right amount is wanted. Hungli is put off by the fellow who is "too clever by half," who uses his wits as a substitute for more substantial virtues.

The man whom Hungli failed to find, among this fragmentary sample at least, was the "great talent," the rare candidate who is destined for a top ministerial post. He often used the term with a negative to derogate a man who was clearly *not* an outstanding talent. Such quality is always more obvious in its absence than in its presence, and "not a great talent" is a fair comment on a man whose most evident trait is lack of genius. Even Chou Yuan-li, who was only a prefect at the time of this audience but who was to rise two decades later to the post of board president, was no "great talent," at least not at the audience I have just cited.

The monarch was concerned with character and talent as, indeed, were the formulaic entries of the routine system. Yet there are striking differences in the way the audience notes portray the ideal official. That image includes qualities of toughness, genuineness, and energy—colored equally by courage and ambition—that we call "gumption." This is the mark of the proud, hard-driving achiever: a leader, not a rule-ridden functionary. Caution and diligence, the marks of the reliable paper-shuffler, are not what Hungli sought for membership in the "club" of higher provincial and capital officials.

The Upper-Level System: "Political Appointments"

The principle of "the higher the post, the less routine the appointment" must be common to all bureaucratic systems. "Political appointments," as we know them, offer the chief executive the chance to install personal friends, or at any rate persons who share his views, in positions of power. Hungli plainly regarded the personnel in higher provincial and capital positions as too important for routine handling. He rejected a proposal to bring provincial treasurers and judges under the Grand Accounting, because he knew that punishing malfeasance in such sensitive posts could not wait for the routine triennial review.[55] Although governors-general and governors, along with the upper crust of capital officials, were, in practice, exempt from the triennial evaluations, they had nevertheless been obliged to offer "self-evaluations" *(tzu-ch'en)* instead. Hungli simply tired of reading these prolix and probably formulaic documents, and in 1752 he abolished them.[56] He would, he announced, personally reward and punish officials on that level whenever he wanted. "The evaluation and selection [of high officials] will be daily borne in Our own breast," and hence for them the triennial rhythm of evaluation was pointless.[57]

Yet bearing such weighty material in his breast was not quite reassuring enough, and six years later he seemed to edge back toward formalism. Although the self-evaluation only produced "an endless procession of documents, with no value for practical government," no evaluation at all would make high officials complacent. Now the Board of Civil Office was to prepare, at the time of the Capital Investigation, one register for capital officials of rank three and up, and one for governors-general and governors, furnished with updated *vitae* for the emperor's reference. He was, however, hardly relaxing his direct control over these political appointments, but rather serving notice to his political appointees that he was not about to let their careers settle into comfortable ruts—to become routinized by default.

> Even though We already have a thorough knowledge of whether they are worthy or not, there may yet be those who advance and retire together, seeking emoluments and behaving like horses loath to leave their stables [that is, are routine careerists]. If such men avoid major gaffes and continue to fill their posts adequately without being regularly evaluated, then when they have hovered around for a long time their official performance cannot but be harmed.

The selection and evaluation of political appointments, both as a formal system and as practical politics, operated by a set of rules that was distinct from the routine system. Although the Board of Civil Office was involved in the process to some extent, the monarch's autocratic power cut across its routine procedures at every step. The higher the official, the less routine the procedures for his appointment and discipline, and the more direct the impact of the autocrat's personal power. Although this is only what one might expect, we need to know more exactly how this personal power was expressed.[58]

Ritual Behavior

The monarch's control of his "political appointees" rested largely on his personal relationship with them. This relationship was a two-way communication, proclaimed by the monarch and acknowledged by the bureaucrat. The monarch's constant and conventional recourse to expressions like "arms and legs, heart and backbone" (the upper echelons) is visible everywhere in the documents.[59] The bureaucratic acknowledgment closed the loop of this dialogue of dependency and control. This acknowledgment shows up pointedly in the ritual that immediately follows an official's audience with the emperor and his assumption of a bureaucratic post: the submission of a "gratitude (hsieh-en) memorial" by the newly appointed official.

In a modern context, the gratitude memorial might seem the most abject of documents. It expresses utter personal dependency. Where is the "status honor" that is supposed to characterize the exalted scholar-bureaucrat? The "gumption" quotient seems low, if not nonexistent. It is an "oriental-despotic" document, a long verbal kowtow. Here is an example from 1769, which is worth quoting whole:

> Wu Ta-shan, Governor-general of Hukuang, respectfully memorializes, humbly expressing gratitude for Imperial Benevolence:
>
> Your humble official's nature is undistinguished, stupid, and base. I have received Your Majesty's munificent benevolence, have been nourished and raised by Your Majesty to the extent of repeatedly being

appointed to provincial office. I am ashamed that I have in no way repaid Your Majesty, but rather my errors have multiplied with time.

Now I have received the extraordinary generosity of Your Majesty's appointment to fill the post of Hukuang Governor-general. On the twenty-sixth day of the twelfth month of last year, I journeyed to the Palace, kowtowed before the Imperial Countenance, and respectfully received Your Majesty's sacred instructions. My feelings on that occasion are eternally engraved upon my inmost parts. Your Majesty's having also conferred on me gifts in rich profusion, Your Majesty's benevolence has exceeded all bounds, and Your Majesty's favor has reached an extreme.

Though even dogs and horses know how to repay their masters, yet I, your humble official, though I have a human heart, have yet dared fail to recompense you by serving you with utmost sincerity. What can I do, but with my whole heart and strength reverently obey Your Majesty's instructions to govern my jurisdiction and, without fraud or concealment, to repay, in all matters great and small, Your Majesty's immense generosity?

This, with your humble official's exceeding gratitude and humble sincerity, I respectfully memorialize, kowtowing, in gratitude for the Imperial Benevolence, humbly praying for Your Imperial Majesty's royal perusal.

(Vermilion: "Noted.")[60]

That this language was repeated, with minor variations, in every gratitude memorial does not justify dismissing it as "mere" ritual. It was the symbolic form of a basic political fact. The fact that it was repeated makes it, like other rituals, more significant rather than less. It was a ritual of largesse and gratitude that sustained the relationship between sovereign and high official.

Even in the ordinary conduct of business, the symbolism of dependency had its place. Operational documents, too, were framed in ritually significant forms. For example, it was normal for a memorialist to quote, in full, the imperial order to which he was responding. This was not only good bureaucratic practice, to keep the documentary chain clear for purposes of reference. As a ritual act, the writer often quoted his master's words at much greater length than his own humble reply.[61] Another common form of verbal prostration occurred when the memorialist humbly quoted the vermilion interlineal scoldings he had received when his memorials were returned.[62]

These documentary rituals reinforced the official's personal link to his sovereign, a relationship first established by the man's appointment. The moving force was reciprocity, as expressed in the gratitude memorial we have just seen. These ritual humiliations were signs, not of degradation, but of special status: in Confucian terms, these gentlemen were not tools. They could be scolded, ridiculed, or punished by their imperial master, as an errant son by a stern father. But the relationship was not abject, because they were presumed to have "human hearts," and hence the capacity to act like men, not machines or dumb animals. Unlike mere clerks, they were neither artifacts of a body of rules nor automatons controlled by routine procedures.

The imperial effort to achieve closer control over bureaucrats had to reach resolutely beyond routine procedures. The audience system, the gathering of confidential evaluations, and the partial separation of top officials from the routine system all played parts in this effort. In Hungli's bureaucracy, the routine components grew weaker as the ranks of the men he was dealing with grew higher. At the very top of the system (the province chiefs and the heads of the administrative boards—the "club,") the grammar of communication was highly personal. The personal relationship was stated and restated, both in operational documents and in ritual instruments such as the gratitude memorials. Dereliction of duty was treated as a personal affront to the monarch, a breach of trust that could only stem from ingratitude. Higher officials in both provinces and capital were, as a result, operating in two modes: they were formally still subject to the standard administrative discipline system *(ch'u-fen)*, by which the monarch could turn them over to the Board of Civil Office for administrative punishment *(i-ch'u)*. In addition, however, they were directly exposed to the attention of the emperor, who used the personal relationship—amply robed in ritual—to goad, to blame, and to frighten.

The personal relationship was played out both in the domain of ritual and in the domain of events. Certain classes of events—preeminently "political crime," as I have defined it—provided the best medium for nourishing the personalistic discipline that bound the upper layers of China's bureaucratic monarchy. It was the sort of occasion Hungli could use to keep his top officials from slipping away from his personal control and into the rhythms of routine and cronyism.

The Operation of Imperial Control in the Soulstealing Crisis

The soulstealing crisis was a particularly suitable context for personalistic discipline because it was so ill founded a case. The imperial spleen could be vented upon provincial officials for failing to turn up master-sorcerers—a failure that was inevitable because no master-sorcerers existed. That the case was so ill founded, Hungli certainly did not know at the time. It would be no more true to say that he "used" political crime than to say that political crime "used" him. Political crime was a context that called forth monarchic behavior of a certain type. That behavior was shaped by long-term structural features of the bureaucratic monarchy. Officials' failure to unearth master-sorcerers was variously attributed to sloth, dithering, coddling incompetent subordinates, Kiangnan decadence, and personal ingratitude. These shortcomings were perennial foci of imperial concern. We have seen how difficult it was for Hungli to cope with them in routine circumstances. The overall impetus of a political crime like soulstealing was to shake bureaucrats out of patterns of routine behavior that they used, so effectively, for their own protection; and to give Hungli a context in which to confront his problems with the bureaucracy head-on.

Cracking Down on Subordinates

We have seen how frustrated Hungli was with governors' failure to use administrative discipline on their subordinates. The image of crafty local officials withholding information from indulgent and credulous province chiefs was an imperial stereotype of bureaucratic behavior. His governors, believed Hungli, compounded laxity by gullibility. Governor Asha, in Honan, who had assured his master that the sorcerers must possess secret techniques to render themselves invisible and escape detection, got back vermilion ridicule: "If *you* think this way, it is no wonder your subordinates do not prosecute the case conscientiously and are deceiving you!"[63] Hungli assumed that withholding information from superiors was standard practice for county officials who sought to avoid trouble, and the belated revelations of the spring queue-clipping scare proved the point. Having embarrassed G'aojin and Jangboo over their failure to report the spring queue-clipping incidents, Hungli berated them for their lax control of local officials. The magistrates of Ch'ang-chou, Yuan-ho, and Wu-hsien who had reported "that there had been no queue-clipping incidents in their jurisdictions" were really "the ultimate in perversity and deceitfulness." G'aojin was ordered to verify the actual number of clipping victims in each county, then impeach the magistrates.[64] The monarch soon had to back off from this stance, however. The chastened Jangboo was planning to impeach the magistrates but leave them on the job to prosecute the case. Hungli now worried that they might then be too intimidated to report anything at all. Although there definitely had been cover-ups by local officials, and cover-ups *for* local officials by province chiefs, wrote Hungli, Jangboo had better hold off on impeachments for the moment. Vermilion: "If you do [impeach them], will they be willing to make any reports? Better just supervise them in prosecuting the case, then impeach them after the criminals are caught. Handling it your way will not solve the problem, and you probably won't catch the chief culprit."[65] The point, however, had been made: provincial supervision of local bureaucrats had to be tightened.

Restating Norms of Official Behavior

Nothing offered surer protection to the local bureaucrat than the boundary around his jurisdiction. He was responsible for everything that went on within it, but it followed that everything outside it was someone else's problem. Yet this routine norm conflicted with the nonroutine side of the provincial official's identity: his master's business was boundless, and as his master's personal servant he was not protected by boundaries in cases affecting dynastic security. Hungli wasted no opportunity to hammer home the point. The master-sorcerer Yü-shih was said to be hiding in Su-chou, Anhwei. Governor Jangboo wrote apologetically that Su-chou, since it was not in Kiangsu, was outside his jurisdiction, and that he was loath to cross the provincial boundary in pursuit. Hungli objected that even in ordinary criminal prosecutions officials cooperated to make arrests across boundaries. In this extraordinary case, how could they use boundaries as an excuse? Provincial officials ought to take "the Dynasty's public business" *(kuo-chia kung-shih)* as their main task. Tender concern for "amity among fellow officials" was not "the Way of public-minded and loyal official service." If all officials were "stymied by bureaucratic obstacles," unable to proceed with urgent business, "what kind of governmental system is that?"[66]

In cases of political crime, bureaucrats found functional boundaries to be no better protection than territorial ones. When Governor Feng Ch'ien wrote that he had entrusted the interrogation of sorcery suspects to his provincial judge, a perfectly reasonable step in normal times, the monarch dressed him down for buck-passing: "What sort of case *is* this, that you have to follow precedent by turning it over to the provincial judge? Ought you not *personally* to conduct judicial investigations every day? The habitual work-style of the provinces is truly hateful!"[67]

Reinforcing the Personal Relationship

Besides the whip of criminal sanctions for outright corruption, the monarch grasped two reins to control his provincial bureaucrats. One was the routine system of administrative discipline, by which he could refer an official's case to the Board of Civil Office for reward or punishment (the *ch'u-fen* system). The other was the nonroutine application of autocratic power, behind which loomed unspecified sanctions ranging from loss of favor to loss of property, freedom, or life. We can assume that the latter was no idle speculation in the official mind: Hungli was known to have repaid serious dereliction of duty, either in waging war or crushing sedition, with brutal severity.[68] In Hungli's rhetoric of personal control, duty neglected was trust betrayed. When the provincial judge of Kiangsu, Wu T'an, admitted that he had failed to inform the Throne about the spring soulstealing cases, the monarch cracked the vermilion whip: "When you were serving in the Board [of Punishments] you were an outstanding official. As soon as you are posted to the provinces, however, you take on disgusting habits of indecisiveness and decadence. It is really detestable . . . you take your sweet time about sending in memorials, and there isn't a word of truth in them! You have really disappointed my trust in you, you ingrate of a *thing (pu-chih-en chih wu)!*"[69]

A natural complement to the gratitude memorial, such rhetoric was, in its milder forms, part of a ritual exchange. A standard response from the culprit would be a conventional expression of fear and humility, such as "I am so fearful that I cannot find peace of mind *(sung-ch'ü nan-an)*" or "I blush with shame and have no place to hide *(k'uei-nan wu-ti),*" conventional expressions that graced hundreds of provincial memorials.[70] Yet royal trust traduced might lead to real terror. Governor Funihan was surely aware of what had happened to his predecessor in Shantung, Juntai, who, sixteen years earlier, had been caught covering up evidence in the Bogus Memorial case of 1751–52. Juntai had failed to pass on information that a copy of the Bogus Memorial had turned up in his province. Because the "memorial" impugned the monarch's personal behavior (and possibly the dynasty's legitimacy), it is not surprising that Hungli vented his fury on this luckless bannerman. The governor had "disgraced his post and shown ingratitude for Our benevolence," and was "wholly ignorant of the sovereign-minister relationship."[71] Hungli jailed the ingrate and confiscated all his property. Political crime subjected the tidy formal garden of bureaucratic life to the harsh gale of autocratic power. That is why the soulstealing case was an imperial issue and not a bureaucratic one.

Bureaucratic Resistance

How the bureaucracy responded to such royal bullying must be teased out of the documents with some care. There seem to have been several varieties of resistance. Some was, no doubt, calculated; some may have been simply the viscosity of bureaucratic procedure that stalled prompt response to urgent demands. Some may have been the disdain of agnostic officials who could not bring themselves to take soulstealing seriously. Some may have reflected fear of how the prosecution might affect bureaucratic careers. And finally, some may have been principled refusal to prosecute innocent commoners on trumped-up charges.

That there was resistance is beyond doubt. It started before Peking got wind of the spring incidents in Kiangnan: these curious affairs were simply not reported to the Throne. Because preemptive control of information did not succeed in keeping the matter quiet, various kinds of damage control followed. Every one of the measures I am about to describe can be explained on other grounds. Taken together, I am persuaded, they indicate a cautious, pervasive resistance to autocratic pressure. That they were concerted is unlikely, that they were deliberate cannot be proved. But neither connivance nor deliberation is needed to make the case. The bureaucratic work-style, which followed well-worn mental tracks, was quite enough to do the trick.

Busy Inaction: Wu Shao-shih in Kiangsi

When someone told Hungli, a year before the soulstealing crisis, that people were referring to his Kiangsi governor, Wu Shao-shih, as "old

Buddha" (a compliment), he was concerned lest the old man had become so passive and indulgent that he could not attend to business.[72] Wu was in fact seventy, the patriarch of a family of noted jurists.[73] So highly did Hungli esteem the family that Wu and his sons, Huan and T'an, had been allowed on two occasions to serve in the Board of Punishments together, postings that would normally have been precluded by the "rule of avoidance" that kept families prudently separated in bureaucratic assignments.

East of Kiangsi's core area, the valley of the Hsin River offered convenient access from neighboring Chekiang, whence rumors of soulstealing seeped into the province as early as mid-June. Governor Wu did not report them. Instead, he told Hungli later, he had "verbally ordered" his subordinates to be watchful for "suspicious persons" traveling about. No arrests were made, and nobody reported any queue-clipping in Kiangsi. Hungli, unwontedly restrained toward this elderly and respected figure, contented himself with a mild rebuke: not reporting the rumors had been "an error on your part." In early October, however, Wu proposed a dragnet more finely meshed than that of any other province: a corps of spies "who would change both their clothing and their surnames" to cover every county and report suspects to officialdom every ten days. Also, every prefecture would appoint special agents to inspect "Taoist and Buddhist temples, as well as shrines and academies, whether busy or secluded." Wu soberly warned his master about practitioners of "deviant ways and black arts": They "establish an organization that purports to burn incense and do good deeds," which "overtly gathers men and women from among the ignorant rustics, but covertly hooks up with desperate scoundrels." Under pretext of avoiding calamities and defending against bandits, they "concoct magic sayings, prepare weapons, and lure followers." All suspicious persons, whether Buddhist monks, Taoist priests, or persons of furtive demeanor or uncertain abode, were to be reported promptly to local officials. (Vermilion: "Probably empty talk. Very hard to believe.")[74]

Indeed, absolutely nothing came of it. With profuse and abject apologies, Wu reported six weeks later (after Hungli had called off the prosecution) that not a single queue-clipper had been found.[75] No documents survive to suggest even a roundup of "usual suspects," like those faithfully reported by governors of neighboring provinces. What can we make of it? Either Wu's dragnet was never deployed, or else it failed to catch plausible suspects. Conspicuously lacking are the torture and perjury we have seen in other provinces. We have to conclude, I think, that Governor Wu was simply not prepared to pursue what he considered a bad case, and that the somber warnings and elaborate preparations he conveyed to the Throne were so much window dressing. Governor Wu got away with it: not only did the sovereign not rebuke him, but the following year he named him president of the Board of Punishments. Shielded by his juristic reputation, and also perhaps by his immediate superior, imperial in-law G'aojin, Wu was not so easily to be disciplined for his unwillingness to play with the team.

Diversion: The Prosecution of the Soochow Sectarians

Wu's Shao-shih's younger son, Wu T'an, was provincial judge of neighboring Kiangsu and, like his father, was a respected legal scholar. He had decided, like his superiors, not to report the spring soulstealing cases to the Throne. He, too, had later been embarrassed by Textile Commissioner Sacai's exposure of the cases and had faced the withering imperial attack that I related earlier. But soon this "ingrate of a *thing*" was able to send his master more creditable news. Around September 28, three weeks after receiving his vermilion scolding, he reported that, although he had caught no soulstealers, he had discovered, through his own investigations, eleven "sutra halls" established by lay Buddhist congregations just outside the Soochow city walls.[76] Two related groups were involved: the Greater Vehicle sect *(Ta-sheng chiao)* and the Effortless Action sect *(Wu-wei chiao)*, the latter of which, it will be recalled from Chapter 6, had been persecuted in Pao-an just a few weeks before. The Wu-wei sect, and possibly the Ta-sheng sect as well, revered the patriarch Lo Ch'ing and had been banned by imperial order since 1727. Now some seventy people were arrested by Wu T'an. Their depositions revealed the astonishing fact that these groups had been in existence, in their present locations, since the year 1677, when the first of their sutra halls had been erected.[77]

We must shift to conjecture here. I infer (though I cannot prove) that proscribed sects of this size could not long have remained unknown to some level of local government in a busy city like Soochow. County functionaries probably had been extorting protection money from them for years. Not by nature secret groups, the sects afforded solace and shelter to Grand Canal boatmen from the grain-tribute fleet, and some of those living in the halls were evidently retired boatmen. The provincial judge, pressured to produce soul-stealers, must in turn have pressed his subordinates for results. Someone down the line must have decided that the secretarians would make a fair substitute. Turning in these inoffensive but vulnerable groups would, for the moment, appease the imperial appetite for prosecutions and would allow the shamefaced Wu T'an to display his attention to duty. Hungli, predictably, responded harshly—toward the sectarians. He ordered that they be treated severely in order to discourage others from joining such sects, and that they be questioned narrowly on possible connections to soulstealing. Wu T'an was to be especially vigilant for "seditious writings" like those unearthed in Pao-an.[78]

Criminal prosecution of the sect also triggered the bureaucratic impeachment of officials who had "failed to investigate" it.[79] Because the sects were deemed to have been active in and around Soochow since 1677, when the first sutra hall was built, a host of former officials of several counties, along with their superiors, were technically accountable for having failed to prosecute it.[80] The cumulative result was laughable. The list of former incumbents to be disciplined retroactively included sixty-eight county magistrates, twenty-two prefects, fourteen circuit-intendants, thirty-two provincial judges, twenty-nine provincial treasurers, twenty-six governors, and fourteen governors-general. Many of course were already dead, and some were excused because they had served in the jurisdiction less than six months. Others were let off because they had taken part in breaking the case. Some had since risen to high position: Yenjišan, former Kiangsu governor, now a grand secretary and grand councillor, was slapped with a fine of nine months' nominal salary, which for a man in his position had about the force of a parking ticket. Though a few lower ranks suffered demotion and transfer, most got off with token penalties. This elaborate impeachment proceeding was an embarrassing farce, yet Wu T'an and other Kiangsu leaders may have accounted it a modest price to pay for relief from Hungli's relentless pressure.

Unanimity: The Chueh-hsing Case

In the matter of the amorous monk of Hunan, whose story I related in Chapter 7, Governor-general Dingcang afforded his sovereign scant satisfaction. After Chueh-hsing had recanted and told the full story of his dalliance with the young wife of innkeeper Liu, he had been absolved of soulstealing charges and had merely been beaten and exiled for adultery. Dingcang returned to his yamen in Wuchang and wrote Hungli on October 31 that no progress had been made in the sorcery prosecution. The monarch was furious. He now understood the reason for Dingcang's conscientious desire to travel more than two hundred miles to be present at the investigation. Vermilion: "You use your tricks and hateful techniques once again to present unanimity in order to close a case *(shen-ch'u wan-shih)*. How can you be said to earn your governor-general's salary? What can be done about a shameless, useless thing like you?"[81] Nothing in the rules required the presence of the governor-general at a provincial trial. We can safely assume, along with Hungli, that provincial officials had presented a united front so that he would have had to discipline the lot of them if the outcome were not to his liking. The record is full of cases in which interrogations were attended by a number of officials on the scene, presumably for safety in numbers. A seamless joint report by high provincial officials would more likely turn aside imperial wrath than a report from an isolated bureaucrat, and would minimize the danger of a discrepant opinion from someone else.[82]

Routinization: Switching to a Safer Track

Karl Mannheim observed that "the fundamental tendency of all bureaucratic thought is to turn all problems of politics into problems of administration."[83] By this he meant that bureaucrats are incapable of seeing beyond their "socially limited horizon," their rationally ordered sphere of work, to the clash of irrationally generated interests in the larger political world. I would credit Ch'ing bureaucrats with more insight and guile, and assume that they were quite capable of purposely redefining political problems as administrative problems.

In the soulstealing case, there are numerous instances in which bureaucrats did their best to channel the monarch's urgent, nonroutine demands into conventional, routine channels. After all, showing attention to duty was the next best thing to achieving concrete results, and a hard-pressed official had many routine activities in which he could busy himself, with minimal risk. For example, the *pao-chia* system of mutual responsibility had long been on the books but was always in need of updating and tightening up. The Nanking provincial treasurer dutifully suggested such a measure during the sorcery prosecution as a way of checking the backgrounds of all commoners in the Nanking area. Hungli saw the suggestion for what it was: a device to seem busy but avoid the unrewarding task of ferreting out soulstealers. Vermilion: "This is all empty talk. The habits of you provincial officials are really hateful."[84] G'aojin himself was not above suggesting an empire-wide re-registration of monks and priests, most of whom were "failed literati" and whose heterodox ways did the populace much harm. G'aojin assured His Majesty that he dared not reply on "empty words." Vermilion: "You have not caught a culprit in ages. How can you say 'no empty words'?" It was easy enough to unleash a routine crackdown on a vulnerable group, and the monarch plainly understood what was going on.[85] A similar proposal, floated by the Chekiang provincial judge, suggested that monks and priests who lacked ordination certificates be required to carry travel passes with them on their wanderings.[86]

By routinizing the search for soulstealers, local bureaucrats were falling back on familiar techniques (such as *pao-chia*) that were not susceptible to short-term evaluation. An official could in any case count on having been transferred before the results could be assessed. The effect would be to divert a case from the emergency channel into the routine channel, where local bureaucrats were less vulnerable. This stratagem was not, however, notably successful in diverting the alert Hungli from his purpose.

The Bureaucratic Monarchy as a Social System

The documentary record of the soulstealing crisis projects a double image. The bolder lines depict the day-to-day prosecution of sorcery. The subtler pattern is the relationship among the writers and readers of documents. In this double image, we perceive the two aspects of the Chinese imperial state: as *instrument* (managing the realm in the interests of its proprietors, the Manchu monarchy and the Sino-Manchu elite); and as *system* (allocating power and status among political actors). The state-as-instrument (I shall call this "the government") fits our commonsense understanding of government: institutions set up to accomplish tasks such as collecting taxes, maintaining order, and waging war. The state-as-system (which I shall call "the bureaucratic monarchy") consists of relationships among men whose careers are measured by prestige and power, mobility and security, within a hierarchical order. Every document generated by an "event"—whether a routine report on taxes or an urgent report on insurrection—must be read both as description of an outer reality and as a reflection of the political needs of its author. ("Political needs," of course, were not necessarily narrow, selfish interests. They might also encompass the writer's principled defense of his institutional turf.) The interaction of men within the state-as-system was not insulated from "events" in the world of action. On the contrary, it was such "events" that made the two aspects of the state meaningful in terms of each other.

"Event" has a slippery meaning to us, but in Chinese bureaucratic practice it was a unit of accountability. It had a beginning (when someone could first be held accountable for it) and an end (when someone could be rewarded or punished for the way he handled it). An official's career was formally measured by his performance, and performance was measured by how well he handled specific tasks. Were taxes collected in full? Were crimes solved on time? Were rebellions forestalled or quelled? Were floods prevented or their victims relieved? A notable success or failure was, in terms of accountability, an "event." It was generally an "event" that gave one official an occasion to impeach another, or to patronize him by pointing to his merits. "Events" were opportunities not only to advance one's own fortunes but also to serve the needs of patrons and clients, and so to embroider the fabric of personal connections that sustained a man in public life.

So besides keeping the realm in order, the government had another role to play: it provided the symbolic resources for the operation of the bureaucratic monarchy. Just as the bureaucratic monarchy lived on the economic surplus of China's society, it depended on society for the "events" that served as raw material for the operation of its internal relationships. The internal machinery of the bureaucratic monarchy processed all such "events" and transformed them into power and status.

Like every other relationship in the bureaucratic monarchy, that between Throne and bureaucracy, the central axis of the system, consumed raw material in the form of "events." The monarch needed concrete occasions to assert his dominance over the bureaucracy, to punish men in his black book and to reward those in his favor. A provincial-level official was not merely a functionary in an organization; his every public act was informed by the personal relationship he bore to his sovereign, a relationship confirmed by an imperial audience when he was appointed, and by regular audiences thereafter. The quality of this personal relationship and its complex interplay with the formal, "objective" structure of bureaucratic government was largely defined by the "events" in which the official participated. Only through "events" did the relationship become part of the documentary record.

Yet the bureaucratic monarchy was not simply a passive receptor of whatever its social environment might provide in the way of "events." Instead, men were capable of some selectivity in which "events" they chose to handle, and indeed in the way they defined them. An actor in this system could shape "events," redefine them, or even manufacture them, if that would redound to his advantage within the system. Similarly, it was possible to screen out "events" that were likely to harm one's interests. Of course, such selectivity could only operate within limits; a major popular uprising could be neither cooked up nor screened out. But both monarch and bureaucrat could use the documentary system to influence the way an event was defined or perceived. The soulstealing crisis could certainly be manipulated this way. Popular panic forced it to the surface of public life. Yet the meaning attached to sorcery by the bureaucratic monarchy was clearly influenced by the needs of the various actors within it. All who handled this "event" appear to have done so with an eye to power and status relations within the official world.

What I am suggesting is that, besides being a genuinely urgent problem for government, the sorcery crisis of 1768 provided an outlet for Hungli's deepest misgivings about the state. To say that Hungli intentionally used the soulstealing crisis to whip his bureaucracy into line would be to reach beyond the evidence. The evidence does show, however, that Hungli was used to thinking about bureaucracy in a language born of his inmost concerns: routinization and assimilation; and that the power of this language—to define and to motivate— grew enormously in an environment of political crime.

The link between sorcery and Hungli's deeper anxieties about the empire is to be seen in his vermilion rescripts. He wrote them quickly: no drafts, no drafters. There, in the bare outcroppings of his thought, are his spontaneous perceptions of the issues before him. The *context* of these rescripts was the prosecution of sorcerers, but the *content* was the control of bureaucrats. Hungli detested sorcery and feared its effects. But his reaction to it was colored by what he thought were the persistent ills of his realm: routinization, assimilation, the baleful effects of Kiangnan culture, all of which mocked royal power. The language by which he goaded his officials to action against sorcery shared the tone, and indeed the vocabulary, of his long-term frustration with the bureaucracy. He could vent this frustration only in the context of concrete events. Now, in the context of this one, a political crime, the vocabulary was about bureaucratic behavior.

Yet how far could the monarch push such a tainted case without raising doubts about his own behavior? As the case collapsed, the Throne had to be shielded from falling debris. Embarrassed and angry, Hungli ended the soulstealing prosecution with a search for scapegoats in the bureaucracy. But he wanted it both ways. Governor Funihan had misled him by suggesting that soulstealers' confessions had been extracted without the use of torture, and the man had to be degraded and humiliated. Other bureaucrats, however, had abused his trust by failing to prosecute the case vigorously enough. This negligence had allowed sorcery to spread around the empire. Only by punishing officials who had shown laxity toward sorcery could he demonstrate, to his descendants no less than to his contemporaries, that he had been right to prosecute the case in the first place.

As a final flourish, the monarch's fury focused on the newly appointed governor of Shansi, Surde, fresh from six years of service as provincial treasurer in Soochow and already under fire for tardy reportage of sorcery cases. He had memorialized on Shansi soul-stealing only after Hungli had raised the matter. Vermilion: "This shows that you haven't rid yourself of the hateful habits of deceit you picked up in Kiangnan."[87] When the case finally collapsed, Surde was singled out for special abuse. He "had served in Kiangsu the longest," and had been "deep-dyed with the ways of the hateful [Kiangnan] clique." When the soulstealing affair first emerged, he did not report it (although he was still serving in Soochow at the time). Later, as Shansi governor, even numerous cases of sorcery did nothing to change his ways. He had "impeded the prosecution most profoundly." Hungli demoted him to the rank of provincial judge and sent him to an unpleasant post in remote Sinkiang.[88] What better place to scourge Kiangnan decadence from a bannerman's soul?

CHAPTER 10

Theme and Variations

Chinese culture was unified but not homogeneous. That, I think, is why there could occur a society-wide experience such as the soulstealing crisis, even while different social groups represented that experience in different ways.[1] We have had occasion to observe the cultural disparities between silk-gowned inquisitor and ragged prisoner. But social distance did not mean mutual incomprehension. Sometimes it meant different configurations of commonly available symbols. Though the "evil arts" were feared and detested by all, the components of sorcery lore were arranged by each social group to fit its own view of the world. That is why an "event" like the sorcery scare could "happen" to both prince and peasant, but to each in his own terms. The different expressions of this event sprang from different social roles and life experiences. Seen in this light, the soulstealing theme was given voice through different stories, each of which expressed the fears of a particular group. The theme they had in common was danger from persons unknown and forces unseen.

The Throne: Shadow and Substance

Trying to plumb Hungli's state of mind, we begin with the fact that soulstealing scares occurred at least twice thereafter: in 1810 and again in 1876. On neither occasion did the court seize the issue and make a national campaign of it. Reigning in 1810 was Hungli's son, Yungyan (the Chia-ch'ing emperor), who refused to get alarmed by rumors of queue-clipping sorcery. Similar oddities had arisen in 1768, he wrote, and his august father had "ordered restraint in prosecuting them"(!). Then they gradually ceased of their own accord. Now Yungyan expressly forbade local officials to "prosecute through implication" (*chu-lien ken-chiu,* to generate a chain of accusations by forcing suspects to reveal their associates, as had been done in 1768, and, later, in the aftermath of the Eight Trigrams revolt of 1813). Instead, they were to make discreet inquiries and secret reports, to avoid "yamen underlings' victimizing innocent people" and stirring up public disorder (as had, in fact, happened at the outbreak of the great White Lotus uprising of 1796). In the end, the affair came to nothing.[2]

The cases of 1876 occurred during the minority of the Kuang-hsu emperor. During this period, China was ruled by a regency in which the dowager empress, Tz'u-hsi, was becoming increasingly powerful. The Ch'ing regime was struggling with the effects of internal rebellions and foreign aggression. One particularly irksome effect was the social conflict between Christian converts and other commoners, which sometimes sparked violent riots. These factors lay in the background of the spring queue-clipping panic that broke out in Nanking and then spread through the Yangtze provinces. Authorities reported that some of those arrested had confessed to being members of sects or of secret societies. The "evil arts" in this case involved attaching human hair to wooden or paper figures, which would then (after suitable incantations) come alive and serve their masters as armed retainers. Some people also believed that queues were being clipped by paper mannikins sent forth by sorcerers. Governor-general Shen Pao-chen believed that these sorcerers came from the White Lotus tradition. Those whose guilt was "proved" were summarily beheaded (an aspect of provincial power that had greatly expanded since the Taiping Rebellion), "in order to settle the minds of the people." The problem for local officials was, as always, to find a middle ground between prosecuting those denounced as sorcerers (and thus risking miscarriages of justice), and letting them go (and thus risking the anger of the people).

Feelings were inflamed by the missionary presence. Many commoners believed that Catholic missions and their Chinese converts were busily engaged in sorcery, and the popular antisorcery movement therefore took on an antimissionary animus. The situation was made worse, according to Shen, when sorcerers or gangsters became

Christian converts to escape prosecution. What the court needed least, at this point, was mob violence against missions, which would provoke foreign powers to intervene. Commoners were therefore warned not to "grasp the wind and seize the shadows" (that is, make up wild unfounded stories). Instructions from Peking forbade official laxity, but they even more forcefully forbade mob action.[3]

On neither occasion did the Throne undertake a campaign remotely resembling Hungli's of 1768, in each case for excellent reasons. But in addition to having reasons *not* to undertake it, the rulers of these later eras evidently lacked good reasons *to* undertake it. We are now left with the question: what was it about Hungli's outlook, or the situation he confronted, that led him to respond to sorcery as he did?

It may be no coincidence that Hungli's two most implacable prosecutions of sedition occurred in the wake of frustrating military campaigns, in which the monarch was deeply chagrined by the performance of his armies. The crisis of 1751–52, which included the Bogus Memorial case and the frantic search for Ma Ch'ao-chu, came shortly after a protracted struggle to subdue the Chin-ch'uan aborigines of western Szechwan. So costly and futile were Ch'ing attacks on the Chin-ch'uan wilderness strongholds that Hungli executed his two top generals for allegedly having botched the campaign. The crisis of 1768 occurred while the campaign against King Aungzeya of Burma seemed hopelessly mired in the malarial jungles, and after Hungli had exposed his own field commanders as incompetents and liars. As the Ch'ing armies floundered, might Hungli's fury and frustration have spilled over into domestic politics?[4]

Though such frustration may have added steam to Hungli's antisorcery campaign, the actual content of the campaign had its own logic. Hungli's fears were part substance, part shadow. The substance was the difficulty of breaking through the bureaucracy's self-serving and routine-ridden habits. The interests of the Throne had to be boosted by repeated injections of autocratic, unpredictable power, which were best administered in the context of political crime. The shadow (and who can certify the unreality of shadows?) was the fear of forces unseen: sorcery, of course, but also the twin menaces of sedition and assimilation. Even as sinicized a Manchu ruler as Hungli could not dissociate sedition from the ethnic factor, and a case involving the symbolism of the queue was a perfect lightning rod for his suspicions. Lurking beside sedition was assimilation, a threat slower-acting but more insidious. Hungli's response was partly cultural (championing Manchu language and history, and launching a literary inquisition to root out supposed anti-Manchu slurs in books all over the empire); and partly political (stamping out "bad practices" characteristic of the worst of the Han bureaucracy).

Kiangnan was the link. From the rich and cultured lower Yangtze provinces, danger was making its way northward through the counties bordering the Grand Canal. In the South, as Hungli saw it, Han bureaucratic culture was to be found at its worst: decadent, refractory, clique-ridden, timid, and mendacious. Sturdy bannermen could fall under its spell, and his harshest language was reserved for Manchu officials who had been bewitched by Kiangnan culture. From Kiangnan was spreading something evil: signaled in the bureaucracy by decadent values, and in the world of shadows by sorcery. It may be objected that Hungli "really believed" in the first danger, but not the second. Yes, he was officially a scoffer: sorcery was bunk, an "absurd" superstition. Yet there are personal notes on memorials that reveal his lively interest in the details of how sorcery was practiced, and to what end.[5] Did he "believe"? Better ask, did the magic of sorcerers seem to him less plausible than the bewitchments of Han culture? Did the theft of men's souls by sorcerers seem less plausible than the theft of Manchu virtue by Han decadence?

Learned and Popular Views of Sorcery

The distinction between popular sorcery beliefs and the Throne's vision of sorcery as sedition recalls the distinction in late medieval and early modern Europe between village sorcery and the "learned" or "diabolic" version propounded by clerical courts. In his study of European witchcraft prosecutions, Richard Kieckhefer writes that most villagers who accused their neighbors of witchcraft did so because they believed these people were harming them by sorcery, but not necessarily through any pact with the Devil.

> The idea of diabolism, developed and elaborated on the Continent, was evidently the product of speculation by theologians and jurists, who could make no sense of sorcery except by postulating a diabolical link between the witch and her victim . . . [T]he charge of diabolism was not even grounded in contemporary popular belief . . . [It] occurred only with extreme rarity in English trials, and when it arose it was clearly the result of learned influence.[6]

Trial judges and other "experts" superimposed the idea of the "demonic pact" upon villagers' simple fears of sorcery. Such men scorned folk beliefs in the "evil eye" and substituted their own finely rationalized vision of life as a struggle between God and the Devil.

Like Europe's ecclesiastical judges, Hungli was imputing to village sorcery a significance that grew from his own fears. Here is another example of how sorcery overspreads social class in a complex, large-scale society. Two or more versions may be current. The Throne's version centered on threats to Manchu hegemony and ultimately to the polity as a whole. The peasant version centered on sudden, random death (by soul-loss) inflicted by strangers. Yet monarch and peasant were not speaking entirely different languages. To Hungli, too, the plotters were outsiders ("treacherous monks" and "disheartened scholars"): outcasts of the Confucian order, of no fixed cultural abode, who were not under the restraints of the Confucian family system (monks who had turned their backs on their parents by refusing to produce heirs) or of the orthodox academic-bureaucratic system (men who had failed the civil-service examinations and turned against the system).

The political behavior of the monarchy in the soulstealing crisis may help us refine our view of the "autocracy" that has been seen as the hallmark of the late empires. That behavior surely reflected the character of Hungli himself. Upon ascending the throne, he swore to seek a middle way between the rule of his grandfather, which he characterized as having been too lenient, and that of his own father, which he saw as too harsh.[7] Such a middle ground he did attain, but in an odd way: he vacillated between extremes of leniency and harshness, so that his "middle way" was really not a constant but an average. Does such behavior suggest an effective autocracy? His vermilion jottings drip pique and petulance. His reactions to threats real or imagined seem obsessive and vindictive. These qualities of the fourth and most glorious Manchu monarch may have made "political crime" a particularly needful ingredient of his personal control.

Yet I cannot help wondering whether China's imperial system itself, by this time, had reached a state in which "political crime" was becoming a necessary part of politics. Steady, methodical, and reliable control of the bureaucracy was by now very difficult for any monarch to sustain. Hungli's father was the last to make a serious attempt at it. Rationalizing the fiscal system, bureaucratizing the control of border areas, firming up the impeachment system, tightening the secrecy of imperial communications: all had been undertaken energetically by Injen, all had stalled or slid backward under Hungli himself. Perhaps it was not simply that he lacked his father's staying power. The bureaucracy was by now so well entrenched, the conquerors so irreversibly sinicized, that routine control was not enough. If this is the case, then political crime may have seemed a fair substitute: mobilizing the bureaucracy around sedition crises like those of 1751 and 1768, intimidating the literati by literary purges like that of the 1770s. Without designing to do so, Hungli may have been led by his vindictive temperament and his taste for political theatrics into relying on such methods to attain what he otherwise could not: monarchic control over a powerful and resourceful elite.

The Common People: Fantasies of Power

Though we have examined the sources of popular soulstealing belief, we surely shall never know what "caused" the soulstealing panic of 1768—if that is even a meaningful question. Clues as to why it happened just then, and in just that way, must be sought in the effects of mid-Ch'ing conditions upon the minds of the common people, as I suggested in Chapter 2. Our study of eighteenth-century society will have to take into account a widespread perception of ambient evil, of unseen forces that threatened men's lives. But what I should like to consider here has less to do with the fear of sorcery as such than with the social nastiness it reveals.

As an overture to China's modern age, the soulstealing panic strikes one particularly sour note to the observer of Chinese society: the widespread release of social hostility in the form of score-settling. This unpleasant quality suffused the case right from the beginning. In Te-ch'ing, the original lair of the soulstealing phantom, the monks at the Temple of Mercy sought to frighten devotees away from their competitors' temple by stirring up fears of sorcery. What is more, they did so by concocting what they knew was a believable story: that one company of masons would attempt to harm their competitors by sorcery. It was a play within a play, both scripts founded on popular fears. To malicious envy, add petty greed: constable Ts'ai's attempt to extort money from the Hsiao-shan monks was built upon his perception of a plausible crime.

Once the state campaign against sorcery began in earnest, there arose splendid opportunities for ordinary people to settle scores or to enrich themselves. Here was a loaded weapon thrown into the street, one that could as well be used by the weak as by the strong, by the scoundrel as by the honest man. Malicious imputation of "soulstealing" was a sudden accession of power in a society where social power, for ordinary people, was scarce. To anyone oppressed by tyrannical kinsmen or grasping creditors, it offered relief. To anyone who feared prosecution, it offered a shield. To anyone who needed quick cash, it offered rewards. To the envious it offered redress; to the bully, power; and to the sadist, pleasure.

Are we glimpsing here the moral nemesis of a society that was becoming impacted by overpopulation, by a worsening ratio of resources per capita, and by declining social mobility? In such an "impacted society" men would come to doubt that they could better their circumstances either by work or by study. Such conditions were made less tolerable by a corrupted and unresponsive judicial system, through which no commoner had reason to hope for redress. In such a world, sorcery was both a fantasy of power and a potential addition to every man's power. Even if soulstealing was never really attempted, it was widely believed that anyone with the right "techniques" could conjure power out of the shadow world by stealing another's soul-force. This fantasy was both fearsome and titillating. Its obverse was the real windfall of power that could be acquired by labeling someone a soulstealer, or by threatening to do so. Both sorcery and accusations of sorcery were projections of powerlessness. To the powerless commoner of a certain type, Hungli's campaign catered generously.[8]

Labeling someone a soulstealer could be done by anyone, in high station or low. Indeed, the scapegoating of monks and beggars involved a certain collusion between monarch and commoner. Hungli was convinced that the sorcery-sedition plot was the work of "traitorous monks," who hired beggars to do their legwork. Against these socially marginal groups, Hungli swung the lash of state power. In so doing, he was reinforcing well-worn stereotypes about men who had rejected the Confucian order and who were ipso facto politically unreliable. Such men were the perfect foil for his fears of sedition. For their part, the commoners were, on their own account, already labeling monks as soulstealers. They, too, had stereotypes ready to hand: monks were dangerous outsiders, possibly polluted by their ritual services to the dead, and habituated to traffic with the spirit world. Hungli's persecution of these vulnerable strangers cannot have been unwelcome to the villagers, who could otherwise expect an agnostic bureaucracy to offer them scant protection against the evil arts.[9]

The impacted society into which this power was injected resembles in one respect twentieth-century America's "zero-sum" society described by Lester Thurow.[10] Both societies find that their major problems can no longer be solved by increased production, but now require "loss allocation." A major difference, however, is that in Thurow's late industrial America, the sense of betrayal is sharpened by the very faith in progress and economic growth that led the West to believe that all difficulties must yield to human effort, with benefit to some and no loss to anyone. In late imperial China, by contrast, nobody had ever imagined that human effort could (or should) yield unlimited progress or growth. But "loss allocation" in a poor agricultural society is a grimmer process than in a rich industrial society, however wide its disparities of income. China entered her modern age crowded, poor, and with little awareness of the real forces that were eroding ordinary people's life chances.

In these conditions emerged the politics of the impacted society. In late imperial China, most people lacked the access to political power that would have enabled them to compete, one interest against another, for social resources. Merely to form groups to promote particular social interests was, for ordinary subjects, politically dangerous. In time, such power would be sought outside the old imperial system; the results would be rebellion and revolution. Meanwhile, power was available to most people only in fantasy, or in the occasional opportunity to exploit such free-floating social power as a state campaign against deviants. Only extraordinary circumstances could give the powerless a sudden opportunity to better their lives or to strike at their enemies. Because the empowerment of ordinary people remains, even now, an unmet promise, it is not surprising that score-settling (the impacted society's most pervasive form of social aggression) is still a prominent part of Chinese life.

The Bureaucracy: Two Cheers

Of the three versions of the soulstealing story, the least spectacular is that of our antihero, the bureaucracy.[11] If these practical, agnostic men feared unseen forces, they were the volatility of the mob and the unpredictability of the monarch, both of which endangered their comfortable establishment. They tried to defeat the first by intimidating those who brought sorcery charges, the second by withholding information from the Throne. Neither stratagem worked, and they were forced to press a campaign on the basis of very unpromising material.

One weapon not in Hungli's armory was the capacity to make common cause with his subjects. Both monarch and villager—each from his separate perspective—feared the soulstealer. Both were quick to hunt for scapegoats among the vulnerable outsiders on the fringes of the Prosperous Age. But to rouse the mob was the last thing in Hungli's mind. It was the panic factor, after all, that constrained him to tread so softly at the outset and to keep his communications in the confidential channel. Basic to the old regime's political outlook was the political passivity of commoners. That explosive combination in which vindictive leader and aroused masses gang up on common enemies (the hallmark of the modern political "campaign") lay far in the future. The eighteenth-century bureaucracy was not exposed to that deadly cross fire. Though they might be picked off one by one by an enraged sovereign, their position as a group was quite secure, and they knew it.

Hungli was quite sure that his province chiefs were not prosecuting sorcery cases vigorously, though they kept assuring him of the contrary. The real story is suggested by the only complete provincial list of arrests that I have been able to retrieve: Governor Asha's accounting of October 21, just two weeks before the campaign ended. In it he offered a county-by-county description of all soulstealing suspects arrested in Honan over a three-month period. Here, indeed, were the usual suspects: a ragtag assortment of vagabonds, beggars, and roving clergy, the everyday fraternity of the open road in late imperial China.[12]

Of a total catch of twenty-five people (in addition to poor monk Hai-yin, whose case I recounted earlier, and whom Asha delicately refrained from including in this list), from the beginning of the campaign until just before its end, eight had been released for lack of evidence and seventeen held for further investigation. This was the paltry result of a three-month prosecution in a province with a population in the neighborhood of twenty million. Was Hungli being unreasonable when he scolded his provincial officials for lax performance?[13]

If there were bureaucratic roadblocks to Hungli's campaign, surely most were built of those "ingrained practices" the monarch most despised: prudential concealment of information, self-protective dithering, cover-ups to protect personal relationships, and an unshakable preference for routine procedures. Even when he intended no special obstruction, the average Ch'ing bureaucrat—with only his everyday venality and mendacity—was a tough nut for any monarch to crack. Yet we know that the ultimate turnabout resulted, not from such ordinary qualities of average bureaucrats, but from a few highly placed ministers who dared to tell Hungli that it was a bad case, based on bad testimony, and that it promised bad trouble unless stopped.

I should not like to suggest that herein lay some "constitutional" check upon arbitrary power. In no reliable way could the Ch'ing monarch be held subject to the law, and there was no reliable civil protection for anyone who got in his way. Even a county magistrate could run his courtroom with only modest danger of being brought to book. Yet in certain extraordinary cases, it was evidently still possible for the highest officials to curb such power by invoking a superior code under which all human governments might be judged. To do so required that they regard themselves as something more than servants of a particular regime. Such self-confidence could persist only among men who believed themselves to be certified carriers of a cultural tradition. In late imperial politics, such gumption was scarce enough, even at the highest levels of ministerial power. It became scarcer yet after the empire collapsed, a century and a half later, along with the social and intellectual systems that nourished that elite self-confidence.

Nobody mourns the old Chinese bureaucracy. The social harm it did, even by the standards of its day, went well beyond the crushed ankles of helpless vagrants. Yet its nature impeded zealotry of any sort, whether for good or for ill. Without that great sheet-anchor, China yaws wildly in the storm. Without a workable alternative, leaders can manipulate mass fears and turn them with terrible force against the deviants and scapegoats of our own day—anyone vulnerable to labeling, either for his social origins or his exotic beliefs—with none to stand between.

ABBREVIATIONS

NOTES

BIBLIOGRAPHY

GLOSSARY

INDEX

ABBREVIATIONS

CC	Chia-ch'ing reign
CL	Ch'ien-lung reign
CPTC	*Chu-p'i tsou-che*
CSK	*Ch'ing shih-kao*
CSL	*Ch'ing shih-lu (Ta-Ch'ing li-ch'ao shih-lu)*
CSLC	*Ch'ing-shih lieh-chuan*
HAHL	*Hsing-an hui-lan*
KCSY	*Kung-chung shang-yü*
KCT	*Kung-chung-tang* (Taipei)
KCTC	*Kung-chung t'ing-chi*
LFTC/FLCT	*Lu-fu tsou-che, fa-lü, ch'i-ta*
SLHK	*Shih-liao hsun-k'an*
SYT	*Shang-yü-tang fang-pen*
TCHT	*Ta-Ch'ing hui-tien*
TCHTSL	*Ta-Ch'ing hui-tien shih-li*
TCLL	*Ta-Ch'ing lü-li*
TCSCSH	*Ta-Ch'ing shih-ch'ao sheng-hsun*
TLTI	*Tu-li ts'un-i*
YC	Yung-cheng reign

Notes

1. Tales of the China Clipper

1. A selection of original documents on this case was published in 1930–31 by the Palace Museum, Peiping, in *Shih-liao hsun-k'an* (Taipei: Kuofeng ch'u-pan-she reprint, 1963). For scholarly treatments of these events, consult the works by de Groot (1882–1910), Entenmann (1974), Kuhn (1987), and Tanii (1987 and 1988) in the bibliography.

2. A Chinese province in Ch'ing times typically contained more people than any single European nation. The twelve provinces affected by the 1768 sorcery scare had a combined population of more than 200 million. Official population figures for 1787 are listed in Ho Ping-ti, *Studies on the Population of China, 1368–1953* (Cambridge, Mass.: Harvard University Press, 1959), 283. Ho believes the population to have been somewhat underregistered (55), so the 1787 estimates may not seriously overrepresent the population in 1768.

3. Robert Fortune, *A Residence among the Chinese: Inland, on the Coast, and at Sea* (London: John Murray, 1857), 359, 363.

4. *Te-ch'ing hsien-chih* (1673), 4.3. The eighteenth-century silk industry is explored in E-tu Zen Sun, "Sericulture and Silk Textile Production in Ch'ing China," in W. E. Willmott, ed., *Economic Organization in Chinese Society* (Stanford: Stanford University Press, 1972), 79–108. See p. 91 on the instability of the silk market and its harmful effects on small producers.

5. The reign-period (1736–1796) of the fourth monarch of the Ch'ing Dynasty was officially called "Ch'ien-lung," or "Heaven's Munificence." (See Chapter 3 on the meaning of this term.) The emperor himself,

whom I have referred to by his personal name, Hungli, is conventionally referred to by historians as "the Ch'ien-lung emperor," or simply as "Ch'ien-lung." To anyone who rightly objects that nobody called him Hungli at the time (his personal name being taboo), I can only say that nobody called him "Ch'ien-lung," either.

To emphasize their ethnic distinction, I have represented all Manchus (including Hungli) by their Manchu personal names, romanized by the Möllendorff system (except that sinicized Manchu names such as Hung Li, which properly would be separated, are represented here as single words for consistency). The glossary gives Chinese ideographs for all Manchu romanizations.

6. This account of events in Te-ch'ing, Hangchow, and Hsiao-shan during the months of January–April 1768 is drawn from a batch of confessions relating to the Chekiang sorcery scare in LFTC/FLCT CL 33. Both the drafts and the edited copies are preserved, with only minor differences between them. These confessions were evidently assembled by imperial order in late August 1768. See also CPTC 853.2 and 853.4 (CL 33.7.1 and .17, Yungde) and KCTC CL 33.7.21, all bearing on Yungde's handling of these cases. For the convenience of specialists who may wish to consult them, documents cited in the notes are dated by the Chinese lunar calendar.

7. *Te-ch'ing hsien hsu-chih* (1808), 10.6. Mason Wu later denied that the water level had presented any unusual difficulty; but that was what he had to say, given the nature of the charges against him.

8. All ages referred to here are calculated in the Chinese style, in which the person is reckoned to have attained one year at birth. The Western calculation would make each man one year younger.

9. For information on this folk practice *(kao yin-chuang)* I am indebted to Professor Li Shih-yü, personal communication.

10. I am not sure why Shen was questioned in Te-ch'ing, rather than in Jen-ho County where the solicitation took place. Perhaps it was because Te-ch'ing was the locus of the intended crime.

11. CPTC 853.2, CL 33.7.1.

12. LFTC/FLCT CL 33.

13. None of the monasteries or temples referred to in the confessions can be identified with certainty in the 1784 edition of the *Hang-chou fu-chih*, which indicates that they were all very minor establishments, probably of the "hereditary" type discussed in Chapter 5. To assume the monastic tonsure (a wholly shaved head) was the first step in entering the clergy.

14. A Jesuit prisoner in Peking in 1785 recorded the circumstances of his interrogation: "The prisoners were led before the tribunal, and while being questioned, were chained with three chains, on hands, feet, and around the neck, and had to kneel bareheaded on the floor before the officials." Bernward H. Willeke, *Imperial Government and Catholic Missions in China during the Years 1784–1785* (Saint Bonaventure, New York: Franciscan Institute, 1948), 138.

15. Thomas Allom, *China: Scenery, Architecture, Social Habits, &c., Illustrated,*

2 vols. (London: London Printing and Publishing Company, [18–?]), II, 85.

16. On government runners, see Ch'ü T'ung-tsu, *Local Government in China under the Ch'ing* (Cambridge, Mass.: Harvard University Press, 1962), 56–73; on runners' "mean" status, see Anders Hansson, "Regional Outcast Groups in Late Imperial China" (Ph.D. dissertation, Harvard University, 1988), 47–49.

17. The lynchers in both cases were arrested and convicted of manslaughter. I have succeeded in locating the original and review judgments only for the An-chi case (*Hsing-k'o shih-shu*, vol. 2772, CL 34.3.29, and vol. 2781, CL 34.6.23).

18. *Chiang-su an-ch'a-ssu lu-ch'eng Ch'ang-chou-hsien na-huo ch'i-kai Ch'en Han-ju teng i-an ch'üan-chüan ch'ao-ts'e*, LFTC/FLCT CL 33.8. The Soochow case is documented by this ninety-page booklet, submitted by provincial authorities to the Grand Council as the complete record of the case of Ch'en Han-ju et al. The interrogation of the suspects by the Grand Council and the Board of Punishments is summarized in LFTC/FLCT CL 33.9.17. Except when another source is cited, all material on the Soochow case comes from these documents. Three similar cases occurred within the province at about the same time: in K'un-shan (April 30), again in Soochow (May 14), and in An-tung (May 28). All involved suspected queue-clippers' being attacked by mobs, placed under arrest, and later released. For reasons of space, I have not related them here. They are summarized in CPTC 855.4, CL 33.7.30 (G'aojin).

19. Persons suspected or accused of crimes were routinely designated "criminals" *(fan)* in official documents. In order to preserve the flavor of this Chinese judicial bias *against* the accused, I have used "criminals," in both direct and indirect quotations, wherever this Chinese term appears.

20. Henry Brougham Loch, quoted in Derk Bodde, "Prison Life in Eighteenth-Century Peking," *Journal of the American Oriental Society* 89.2 (1969): 329.

21. Quoted in Bodde, "Prison Life," 320.

22. LFTC/FLCT CL 33.9.17 (Fuheng).

23. Clyde Kluckhohn, *Navaho Witchcraft* (1944; reprint, Boston: Beacon Press, 1967), 116.

24. "Introduction," in John Middleton and E. H. Winter, eds., *Witchcraft and Sorcery in East Africa* (London: Routledge and Kegan Paul, 1963), 21.

25. John Beattie, "Sorcery in Bunyoro," in ibid., 27–55.

26. CPTC 865.1, CL 33.7.15 (Dingcang). The reader may wonder at the term "panic." I have used it advisedly, because that is what Western observers called it when they saw it on other occasions. A correspondent of the *North China Daily News* who witnessed a queue-cutting scare in 1876 (see Chapter 10) wrote that the "commotion which has been witnessed here [Wuchang] since Friday last" was caused by a belief that queue-clippers were abroad, and that their victims would die within three days: "The news spread like a panic through the city . . . Grave men are to be seen walking along the streets with their tails hanging down over

their shoulders in front. Others are tenderly carrying them in their hands, and evince considerable anxiety on the appearance of a foreigner or any suspicious-looking character . . . [N]early all the children carry [a magical charm] in a red bag at the lapel of their dress or have it written on a piece of yellow cloth and tied into their hair." August 4, 1876, p. 119.

2. The Prosperous Age

1. Scholarship on these trends is ably synthesized in Susan Naquin and Evelyn S. Rawski, *Chinese Society in the Eighteenth Century* (New Haven: Yale University Press, 1987).
2. A recent bibliography lists, on the subject of China's late imperial economic development (called at one time "sprouts of capitalism"), 565 articles, 26 monographs, and 7 documentary collections published in mainland China between 1951 and 1984. T'ien Chü-chien and Sung Yuan-ch'iang, eds., *Chung-kuo tzu-pen chu-i meng-ya* (Chengtu: Pa-shu shu-she, 1987), 1016–1063.
3. Naquin and Rawski, *Chinese Society,* 100.
4. The works of William S. Atwell have led the way to understanding the role of monetized silver in the late Ming economy. See especially his "Some Observations on the 'Seventeenth-Century Crisis' in China and Japan," *Journal of Asian Studies* 45.2 (1986): 224, and "Notes on Silver, Foreign Trade, and the Late Ming Economy," *Ch'ing-shih wen-t'i* 3.8 (1977): 5; on the money supply and its effects in the seventeenth century, see Frederic Wakeman, Jr., "China and the Seventeenth-Century Crisis," *Late Imperial China* 7.1 (1986): 1–26; on the Ch'ing money supply in general, see Hans-Ulrich Vogel, *Central Chinese Monetary Policy and Yunnan Copper Mining during the Early Ch'ing, 1644–1800* (Cambridge, Mass.: Council on East Asian Studies, Harvard University, forthcoming); and Lin Man-houng, "Currency and Society: The Monetary Crisis and Political-Economic Ideology of Early Nineteenth-Century China" (Ph.D. dissertation, Harvard University, 1989).
5. Naquin and Rawski, *Chinese Society,* 222.
6. The regional-systems analysis, worked out by G. William Skinner, is the most influential modern effort to make sense of the functional divisions of the Chinese economy and to relate these divisions to the political-administrative system. See, for example, Skinner's "Regional Urbanization in Nineteenth-Century China" in his (edited with Mark Elvin) *The City in Late Imperial China* (Stanford: Stanford University Press, 1977), 211–252.
7. Liu Shih-chi, *Ming Ch'ing shih-tai Chiang-nan shih-chen yen-chiu* (Peking: Chung-kuo she-hui k'o-hsueh ch'u-pan-she, 1988), 61.
8. Liu Shih-chi (ibid., 63), quoting Ts'ai Shih-yuan, who is arguing that government restrictions on rice export from Fukien should be lifted. The stability of rice prices was, unfortunately, not to last long.
9. Liu Shih-chi (ibid., 17), quoting a gazetteer from the Sung-chiang area.

10. The classic description of the "standard marketing community" is based on fieldwork by G. William Skinner in the Chengtu plain. Although it has had to be modified somewhat for other regions, the "marketing community" is a concept that has been borne out by historical study of earlier periods. Skinner, "Marketing and Social Structure in Rural China (Part I)," *Journal of Asian Studies* 24.1 (1964): 3–43.
11. Naquin and Rawski, *Chinese Society,* 114–123.
12. The emancipation decrees are summarized in TCHTSL 158.30b ff. See also Hansson, "Regional Outcast Groups"; Naquin and Rawski, *Chinese Society,* 100; and Philip A. Kuhn, "Chinese Views of Social Classification," in James L. Watson, ed., *Class and Stratification in Post-Revolution China* (Cambridge: Cambridge University Press, 1983), 22–23.
13. Naquin and Rawski, *Chinese Society,* 121.
14. TCHTSL 158.32.
15. TCHTSL 158.32b–33.
16. Yeh Hsien-en, *Ming-Ch'ing Hui-chou nung-ts'un she-hui yü tien-p'u-chih* (Anhwei: Hsin-hua shu-chü, 1983), 291.
17. Quoted in Ch'üan Han-sheng, "Ch'ien-lung shih-san-nien ti mi-kuei wen-t'i," in his *Chung-kuo ching-chi-shih lun-ts'ung* (Hong Kong: Hsin-ya yen-chiu-so, 1972), 560.
18. Wang Hui-tsu, *Pin-t'a meng-hen lu, hsia,* CL 57, quoted in Lin Man-houng, "Currency and Society," 294.
19. Lin Man-houng, "Currency and Society," 267.
20. P'eng Hsin-wei, *Chung-kuo huo-pi shih* (Shanghai: Ch'ün-lien ch'u-pan-she, 1958), 605.
21. Wang Hui-tsu, *Pin-t'a meng-hen lu, hsia,* CL 59, quoted in Lin Man-houng, "Currency and Society," 294.
22. Lin Man-houng, "Currency and Society," 295.
23. Although P'eng's chart (see text at note 20) shows the negative silver balance beginning in the period 1821–1830, this figure (from East India Company records) does not include the brisk opium-smuggling business, so the reversal probably began at least a decade earlier.
24. An independent department can be considered a county-scale unit, though it ranked slightly higher in the administrative hierarchy.
25. *Kuang-te chou-chih,* 1881 ed., 50.13; *An-chi hsien-chih,* 1871 ed., 8.29; Steven C. Averill has described immigration to Kiangsi, which seems analogous to the process in Kuang-te and neighboring areas, in "The Shed People and the Opening of the Yangzi Highlands," *Modern China* 9.1 (1983): 84–126.
26. *Kuang-te chou-chih,* 1881 ed., 24.10b. To be sure, a plea for tax remission paints the bleakest picture. Yet events a generation later, on the eve of the soulstealing panic, afford only too vivid a confirmation of its general accuracy, as will be seen in the discussion of beggars later in this chapter.
27. Yeh, *Ming-Ch'ing Hui-chou,* esp. 232–302.
28. A report in 1843 notes that migrants from the poorer southeast prefectures of Chekiang were flooding into the hills of the Kuang-te–Hui-chou region and living as "shed people" *(p'eng-min)* on waste land. Many

immigrants could find no work and probably formed a pool for the kind of roving beggar-desperados found in eighteenth-century Kuang-te, described below. TCHTSL 158.29b.

29. Wang Shih-to, *Wang Hui-weng i-ping jih-chi* (1936; reprint, Taiwan: Wen-hai ch'u-pan-she, 1967), 1.13, 2.10.

30. *Chi-ch'i hsien-chih*, 1755 ed. (Taipei: T'ai-pei-shih Chi-ch'i t'ung-hsiang hui, 1963), 83.

31. Tanii Toshihito extracts, from literati essays, an impressive picture of the crush of travelers on China's roads during the eighteenth century. His main point is how easy it was for queue-clippers to move around, and how hard it was for the authorities to identify and catch them. "Kenryō jidai no ichi kōiki hanzai jiken to kokka no taiō: katsuben'an no shakaishiteki sobyō," *Shirin* 70.6 (November 1987): 33–72.

32. Ho, *Studies on the Population of China*, 278. Ho's remains the standard work.

33. On migration and its effects, see ibid., chaps. 6–8.

34. A mid-nineteenth-century Ch'ing governor recalled hearing from elders in his home town in Chihli (Pao-ting Prefecture) that "in former times" one might see only a few homeless vagrants in a village or market town, and everyone laughed at them and despised them. "But now [that is, around 1830] a community of a hundred might have ten or more, and this was their normal condition." Quoted in P'eng Tse-i, "Ya-p'ien chan-hou shih-nien-chien yin-kui ch'ien-chien po-tung-hsia ti Chung-kuo ching-chi yü chieh-chi kuan-hsi," *Li-shih yen-chiu*, no. 6 (1961): 63. These conditions arose from the economic crisis caused by the silver shortage of that period.

35. I use the terms "clergy" and "clerical" in this book to avoid the clumsy expression "ritual specialist" (though I sometimes use that term as well). In late imperial China, most ritual specialists were not comparable to the Western clergy, in that they did not "belong" to any ecclesiastical order. Nor did they all practice their specialty as a "calling" or to the exclusion of other pursuits. In the case of people broadly considered "Buddhists," there was a large intermediate group of novices who were not full members of the *sangha* and might never be unless they became formally ordained. Most "monks" did not live in the big, well-regulated elite monasteries, but rather in small temples in or near lay communities. As for "priests" who were roughly in the Taoist tradition, most were neither full-time practitioners nor inhabitants of religious establishments of any sort. Many "monks" and "priests" performed ritual services at community temples of the eclectic "popular religion" rather than at exclusively "Buddhist" or "Taoist" establishments. In short, some religious practitioners lived much more closely regulated lives than others. There was a vast distance between the small, highly trained monastic elite and the mass of relatively unregulated "monks." Official documents refer to "Buddhist monks" or "nuns" (*seng* or *ni*) and "Taoist priests" (*tao*) as a kind of shorthand to describe a wide variety of people who in dress, tonsure, and behavior identified themselves with one or another

of the major religious traditions. Officials were compelled to classify people, though the results should not be taken literally. In old China, the distinction between "clergy" and "lay" was much hazier than in the West. For general discussions of this subject, refer to works by Prip-Møller, Schipper, Thompson, Watson, Welch, and Wolf in the bibliography.

36. SYT CL 33.7.20 (Fuheng).
37. On the crowded North China plain, about one hundred miles southwest of Peking.
38. The grand councillors turned the matter over to the Chihli provincial authorities, who searched all the temples and monasteries Li had mentioned. They found "Buddhist and Taoist scriptures," but no drugs, charms, or sorcery manuals. Every one of the persons Li had mentioned in his story was arrested and taken to Ch'eng-te for interrogation. Eventually Li and all the others were exonerated and sent home.
39. CSL 790.10, CL 32.intercalary 7.17.
40. One problem was that the routinization of reporting procedure (reports being transmitted through the provincial bureaucracy to the Board of Rites, rather than being memorialized by provincial officials to the Throne) gave local officials the impression that the exercise was entirely formulaic. Ironically, this routinization had been mandated in 1674 by order of Hungli's grandfather. The removal of the imperial factor (taking the Throne out of the information path) meant that the whole system became a dead letter. CPTC 864.6, CL 33.8.13.
41. Hungli rejected the idea. Such a superficial measure would miss the heart of the problem, reads his vermilion comment (it is unclear what he thought the heart of the problem was). Furthermore, this was not the time (evidently fearing to stir up commotion among the clergy just as the antisorcery campaign was gaining ground): "We'll discuss it after the case is over." A similar proposal was offered by Hui Yueh-li, the Che-kiang provincial judge, who observed that very few monks today had ordination certificates. Hui suggested requiring travel passes for all clergy. CPTC 864.12, CL 33.9.2. This proposal, like G'aojin's, was a characteristic response from the provincial bureaucracy: sooner than institute rigorous investigations, it was better to routinize the whole problem by instituting regular documentary procedures. This sort of response is analyzed further in Chapter 9.
42. Present-day official attitudes toward beggars are still heavily freighted with concerns for public security, as well as moral cant. I am indebted to Susan Naquin for the following reference from the *China Daily*: "*Beggars Threaten Social Order.*" Although beggars were said to have decreased in number, there remained an estimated 670,000 nationwide in 1987, which was supposedly a decrease of 37 percent since 1979. These people "pose a hazard to the social order and should arouse wide social concerns . . . Only 20 percent of those who beg do so because of natural disasters or the misfortunes of their families. Most see begging as an easy way to make money; others are playing truant or escaping from forced mar-

riages arranged by their parents. Some are mental patients forsaken by their families . . . In Guangzhou City in 1987, 35 percent of the beggars were also criminals," according to a report in *People's Daily. China Daily* (Peking), May 16, 1988.
43. CPTC 865.5, CL 33.8.19 (Min O-yuan).
44. If Min's program was actually authorized, however, I have not found the edict.
45. CSL 813.15b, CL 33.6.22.
46. Tanii Toshihito quotes a travel account by Sun Chia-kan (1721) about destitute men who became monks in order to survive. "Kenryō jidai," 60.
47. This last reference is from Nathaniel Gist Gee, *A Class of Social Outcasts: Notes on Beggars in China* (Peking: Peking Leader Press, 1925). On beggar typologies, see also Jean-Jacques Matignon, "Le mendiant de Pékin," in *Superstition, crime, et misère en Chine*, 4th ed. (Lyons: Storck, 1902), 207–246; and Hsu K'o, *Ch'ing-pai lei-ch'ao* (Shanghai, 1928; reprint, Peking: Hsin-hua shu-chü, 1986), 5473.
48. An annotation by "Hsien-fang" to P'u Sung-ling, *Liao-chai chih-i*, ed. Chang Yu-ho (Shanghai: Ku-chi ch'u-pan-she, 1978), 131–132.
49. David C. Schak, *A Chinese Beggars' Den: Poverty and Mobility in an Underclass Community* (Pittsburgh: University of Pittsburgh Press, 1988), 26.
50. Hsu, *Ch'ing-pai lei-chao*, 5475.
51. Ibid.
52. CSL 787.2, CL 32.6.17.
53. *Hsing-k'o shih-shu*, vol. 2773, CL 34.5.3 and 5.4. The first case took place in Kwangsi, the second in Shensi.
54. Such research would require a large-scale longitudinal study of the chronological records of the Board of Punishments, the *Hsing-k'o shih-shu*, which are kept at the First Historical Archives, Peking. It takes little research to show that social hostility to beggars is rising in American society. Consider a 1988 story from New York City: "The number of panhandlers appears to have multiplied over the last year and their methods have become increasingly aggressive, even intimidating." One New Yorker admitted that beggars provided "a new target for my homicidal fantasies." Even hardened city residents who habitually refuse beggars suffer "some psychological cost . . . A tiny little low-scale war is going on inside. Sometimes it comes out as anger." Fox Butterfield, "New Yorkers Turning Angry with More Beggars on Street," *New York Times*, July 29, 1988, 1.
55. For a recent "anxiety" explanation, see Brian P. Levack, *The Witch-Hunt in Early Modern Europe* (London: Longman Group, 1987), 140–142.

3. Threats Seen and Unseen

1. On the Yung-cheng succession, see Silas H. L. Wu, *Passage to Power: K'ang-hsi and His Heir Apparent, 1661–1722* (Cambridge, Mass.: Harvard University Press, 1979). On Injen's reign, the major work is Feng Erh-k'ang, *Yung-cheng chuan* (Peking: Jen-min ch'u-pan-she, 1985).

2. CSL 2.5b, YC 13.9.3.
3. In fiscal affairs, for instance, Madeleine Zelin's study of Injen's ration-alization of provincial finance shows how new factors, such as inflation, introduced problems into local government that were beyond the powers of the new surtax system to remedy. *The Magistrate's Tael: Rationalizing Fiscal Reform in Eighteenth-Century Ch'ing China* (Berkeley: University of California Press, 1984), 291–298.
4. On Hungli's biography, begin with Fang Chao-ying's essay in Arthur W. Hummel, *Eminent Chinese of the Ch'ing Period*, 2 vols. (Washington, D.C.: Government Printing Office, 1941), 369–373. A sensitive study of aspects of Hungli's character and training is Harold L. Kahn, *Monarchy in the Emperor's Eyes: Image and Reality in the Ch'ien-lung Reign* (Cambridge, Mass.: Harvard University Press, 1971).
5. The communication system and the "vermilion" component of it are discussed in Chapter 6.
6. It is unknown when Manchu men adopted their characteristic shaved forehead and queue. It was presumably a convenient headdress for a hard-riding warrior people: no frontal hair to obstruct the eyes while shooting.
7. Frederic Wakeman, Jr., *The Great Enterprise: The Manchu Restoration of Imperial Order in Seventeenth-Century China* (Berkeley: University of California Press, 1985), 416–422, 646–650, 868, and elsewhere.
8. *To-erh-kun she-cheng jih-chi* (entry for June 22, 1645), quoted in Shan Shih-yuan, "Ch'ing-tai Ch'i-chü-chu," in *Ch'ing-tai tang-an shih-liao ts'ung-pien* (Peking, Chung-hua shu-chü), vol. 4 (1979): 260.
9. CSL.SC 17.7b–8b.
10. TLTI 2.17, 3.558.
11. Frederic Wakeman, Jr., "Localism and Loyalism during the Ch'ing Con-quest of Kiangnan: The Tragedy of Chiang-yin," in Frederic Wakeman, Jr., and Carolyn Grant, eds., *Conflict and Control in Late Imperial China* (Berkeley: University of California Press, 1975), 43–85.
12. This episode is drawn from *Hsing-k'o t'i-pen, hsu-fa* 0004.
13. The Han-ch'uan case is from *Hsing-pu t'i-pen, hsu-fa* 469.7 (February 28, 1648) and 469.16 (1648, exact date missing).
14. "In ritual situations: long hair = unrestrained sexuality; short hair or partially shaved head or tightly bound hair = restricted sexuality; close shaven head = celibacy." Leach makes the point even more apposite by citing the psychiatrist Charles Berg on the subject of seventeenth-century England: Cavaliers (long hair, sexual license, lack of self-discipline) versus Roundheads (short hair, sexual restraint, rigorous self-discipline). Edmund R. Leach, "Magical Hair," *Journal of the Royal Anthropological Institute* 88 (1958): 153–154. Christopher R. Hallpike rejects Leach's association of short hair and sexual restraint, but his own hypothesis strongly supports the theme of social discipline: "Cutting the hair equals [i.e., is symbolically associated with] social control." "Social Hair," *Man* 4 (1969): 261.
15. Wakeman, *The Great Enterprise*, 646–650.
16. On the third-century penal code, see A. F. P. Hulsewe, *Remnants of Ch'in*

244 · Notes to Pages 59–64

Law (Leiden: E. J. Brill, 1985). I am indebted to Robin Yates for this reference.

17. Chao Shu-ch'iao, T'i-lao pei-k'ao (1893), 2.6b.

18. There are stories of anti-Ch'ing resistance fighters cutting off the queues of peasants who had submitted to the Manchu decree. See Wakeman, The Great Enterprise, 765n, 807.

19. A modern analogue to the tonsure requirement is the nationwide change of dress style imposed (by ideological pressure) by the Communist conquerors in 1949. The "Sun Yat-sen jacket" (wrongly called the "Mao jacket" in the West) and the Russian-style worker's cap were an unmistakable restatement of the idea that the conquered must signify submission by adopting the styles of the conquerors.

20. See Pamela K. Crossley's important study, "Manzhou yuanliu kao and the Formalization of the Manchu Heritage," Journal of Asian Studies 46.4 (1987): 761–790.

21. Ch'en Tung-lin and Hsu Huai-pao, "Ch'ien-lung-ch'ao i-ch'i t'e-su wen-tzu-yü: 'wei Sun Chia-kan tsou-kao an' k'ao-shu," Ku-kung po-wu-yuan yuan-k'an, no. 1 (1984): 3–10. Documents on this case are preserved under various categories in the First Historical Archives, Peking.

22. According to an archival document cited by Ch'en and Hsu, "Ch'ien-lung-ch'ao," 9.

23. CSL 414.14, CL 17.5.9. Hungli found certain phrasing in Ma Ch'ao-chu's proclamations to be similar in "spirit and intent" to the Bogus Memorial.

24. Ch'en and Hsu, "Ch'ien-lung-ch'ao," 4. The notorious case was that of Tseng Ching, a Hunanese scholar who in 1728 had plotted to overthrow the regime, was granted amnesty by Hungli's father, but was later put to death (by slow slicing) by Hungli himself after he ascended the throne. See Hummel, Eminent Chinese, 747; CSL 9.10b.

25. Suzuki Chūsei, "Ch'ien-lung shih-ch'i-nien Ma Ch'ao-chu ti fan-Ch'ing yun-tung: Chung-kuo min-chung ti wu-t'o-pang yun-tung ti i-li," in Ming-Ch'ing shih kuo-chi hsueh-shu t'ao-lun-hui lun-wen-chi (Tientsin: Jen-min ch'u-pan-she, 1982), 698–714.

26. Suzuki Chūsei pieced this picture together from numerous "confessions," now in the Grand Council archives in the National Palace Museum, Taipei. I have also seen abundant documents on the Ma Ch'ao-chu case in the First Historical Archives, Peking.

27. CSL 413.19b.

28. CSL 414.2. The magistrate had reported that the group were merely "poor peasants" trying to make a living in the mountains—an assertion that we cannot wholly discount, in view of the methods by which "confessions" were constructed; more on this later.

29. In the Peking imperial archives I came across a provincial report to the Throne, dated seventeen years later, stating that no trace of Ma had yet been found. Such reports evidently had to be turned in annually. Hsing-k'o shih-shu, vol 2771, CL 34.3.5.

30. CPTC 836.1, CL 17.4.8 (Yungcang). Governor-general Yungcang seems

to be quoting the confessions directly. Neither the inquisitors nor the memorialist himself would have had a motive for inserting such wording into the confessions; on the contrary, the usual pattern was for local inquisitors to downplay evidence of a direct challenge to Manchu rule.

31. CSL 414.14, CL 17.5.9.
32. Ibid.
33. CSL 413.9–12.
34. Hsiao I-shan, *Ch'ing-tai t'ung-shih*, 5 vols. (Taipei: Commercial Press, 1967), II, 17–18; the same view is taken by Fang Chao-ying in Hummel, *Eminent Chinese* (s.v. O-erh-t'ai).
35. Hu's doom was announced to an extraordinary convocation of high court officials on April 23, 1755. Hungli's edict (open-channel) is recorded in CSL 484.17b.
36. Hsiao, *Ch'ing-tai t'ung-shih*, II, 21.
37. These figures are taken from what must now be considered the authoritative count, from internal Manchu documents. An Shuang-ch'eng, "Shun-K'ang-Yung san-ch'ao pa-ch'i ting-e chien-hsi," *Li-shih tang-an* 10.2 (1983): 100–103.
38. Naquin and Rawski, *Chinese Society,* 141.
39. Mongolian, too, was falling into disuse among bannermen in Peking; by 1765, Hungli was outraged to discover that the "Mongolists" at the Imperial Academy could not speak the language. CSL 737.18b, CL 30.5.28.
40. Naquin and Rawski, *Chinese Society,* 18.
41. CSL 664.3, .9 (1762). The chief culprit was stripped of banner status and sent to slavery in Ili.
42. CSL 685.1b (1763) Hungli was even embarrassed by the "disgraceful" conduct of members of the Imperial Clan, arrested for drunken brawling in Peking. CSL 694.16 (1763).
43. CSL 736.3 (1765).
44. CSL 695.5 (1763).
45. CSL 734.5b (1765)
46. Hungli related that he had placed great trust in Yang Ying-chü, but saw discrepancies in his memorials. He feared that Yang's illness had permitted him to be deceived by others. He therefore sent Fulinggan, along with an imperial physician, to the front to examine Yang's medical condition. "We issued a decree to Fulinggan to take advantage of being on the spot to visit the military camps and to report to Us the true state of affairs." Fulinggan's investigations revealed that Yang had been deceived by the Burmese, who had thereby advanced into Ch'ing territory; and that Li Shih-sheng's battle reports were completely false. His suspicions vindicated, Hungli added a colorful touch to downplay the importance of Fulinggan's spying: Yang's mendacity had been "revealed to Us by Heaven." No one had previously denounced him. Though Fulinggan had intended to wait until he returned to the capital to report in person, "We repeatedly sent decrees questioning him; only then did he tell all that he knew . . . This was entirely due to the divine protection

of the Powers Above, which guided my understanding and enabled me to have foreknowledge of the truth and falsity of the case . . . It was by no means because of Fulinggan's memorials." Fulinggan's secret memorials, originally written in Manchu, were now to be "translated and sent to the Grand Secretariat," and then published throughout the empire. CSL 781.18b, CL 32.3.24.

47. For a discussion of the Kiangnan problem in the early Ch'ing, see Frederic Wakeman, Jr., "The Evolution of Local Control in Late Imperial China," in Wakeman and Grant, eds., *Conflict and Control,* 9–13.

48. Hungli liked to point out to Kiangnan officials that "previously" they had been conscientious administrators, until they took office in that deeply corrupt environment. Even a trusted old servant like G'aojin, governor-general of Liangkiang, was heaped with such abuse. CSL 751.6 (1766).

49. CSL 670.5 (1762).

50. There remains, of course, the nagging question of Hungli's "real" state of mind about Han culture. The avid connoisseur of Chinese art, the prolific composer of Chinese poetry (whether his own or his ghostwriter's hardly matters), the imitator of Chekiang pavilions, and the patron of the most recondite of Chinese scholarship: is this the same man who so scorned the decadence of Kiangnan? Hypocrisy would be an easy answer, but I think the truth lies elsewhere. Hungli was playing a double role: as cosmopolitan monarch in the Chinese manner; and as chief of a minority conquest group. One is reminded of an American presidential candidate who, upon entering the Oval Office, immediately finds himself compelled to go beyond the concerns of the faction that got him elected and appear to be "president of all the people." The rhetoric grows blander, the images more conventional. Does this mean that the man is "really" one thing but feigning something else? Or are these roles amalgamated, internalized, as a necessary mental qualification for the job? He can still shift tactically from one rhetorical context to another, of course, as the occasion requires.

4. The Crime Defined

1. CSL 812.18, CL 33.6.12. Emphasis added. The letter was actually dispatched on July 26, 1768. On the imperial communication system, see Chapter 6.

2. We have to assume that Funihan's sources at court sent word to him no later than July 6 that such information was in Hungli's possession. The court letter was dated July 25 and actually dispatched July 26. Funihan's July 24 memorial on the subject was probably not received in Peking before the twenty-ninth, the day it was seen by Hungli. *Sui-shou teng-chi* CL 33.6.16. I have not been able to identify Funihan's informant at court.

3. See the route of eighteenth-century travelers traced by Tanii, "Kenryō jidai," 55.

4. The confessions related here were summarized in CPTC 852.1, CL 33.6.11 (Funihan), and supplemented eight days later by transcripts of further interrogations, CPTC 852.6 and LFTC/FLCT CL 33.6.29 (Funihan).
5. The transcripts *(kung-tan)* of the confessions, originally enclosed with this memorial, have not been preserved, but I have consulted the transcripts of interrogations made eight days later.
6. CPTC 852.6, CL 33.6.29 (Funihan), enclosed confessions (now filed separately in LFTC/FLCT, box 51) of Han and the other queue-clippers discussed below.
7. CSL 813.1b–3, CL 33.6.16.
8. The edition of the *Ch'ing Code* referred to here is Yao Yü-hsiang, ed., *Ta-Ch'ing lü-li hui-t'ung hsin-tsuan* (TCLL) (Peking, 1873; reprint, Taipei: Wen-hai ch'u-pan-she, 1964). How the state actually applied the *Code* to sorcerers is examined through cases in the *Conspectus of Penal Cases (Hsing-an hui-lan)* (HAHL) (Shanghai: T'u-shu chi-ch'eng chü, 1886) and interpretations in Hsueh Yun-sheng, *Tu-li ts'un-i* (TLTI), ed. Huang Ching-chia (Taipei: Ch'eng-wen ch'u-pan-she, 1970). Statute and substatute numbers given here are those in TLTI. I shall refer where possible to the translations of selected cases by Derk Bodde and Clarence Morris in *Law in Imperial China, Exemplified by 190 Ch'ing Dynasty Cases* (Philadelphia: University of Pennsylvania Press, 1967). An excellent early study is É. T. Williams, "Witchcraft in the Chinese Penal Code," *Journal of the North China Branch of the Royal Asiatic Society* 38 (1907): 61–96.
9. The *T'ang Code* includes all but "extracting vitality," which was a Ming addition. In place of "extracting vitality," the *T'ang Code* forbids "dismemberment" *(chih-chieh)*, a crime against the spirit of the murder victim. See TLTI 17; Lin Yung-jung, *T'ang Ch'ing lü ti pi-chiao chi ch'i fa-chan* (Taipei: Kuo-li pien-i-kuan, 1982), 546. J. J. M. de Groot renders *yen-mei* as "spirits in subjection" or "spirits in the power of sorcerers." These are demons a sorcerer has evoked by "written orders sent into the world of spirits" (that is, by charms). *The Religious System of China*, 6 vols. (Leiden: E. J. Brill, 1892–1910), V, 887, 905. On "biodynamic" sorcery, see Chapter 5.
10. TCLL 15.12, TLTI 421; this is a Ming statute, revised in 1727.
11. TCLL 15.12b.
12. HAHL 10.22b–32, HAHL *hsu-pien* 7.103.
13. HAHL 10.22b–23. In neither case was the statute applied analogically. The second defendant received a reduced sentence because his sexual "delusion" involved "only a monk" and not a real woman.
14. TCLL 16.31.
15. TLTI 441; I have not located the case that gave rise to this substatute.
16. TLTI 567, TCLL 22.10–11. The statute is as historically deep as the "Ten Abominations," dating back to the seventh century (Lin Yung-jung, *T'ang Ch'ing lü*, 713). The T'ang penalty, however, is only strangulation.
17. HAHL 12.21.

18. TCLL 25.68; TLTI 828.
19. In contemporary popular usage in Taiwan, the term *jen-yao* denotes a male prostitute. I have not been able to determine whether sexual deviance was its principal content in Ch'ing times.
20. TCLL 25.69; Bodde and Morris, *Law in Imperial China*, 327–330, overlooks the "extracting vitality" element.
21. TCLL 25.70.
22. TLTI 828.
23. The "Commentary" specifies that inserting slivers of peach and ailanthus wood into someone's grave in order to spoil its geomantic properties *(p'o feng-shui)* should be punished by analogy to clause 3 of this statute (inflicting curses in order to kill or injure).
24. TCLL 25.72–75.
25. TCLL 16.31.
26. CSL 813.1b–3 (court letters of July 29, 1768).
27. I have not recovered the original report that tells how this was done.
28. CSL 666.1b, CL 27.71.
29. CPTC 864.11, CL 33.9.1, relating events of early August.

5. The Roots of Sorcery Fear

1. Hsu K'o, *Ch'ing-pai lei-ch'ao* 73.68.
2. Ibid., 84.29–30.
3. P'u Sung-ling, *Liao-chai chih-i*, ed. Chang Yu-ho (Shanghai: Ku-chi ch'u-pan-she, 1978), 663–665.
4. See E. E. Evans-Pritchard, *Witchcraft, Oracles, and Magic among the Azande* (Oxford: Clarendon Press, 1937).
5. "Religion" is not a unified Chinese concept, either, but that does not mean it is an unsuitable subject for us to study in a Chinese setting, if we believe that it is important to our understanding either of China or of religion. We do, of course, have to be careful not to impose upon it meanings that do violence to the evidence.
6. The closest is Sawada Mizuho, *Chūgoku no juhō* (Tokyo: Hirakawa shuppansha, 1984), which organizes a marvelous assemblage of Chinese writings about magic. J. J. M. de Groot, *The Religious System of China*, 6 vols. (Leiden: E. J. Brill, 1892–1910), particularly volumes 5 and 6, contains a wealth of material based on both fieldwork and Chinese sources.
7. Myron L. Cohen points out that Chinese belief virtually requires a plurality of souls because of the overlap of two views of the dead: the ancestral cult, and the Buddhist overlay associated with judgment and reincarnation. "Souls and Salvation: Conflicting Themes in Chinese Popular Religion," in James L. Watson and Evelyn S. Rawski, eds., *Death Ritual in Late Imperial and Modern China* (Berkeley: University of California Press, 1988), 180–202. Whether one adopts a primarily metaphysical or a social-contextual approach to the "number" question is not crucial to the discussion here, which deals with the problem of separability, whether of the entire soul or part of it, from the living body.
8. Yü Ying-shih, "'O Soul, Come Back!' A Study in the Changing Concep-

tions of the Soul and Afterlife in Pre-Buddhist China," *Harvard Journal of Asiatic Studies* 47.2 (1987): 374–375.

9. De Groot, *The Religious System of China*, IV, 92.
10. A soul-separating "fright" is called *ching* or *haak-ts'an* (Cantonese; = *hsia-ch'in*, Mandarin). Stevan Harrell, "The Concept of Soul in Chinese Folk Religion," *Journal of Asian Studies* 38 (1979): 524; Marjorie Topley, "Chinese Traditional Ideas and the Treatment of Disease: Two Examples from Hong Kong," *Man* 5 (1970): 429–436.
11. Yü, "'O Soul, Come Back!'" 365.
12. Ibid., 375. The ritual of recall has survived in popular culture until recent times. De Groot describes a nearly identical ceremony in Amoy, used to call back the soul of a child who is unconscious or suffering convulsions. *The Religious System of China*, I, 234–235.
13. Harrell, "The Concept of Soul," 525, citing Emily M. Ahern, *The Cult of the Dead in a Chinese Village* (Stanford: Stanford University Press, 1973). A Cantonese "soul-travel" episode is described in detail in N. B. Dennys, *The Folk-lore of China, and Its Affinities with That of the Aryan and Semitic Races* (London: Trübner and Co., 1876), 59–61. De Groot cites fictional sources to show that gifted persons could send their souls from their bodies "especially with the aim to see hidden things." *The Religious System of China*, IV, 103–106.
14. Nathan Sivin points out that the Chinese distinction between death and sleep is not a sharp one. Death is simply a failure to wake up. The term *ssu* ("death") is commonly used to mean "unconscious." Personal communication, December 24, 1988.
15. P'u, *Liao-chai chih-i* (234), contains a story in which lovesickness was thought responsible for a young man's soul-loss.
16. Harrell, "The Concept of Soul," 525, citing Arthur P. Wolf, "Gods, Ghosts, and Ancestors," in Arthur P. Wolf, ed., *Religion and Ritual in Chinese Society* (Stanford: Stanford University Press, 1974), 131–182.
17. De Groot, *The Religious System of China*, I, 243–244.
18. Ibid., V, 470.
19. Harrell, "The Concept of Soul," 525.
20. Henry Dore [Henri Doré], *Researches into Chinese Superstitions* (Shanghai: T'usewei Printing Press, 1918), V, 472.
21. Shen Te-fu, *Wan-li yeh-huo-p'ien* (Peking: Chung-hua shu-chü, 1980), 753. The leader of a sixteenth-century rebellion, a woman named T'ang Sai-erh, was a White Lotus sectarian who was believed to practice sorcery by enlivening "paper men." *Dictionary of Ming Biography, 1364–1644*, 2 vols., ed. L. Carrington Goodrich and Chaoying Fang (New York: Columbia University Press, 1976), 1251.
22. Classical texts had magical force, quite apart from their doctrinal content. See de Groot, *The Religious System of China*, VI, 1011, on the use of the *I-ching* and other classics as protection against demons.
23. Yuan Mei, *Tzu pu-yü* (Shanghai: Chin-chang t'u-shu-chü, 1914), 2.15b; a translation of this story appears in de Groot, *The Religious System of China*, V, 893.
24. De Groot, *The Religious System of China*, V, 920.

25. Ibid., V, 926.
26. Ibid., V, 871.
27. Lo Kuan-chung and Feng Meng-lung, *P'ing-yao chuan* (reprint, based on an 1830 ed., Shanghai: Ku-tien wen-hsueh ch'u-pan-she, 1956), 52.
28. Leach's hypothesis is "that head hair is a visible symbolic displacement of the invisible genitals." "Magical Hair," 153. See also Chapter 3, note 14.
29. Leach, "Magical Hair," 160.
30. Paul Hershman, "Hair, Sex, and Dirt," *Man* 9 (1974): 277, 289. Hershman writes (275) that a symbol "gains its power" by its deep psychological connections (e.g., hair = genitals), but then becomes a free-floating unit of meaning in a ritual situation. Its meaning within a ritual context is related to, but not necessarily the same as, its root meaning.
31. James L. Watson, "Of Flesh and Bones: The Management of Death Pollution in Cantonese Society," in M. Bloch and J. Parry, eds., *Death and the Regeneration of Life* (Cambridge: Cambridge University Press, 1982), 173. Why *married daughters* do this remains obscure, unless it is to reinforce affinal ties.
32. There is widespread evidence of keeping disciples' hair. CPTC 858.3, CL 33.7.26 (Liu T'ung-hsun et al.), is an example. On "linking destinies," see CPTC 866.6, CL 33.9.15 (Surde). That soul-force was increased by the number of persons from whom one had acquired hair, rather than the amount of hair per se, is suggested by the "ten-thousand-soul bridge" that master-sorcerer Ming-yuan was planning to construct (see Chapter 4).
33. De Groot, *The Religious System of China*, VI, 931.
34. On charms, see Dore, *Researches into Chinese Superstitions*, III, 255, V, 500–509; and de Groot, *The Religious System of China*, VI, passim.
35. Dennys, *The Folk-lore of China*, 82–83.
36. Wu Jung and Chang Yen, comps., and Chou Yen, ed., *Lu-pan-ching chiang-chia-ching* (Shanghai: Sao-yeh shan-fang, 1909), 4.3b–4. The material quoted here is from an appended section entitled "Mi-chueh hsien-chi," the origin of which is not given. The work as a whole dates from the mid-fifteenth century but incorporates earlier material. On the history and character of this book, see Klass Ruitenbeek, "Craft and Ritual in Traditional Chinese Carpentry," *Chinese Science* 7 (December 1986): 13–16. This book was thought to have such magical power that when a bookseller sold a copy, he always faced away from the book. Once you had looked at the book, you had to inflict magical harm on someone, otherwise you would suffer harm yourself. Ts'ao Sung-yeh, "Ni-shui mu-chiang ku-shih t'an-t'ao," *Min-su* (Kwangchow), 108 (April 1930): 1.
37. Further tips on how to defeat builders' sorcery are quoted by Sawada Mizuho from popular lore in fiction and literati essays: *Chūgoku no juhō*, 213–237. For instance (218), if you find a baneful object in your bedroom, "do not touch it, but fry it in hot oil and then throw it in the fire. The carpenter will either die or become ill." Sometimes the curse was

unintended: an inhabitant of a house began to "cough up blood," after which it was discovered that a carpenter had injured his hand while raising a roof-beam and his blood had soaked into the wood (230).

38. C. K. Yang, *Religion in Chinese Society: A Study of Contemporary Social Functions of Religion and Some of Their Historical Factors* (Berkeley: University of California Press, 1961), 134–135, 156–158.

39. I have benefited from reading an unpublished paper by Kristofer Schipper: "On Chinese Folk Religion" (n.d.). I am also grateful to Nathan Sivin for extensive remarks on this subject (personal communication, December 24, 1988).

40. Yang, *Religion in Chinese Society*, 188–189; TCHTSL 501.2. I owe thanks to Susan Naquin for sharing with me her extensive notes on the Ch'ing clergy.

41. These officers were called *seng-lu-ssu* (for Buddhists) and *tao-lu-ssu* (for Taoists). TCHTSL 501.5. In 1773 the supervision of these offices was turned over to the Imperial Household Department, for reasons unclear. TCHTSL 1219.3.

42. Personnel of these offices were to be reported by provincial governors or commanders-in-chief to the Board of Rites, which would then transmit the lists to the Board of Civil Office to be inscribed in registers. The whole system was delegated to the provincial bureaucracy and the two boards; the old Ming practice of reporting lists of personnel to the Throne was discontinued. All this was evidently intended to routinize the procedures and generate less paperwork for the Throne. TCHTSL 501.6.

43. TCHTSL 501.5–8.

44. TCHTSL 501.8b–11. The term used here for Buddhist secular clergy (*ying-fu seng*) is obscure and may be a localism. De Groot (*Sectarianism*, 127) links the term to a Yogic sect, but I can find no confirmation of this in standard reference works on Buddhism. The term for secular Taoists is *huo-chü tao-shih*. Hungli's edict against the secular clergy may have been inspired by a Ming pronouncement four centuries earlier. J. J. M. de Groot, *Sectarianism and Religious Persecution in China* (Amsterdam: Johannes Muller, 1903–1904), 121.

45. KCT CL 33.1.18 (374) and CL 33.2.13 (644).

46. P'u, *Liao-chai chih-i*, 131. In this most popular collection of supernatural tales, the one story in which a monk uses sorcery to harm a niggardly donor stands out as an exception (194–199).

47. The actual practice of Buddhism and the life of the Buddhist clergy in late imperial times still await research. In the discussion that follows, I am falling back on fieldwork that reveals conditions in the early twentieth century. Though this solution is far from satisfactory, it has the merit of dealing with practice rather than with prescription. Furthermore, I am assuming that the aspects of clerical life I am discussing here probably changed rather slowly. I rely mainly on Johannes Prip-Møller, *Chinese Buddhist Monasteries: Their Plan and Its Function as a Setting for Buddhist Monastic Life* (Copenhagen, 1936; reprint, Hong Kong: Hong Kong

University Press, 1967), chap. 5; and Holmes Welch, *The Practice of Chinese Buddhism, 1900–1950* (Cambridge, Mass.: Harvard University Press, 1967), esp. chaps. 9–10.

48. Welch, *The Practice of Chinese Buddhism*, 207–210.
49. On Taoist healing exorcism, see Michael Saso, "Orthodoxy and Heterodoxy in Taoist Ritual," in Wolf, ed., *Religion and Ritual in Chinese Society*, 329–335.
50. *Yung-chia hsien-chih*, 1882 ed., 6.12, quoting Hsiang Ou, *Tung-ch'iao Hsiang-shih chia-hsun*. I have not been able to date Hsiang Ou's work.
51. James L. Watson, "Funeral Specialists in Cantonese Society: Pollution, Performance, and Social Hierarchy," in Watson and Rawski, eds., *Death Ritual in Late Imperial and Modern China*, 118.
52. Macfarlane's point is that "they are more likely to be accused of sorcery than witchcraft, for they are not a perennial, secret, inside challenge to a group, but just passing threats." The distinction here concerns the presence in "witches" of the innate malevolence (i.e., a motive for injuring particular people) that can only result from living together a long while. *Witchcraft in Tudor and Stuart England: A Regional and Comparative Study* (London: Routledge and Kegan Paul, 1970), 229.
53. The view that community tension lies behind witchcraft scares offers no help in the case of sorcery, when suspected sorcerers come from outside the community, as in the Chinese case, and are complete strangers to their victims. For a leading "social tension" view, see Max G. Marwick, *Sorcery in Its Social Setting* (Manchester: Manchester University Press, 1965), and for a critique, Christina Larner, *Witchcraft and Religion: The Politics of Popular Belief* (Oxford: Basil Blackwell, 1984), 50–51.
54. Robert P. Weller, "Bandits, Beggars, and Ghosts: The Failure of State Control over Religious Interpretation in Taiwan," *American Ethnologist* 12 (1985): 49–55.
55. Jack Potter, "Cantonese Shamanism," in Wolf, ed., *Religion and Ritual in Chinese Society*, 206–231.
56. The one big exception would seem to be geomancy, or grave magic, which is sometimes used as a weapon in community conflict: one group of agnates aligns ancestral bones to generate magic that favors its own lineage branch over another. This view is offered by Maurice Freedman; see, for instance, "Ancestor Worship: Two Facets of the Chinese Case," in *The Study of Chinese Society: Essays by Maurice Freedman*, sel. and ed. G. William Skinner (Stanford: Stanford University Press, 1979), 296–312, originally published in 1967. On the use of grave magic in community conflict, see also Steven J. Bennett, "Patterns of Sky and Earth: A Chinese Science of Applied Cosmology," *Chinese Science* 3 (1978): 1–26, at 22.
57. Schak, *A Chinese Beggars' Den*, 63. This outstanding ethnography is rich in data from nineteenth- and twentieth-century observers as well as from the author's own fieldwork on Taiwan. See especially chapter 3.
58. Ibid., 59.

6. The Campaign in the Provinces

1. Except for the metropolitan province of Chihli, which had only a governor-general.

2. On the upper layers of the provincial bureaucracy, see Fu Tsung-mao, *Ch'ing-tai tu-fu chih-tu chih yen-chiu* (Taipei: Kuo-li cheng-chih ta-hsueh, 1963).

3. The median time of service in the provincial bureaucracy in 1768 varied in proportion to rank and reflected the normal promotion pattern: for governors-general, 11 years; for governors, 9.5; for provincial treasurers, 5; and for provincial judges, 2.5.

4. Based on the provincial estimates for 1787 in Ho, *Studies on the Population of China*, 283, and Brian R. Mitchell, *European Historical Statistics, 1750–1975*, 2nd rev. ed. (New York: Facts on File, 1981). The European figures are from censuses of 1801.

5. Taking the governors-general and governors serving in 1768, the average length of time served in a single post (since attaining governor's rank) was 3.5 years for governors-general and 2.2 years for governors. The figure for governors-general is somewhat skewed upward by the unusually long tenure (nineteen years) of Fang Kuan-ch'eng as governor-general of Chihli. All my statistics on the bureaucracy are calculated from Ch'ien Shih-fu's comprehensive charts in *Ch'ing-tai chih-kuan nien-piao*, 4 vols. (Peking: Chung-hua shu-chü, 1980).

6. The average number of governors per province who served during Hungli's thirty-third year was 2.5. Some provinces witnessed a bewildering succession of chief executives: Shantung saw four governors that year, and Fukien five. During the mid-eighteenth century, it was not unusual for three governors to serve in a province during a single year. The year 1768 was one of particularly rapid turnover, due partly to the disruption caused by the soulstealing crisis itself.

7. See the cases of Wu Shao-shih and Wu T'an in Chapter 9.

8. Authoritative studies of the communications system are John K. Fairbank and Teng Ssu-yü, "On the Transmission of Ch'ing Documents" and "On the Types and Uses of Ch'ing Documents," *Harvard Journal of Asiatic Studies* 5 (1940): 1–71, and 6 (1941): 135–246; Silas H. L. Wu, "The Memorial Systems of the Ch'ing Dynasty (1644–1911)," *Harvard Journal of Asiatic Studies* 27 (1967): 7–75; Chuang Chi-fa, *Ch'ing-tai tsou-che chih-tu* (Taipei: National Palace Museum, 1979); Beatrice S. Bartlett, "The Vermilion Brush: The Origins of the Grand Council System" (Ph.D. dissertation, Yale University, 1980); and Bartlett, "Ch'ing Palace Memorials in the Archives of the National Palace Museum," *National Palace Museum Bulletin* (Taipei) 13.6 (1979): 1–21.

9. By regulation, all vermilion-endorsed memorials had to be sent back to the palace for storage, which is why we have them at our disposal in Peking and Taipei today.

10. Such as expressions of gratitude for appointments; see Chapter 9.

11. Upon G'aojin's death in 1779, Hungli's funerary poem particularly

praised his rise from the lower ranks. CSLC 23.8–13; Hummel, *Eminent Chinese*, 411, 413. On G'aojin's family background, see Jonathan D. Spence, *Ts'ao Yin and the K'ang-hsi Emperor: Bondservant and Master* (New Haven: Yale University Press, 1966), 16.

12. CSL 813.30b. The memorial is excerpted here, along with the vermilion rescript, but I have not found the original memorial.

13. Jangboo himself was to die in prison eleven years later, convicted of corruption. CSLC 23.41–44

14. CSLC 16.44b; Hummel, *Eminent Chinese*, 413. Documents on the Yangchow case begin in CSL 813.19b, CL 33.6.25.

15. CPTC 853.3, CL 33.7.10; CPTC 862.2, CL 33.7.14 (Jangboo).

16. KCTC 27, CL 33.7.15. Jangboo hastened to assure Hungli that he was preparing to impeach all subordinates who had suppressed information on the spring incidents or released queue-clipping criminals. The emperor replied that, on second thought, impeachments had better wait until after the case was solved—or nobody would be prepared to report events that might implicate him in previous laxity! Here was a classic limitation on bureaucratic discipline: impeachments for withholding information would only result later in *less* information being revealed. CPTC 862.2, CL 33.7.14 (Jangboo).

17. KCTC CL 33.7.9. Though suspicions may arise here that Hungli was using the soulstealing crisis to divert attention from a scandal that smirched imperial in-laws, it seems not to have been so. G'aoheng and the other culprits had already been delivered to the Grand Council for trial, which ended in their conviction and execution.

18. Vermilion on CPTC 853.5, CL 33.7.18 (Jangboo).

19. CPTC 854.2, CL 33.7.15 (G'aojin); KCTC CL 33.7.18.

20. SYT CL 33.7.20.

21. CPTC 853.5, CL 33.7.18 (Jangboo).

22. On the development of this institution, see Spence, *Ts'ao Yin and the K'ang-hsi Emperor*, 82–89.

23. CSK 325.10864.

24. SYT CL 33.7.11. Rainfall and grain prices were considered particularly sensitive intelligence because they were indexes of the popular temper and hence affected state security.

25. CPTC 862.3, CL 33.7.18 (Sacai).

26. KCT, vol. 30, p. 248, CL 33.4.1 (Jangboo).

27. CSL 815.39b, CL 33.7.24.

28. CPTC 862.5, CL 33.7.26 (Jangboo).

29. CPTC 857.3, CL 33.7.26 (Jangboo).

30. The descendants of the uncles of the dynastic founder, Nurhaci, bore the prefix Gioro *(chueh-lo)* before their personal names. They were more distantly related to the royal line than Imperial Clansmen *(tsung-shih)*.

31. *Kuo-ch'ao ch'i-hsien lei-cheng, ch'u-pien* (1884–90; reprint, Taipei: Wen-hai ch'u-pan-she, 1966), 290. 14–15b. Biographical writings on Yungde are sparse, which perhaps reflects his contemporaries' estimate of him.

32. CPTC 853.2, CL 33.7.1 (Yungde).

33. Ibid.
34. We do not know the exact date these documents were forwarded, but they were certainly on Hungli's desk before September 1. These are the confessions referred to in Chapter 1, note 6.
35. KCTC CL 33.7.21.
36. CPTC 856.1, CL 33.8.2 (Funihan).
37. CPTC 851.1, CL 33.8.2 (Funihan).
38. CPTC 852.1, CL 33.6.11 (Funihan).
39. CPTC 854.2, CL 33.7.15 (G'aojin).
40. CPTC 854.2, CL 33.7.15 (G'aojin). G'aojin evidently received the Suchou report even as he was composing his memorial and appended it as a happy ending to an otherwise discouraging story.
41. CSL 815.46b–47, CL 33.7.26.
42. CSL 815.57, CL 33.7.27.
43. Some minor details of this story are filled in from later documents. See LFTC/FLCT CL 33.9.5 (Liu T'ung-hsun et al.) and CPTC 854.9, CL 33.8.17 (Dingcang).
44. CPTC 865.1, CL 33.7.15 (Dingcang).
45. On the Meng Shih-hui case: CPTC 859.1, CL 33.6.20; CPTC 851.1, CL 33.7.4 (Fang Kuan-ch'eng); SYT CL 33.6.22; LFTC/FLCT CL 33.7.11 (Liu T'ung-hsun and Liu Lun); CSL 813.15–15b (CL 33.6.22 and 23, drafted by Fuheng et al.); SYT CL 33.7.20 (Fuheng).
46. CSL 813.15b, CL 33.6.22.
47. KCTC and SYT CL 33.7.12.
48. Hummel, *Eminent Chinese*, 252.
49. SYT CL 33.7.20.
50. CPTC 858.1, CL 33.7.17 (Liu T'ung-hsun et al.).
51. CSL 815.5–6b, CL 33.7.18; CPTC SLHK 187–188, CL 33.7.26 (Toendo).
52. *Chien-kuai pu-kuai, ch'i kuai tzu-pai.*
53. CSL 815.5–6b, 7b–9, CL 33.7.18–19.
54. CPTC 858.2, CL 33.7.23 (Liu T'ung-hsun et al.).
55. SYT CL 33.7.8, CSL 814.17.
56. The career of Asha (ca. 1710–1776) illustrates how the Manchu elite was able to preserve itself by keeping mediocre men in high provincial office even when they were well-known incompetents. Asha belonged to one of the Upper Three Banners (those attached to the monarch himself, and in whose personnel the monarch reposed special trust). In 1726, probably in his late teens, he obtained a staff position in the Grand Secretariat directly from one of Peking's special schools for bannermen's children *(kuan-hsueh)*. After his apprenticeship in the lower ranks of the capital bureaucracy, he was sent in 1745 to Kansu as provincial treasurer. Four years later he was elevated to the plush job of governor of Kiangsi, where he reportedly pleased his royal master with suggestions for minor improvements in military training routines. The following year he was transferred to the governorship of Shansi, where he blotted his copybook by forcing wealthy households in a famine area to pay "relief" funds

directly into a local government treasury. Hungli, no doubt reflecting the outrage of the Shansi elite, was furious; the action was "vile and erroneous" and Asha was "unworthy of the post of Governor." He was stripped of his office and given a minor job in the Board of Civil Office. By 1755, with brevet rank of provincial treasurer, he was assigned to the Zungaria border camps as supply officer. Somehow, within the year, he obtained a recommendation for "military merit," whereupon he was made Kiangsi governor again in 1757, back where he had started eleven years earlier.

After he had served but three years, a Grand Council commission convicted him of bribery and extortion and sentenced him to death by strangulation, but Hungli quickly reprieved him. Holding brevet third rank, he was sent off to Urumchi to redeem himself. Two years later he was again promoted to top provincial office, first in Kwangtung and then in Honan, where we now find him. Late in his career, after Asha submitted a memorial that Hungli considered "idiotic and laughable," the emperor finally decided that he "lacks those Manchu qualities of courage, sincerity, and simplicity"—"how can We expect him to change?" He was now sent to Ili, at his own expense, to redeem himself by frontier service. Four years later he was recalled to Peking to serve on the Grand Council staff and was shortly made a censor. Assigned to aid in the suppression of the Wang Lun uprising in 1775, he was denounced for cowardice and again disgraced but allowed to keep his job. The same year, Hungli accorded him the privilege of riding horseback within the palace grounds (an honor reserved for distinguished elderly capital officials), and in 1776 he soared to the posts of acting president of the Board of Civil Office, and then director-general of Grain Transport! When he died, later the same year, he was canonized as "Correct and Reverent." CSK 337.11050; CSLC 22.43b.

57. The Honan scare and the Hai-yin story are in CPTC 861.1–3, 6, CL 33.7.13–8.11; CSL 815.14b, CL 33.7.20.
58. CSL 815.14b, CL 33.7.20.
59. CPTC 861.2, CL 33.7.24 (Asha).
60. CPTC 861.3, CL 33.8.1 (Asha).
61. CPTC 861.6, CL 33.8.11; CSL 816.20–22, CL 33.8.9. Hungli's characterization of Asha as a formerly "conscientious official" must be taken as conventional rhetoric in the light of the governor's actual service record; see note 56.
62. Funihan conceded that belief in "whole-queue" prophylaxis was common in Shantung. CPTC 860.7, CL 33.8.2.
63. CSL 815.53; this court letter is dated 7.27 in the SYT, but 7.25 in the CSL.
64. Susan Naquin, *Shantung Rebellion: The Wang Lun Uprising of 1774* (New Haven: Yale University Press, 1981), 48; Daniel Overmyer, *Folk Buddhist Religion: Dissenting Sects in Late Traditional China* (Cambridge, Mass.: Harvard University Press, 1976), 113–114.
65. SYT CL 33.8.9; this was a secret "in-house" order to the Grand Council;

secret court letters were to be sent to Chihli officials. Pao-an was subject to Hsuan-hua Prefecture, and the sect is sometimes referred to in documents as being in Hsuan-hua.

66. "Disasters and good fortune" *(huo-fu)* is the phrase used by the *Ch'ing Code* to mean illegal prophecies about high-level political events. TCLL 16.11. On P'u-ming and the millenarian visions associated with his tradition, see Richard Shek, "Millenarianism without Rebellion: The Huangtian Dao in North China," *Modern China* 8.3 (1982): 305–336.
67. SYT CL 33.8.16.

7. On the Trail of the Master-Sorcerers

1. SYT CL 33.8.12.
2. *Kuo-ch'ao ch'i-hsien lei-cheng ch'u-pien* 173.34.
3. CPTC 866.3, CL 33.8.23 (Mingšan).
4. CPTC 860.3, CL 33.7.28 (Yang Hsi-fu). Boat-troopers were specialized detachments of soldiers assigned to grain transport on the Grand Canal.
5. I suspect this is an exorcism ritual in which paper representations of the offending entity are burned as homeopathic magic.
6. CPTC 860.4, CL 33.8.2 (Funihan).
7. KCTC CL 33.8.4.
8. SYT CL 33.8.5.
9. CPTC 860.6, CL 33.8.9 (Funihan).
10. CPTC 864.5, CL 33.8.24 (Yungde).
11. This substatute, 162.04 in the *Ch'ing Code,* also proscribes a kind of "farmer's almanac" *(Ti-mou-ching)* that, among other things, predicts natural disasters. It was listed as a "book of sorcery" *(yao-shu)* by Hungli in 1744, because natural disasters were believed to be omens of dynastic collapse. See TLTI 423.
12. In Taoist mythology, the Immortals dwelt on an island in a vast ocean.
13. This is actually not a substatute, but a statute *(lü),* number 178 in the *Ch'ing Code,* under "Ceremonies," TLTI 441. Wang's case does not fit neatly under the statute, which refers to sorcerers' practice of their art "in the households of . . . officials." The statute specifically exempts those "prognosticating according to canonical [i.e., Confucian] texts." The official commentary, added in 1646 to this inherited Ming statute, specifies that the prognostication of "disasters or good fortune" has strictly political significance: it bears on the dynasty's legitimacy and longevity.
14. A similar roundup of monks, beggars, and other suspicious characters was going on in Kiangsu, directed by the chastened G'aojin and Jangboo, who now smothered Hungli with names and details. CPTC 856.2, CL 33.8.7; CPTC 862.12, CL 33.8.20.
15. CSL 815.53, CL 33.7.25.
16. Material on the Chueh-hsing case: CPTC 865.14, CL 33.8.27; CPTC 865.16 and 865.19, CL 33.9.11; CSL 818.25b, CL 33.9.11; LFTC/FLCT CL 33.9.18.
17. CSLC 17.39b–41b.

18. Emphasis added. Hungli was referring here to his decree of September 7—see Chapter 6.
19. CSL 817.16b, CL 33.8.22 (to governors in the affected provinces); CSL 817.24, CL 33.8.25 (to all province chiefs in the empire).
20. *Wu wang-yeh t'i seng* was probably a reference to a local cult of the popular religion, which originated in Tainan, Taiwan (then part of Fukien), and spread to many other locations. See Schipper, "On Chinese Folk Religion," 6.
21. CPTC 853.5, CL 33.7.18 (Jangboo); CPTC 856.2, CL 33.8.7 (Yungde); CPTC 853.18, CL 33.8.29 and CPTC 853.19, CL 33.9.17 (Feng Ch'ien). Christina Larner recounts the use of sleep deprivation in seventeenth-century Scottish witchcraft interrogations. *Enemies of God: The Witch-hunt in Scotland* (Baltimore: Johns Hopkins University Press, 1981), 107.

8. The End of the Trail

1. CPTC 866.2, CL 33.8.22 (Syda and Surde; also CSL 816.7b, 817.37). The law specified that a false accuser was to receive the same penalty that would have been meted out to the intended victim—in this case, death by slow slicing.
2. Han bannermen were to be reduced to cut back on the escalating cost of their stipends.
3. SYT CL 33.8.10 (Fuheng et al.).
4. CSL 816.23, CL 33.8.10.
5. CPTC 861.10, CL 33.9.11 (A-ssu-ha).
6. CPTC 862.28, CL 33.10.17 (Jangboo).
7. CPTC 854.4, CL 33.7.30 (G'aojin).
8. Emphasis added.
9. For economy of presentation, I have assembled the above account of Chang Ssu's interrogation from the records of several days' court sessions. All translations are, however, integral. CPTC 854.5, CL 33.8.3 (G'aojin); CPTC 863.6, CL 33.8.14 (Jingšan); CPTC 854.12, CL 33.12.7 (G'aojin); LFTC/FLCT CL 33.9.5 (Liu T'ung-hsun et al.); LFTC/FLCT CL 3.9.11 and CL 33.9.17 (Liu Lun et al.).
10. LFTC/FLCT CL 33.9.8 (Liu Lun et al.). Emphasis added.
11. LFTC/FLCT CL 33.9.2 (Liu T'ung-hsun et al.). I have not recovered the document in which Han replied.
12. The following details of T'ung-kao's recantation are all from Fuheng's written report of October 25. SYT CL 33.9.15.
13. The Chinese practice of keeping large numbers of prisoners in a single cell must have made for a lively prison culture of shared misery. Stories of all kinds, including sorcery lore, were presumably a common diversion for inmates undergoing the common torments of jail life, described in Chapter 1. (Bodde, "Prison Life," 317, describes the practice of large-group confinement.) The "stupefying powder" must have been part of this prison scuttlebutt, too. Yet we cannot entirely rule out the possibility

that there may have been certain preparations capable of inducing something like stupefaction. Peter Goldman, M.D., Professor of Clinical Pharmacology, Harvard Medical School, writes (personal communication, June 13, 1989): "Current experience with cocaine powder shows that pharmacological effects can occur rapidly when drugs make contact with the nasal mucosa." One of his correspondents, a specialist at the Chinese Academy of Medical Sciences, suggests that a powder might have been concocted from various flowers or seeds containing atropine or scopolamine. This Chinese informant also recalls that his father often warned him, when a small boy, not to venture out in the evenings "because I might meet some sorcerers" who would "take me away by sprinkling me with some powder." Later he learned that the powder consisted of the flower of Solanacia plants (a narcotic herb). Dr. Goldman points out, however: "A purely pharmacological explanation for the legend is not tenable, however, until it can be explained how the sorcerer can insert a powder into the nose of an unwilling victim without getting enough of the powder on himself to produce the same symptoms."

14. The Board of Punishments had recommended that the runners be sentenced to strangulation for falsely implicating an innocent party. This would be in keeping with the punishments recently meted out to Ts'ai Jui, the county constable who had victimized the Hsiao-shan monks, and Chang Erh, who had attempted to frame his creditor. Funihan objected that these two cases had involved malicious intent, whereas the two runners had nothing against T'ung-kao. They should receive lesser penalties of beating and banishment. CPTC 856.12, CL 33.11.16 (Funihan). I have not recovered the document that resolved this question.

15. KCTC CL 33.7.18; CPTC 852.5, CL 33.8.5 (Liu T'ung-hsun et al.); LFTC/FLCT CL 33.9.11 (Liu Lun et al.).

16. *Chüan* 43 of the *Ch'in-ting li-pu tse-li* (Peking, 1749) specifies the penalties for officials who wrongfully use torture. They are almost wholly in the administrative channel (dismissal, demotion, or fines). The only offense punishable by criminal sanctions is use of a certain kind of "casket bed" *(hsia-ch'uang)* for pressing a prisoner.

17. "Instructed confessions" *(chiao-kung)* were sternly forbidden in imperial instructions to provincial officials; for instance, CSL 815.38b, CL 33.7.24 (to Sacai).

18. CSL 818.7b, CL 33.9.4.

19. KCTC 815.6b, CL 33.7.21; CPTC 852.3, CL 33.7.23 (Liu T'ung-hsun).

20. CPTC 854.4, CL 33.7.30 (G'aojin).

21. CPTC 852.5, CL 33.8.5 (Liu T'ung-hsun et al.).

22. CSL 816.25, CL 33.8.11 (to Wu T'an).

23. CSL 817.24, CL 33.8.25.

24. LFTC/FLCT CL 33.9.2 (Liu T'ung-hsun et al.); LFTC/FLCT CL 33.9.8 (Liu Lun et al.).

25. CSL 818.15, CL 33.9.7 (October 17, 1768). Emphasis added.

26. CSL 818.16b, CL 33.9.7.

27. Hummel, *Eminent Chinese*, 533.
28. On Liu's customary journeys to Ch'eng-te, see, for example, SYT CL 30.9.5 and CL 33.8.28.
29. The movements of grand councillors during this period can be traced by examining the signatories of court letters copied into the SYT.
30. KCTC CL 33.9.24 (the court letter) and CSL 819.15b (the open edict).
31. KCTC 270, CL 33.9.24.
32. CPTC 860.12, CL 33.10.5. Here was more than a little hypocrisy, considering that Hungli's earlier doubts about "seeking-by-torture" stemmed from the unreliable information it produced. Vermilion on CPTC 854.2, CL 33.7.15 (G'aojin).
33. CSL 819.15b, CL 33.9.24. Those punished included Magistrate Tu, who had released the beggars of Soochow for lack of evidence. *Li-k'o t'i-pen* (civil government, impeachment, packet 72), CL 33.11.15.
34. CSK 477.13023.
35. The statement appears twice in Funihan's memorial of September 1. CPTC 860.2, CL 33.7.21.
36. SYT CL 33.11.23 (December 31, 1768). Funihan was not called to account until two months after the interrogations were over. For clarity of presentation, I am treating these events in conjunction with the October investigations.
37. CPTC 852.9, CL 33.11.27 (December 19, 1768) (Funihan).
38. The analogy is the Bogus Memorial case, in which the then Shantung governor, Juntai had also committed what might be called an "information crime" by failing to report material evidence. KCTC CL 33.12.5. The emperor's injunction to "do your utmost" is in CSL 813.15b, CL 33.6.23. Another governor, Ch'eng T'ao of Hunan, was also demoted to the rank of provincial treasurer for a similar case involving a cover-up of torture in securing a confession. KCTC CL 33.12.5.
39. LFTC/FLCT CL 33.9.17 (Fuheng).
40. LFTC/FLCT CL 33.9.17 (Fuheng).
41. SYT CL 33.9.28 (Fuheng et al.).
42. The "Temple of Mercy" case was originally unearthed by Yungde; it was later confirmed by Jangboo's agents who were following up leads in Chekiang. CPTC 853.24, CL 33.9.4 (Yungde); CPTC 862.19, CL 33.9.8 (Jangboo); LFTC/FLCT CL 33.9.17; SYT CL 33.9.17; CPTC SLHK 181, CL 33.10.25 (Jangboo).
43. Some "business" aspects of temples and monasteries are discussed in Welch, *The Practice of Chinese Buddhism*, 191–205.
44. The local terms were *mai-sang* (bury funerary magic) or *mai-sha* (bury baleful magic). *Sha* meant the baleful spiritual emanations from corpses. Both expressions meant magic that spread death pollution.
45. SYT CL 33.9.17 (Fuheng).

9. Political Crime and Bureaucratic Monarchy

1. Parts of this chapter were published in my "Political Crime and Bureaucratic Monarchy: A Chinese Case of 1768," *Late Imperial China* 8.1 (June 1987): 80–104; used by permission of the Society for Ch'ing Studies.
2. See the works by Li Kuo-ch'i, Metzger, Ocko, and Watt in the bibliography.
3. See the works by Bartlett, Chuang, Spence, and Silas H. L. Wu in the bibliography.
4. In describing such an integrated "system," if one existed, we would have to avoid the temptation of reasoning away the arbitrary component of autocracy by asserting any of the following: (1) that what seems to be "arbitrary" is actually the conventionalized activity of a monarch who is himself a mere instrument of the rules, or of conventional values; (2) that monarchs were largely manipulated by their advisory staffs, who presented them with few real options for independent action; or (3) that monarch and bureaucrat were products of a single social system, so that any apparent contradiction between their roles is illusory.
5. Max Weber, *Economy and Society: An Outline of Interpretive Sociology*, ed. Guenther Roth and Claus Wittich (Berkeley: University of California Press, 1978), 1048.
6. Ibid., 993.
7. Ibid., II.
8. Weber, *The Religion of China* (Glencoe, Ill.: Free Press, 1959), 59.
9. Weber, *Economy and Society*, 818.
10. Ibid., chaps. 3, 8, 12.
11. Hans Rosenberg, *Bureaucracy, Aristocracy, and Autocracy: The Prussian Experience, 1600–1815* (Cambridge, Mass.: Harvard University Press, 1958), 38–41.
12. Ibid., chap. 2.
13. Ibid. 175.
14. Michel Crozier's classic description of power relationships in bureaucracies illuminates the Chinese case: "To achieve his aims, the manager has two sets of conflicting weapons: rationalization and rule-making on one side; and the power to make exceptions and to ignore the rules on the other. His own strategy will be to find the best combination of both weapons . . . *Proliferation of the rules curtails his own power. Too many exceptions to the rules reduce his ability to check other people's power* " (emphasis added). *The Bureaucratic Phenomenon* (Chicago: University of Chicago Press, 1964), 163–164.
15. As Crozier puts it, the bureaucrats' "struggle against centralization is not directed toward helping the organization to adapt better to the challenge of the environment, but rather toward *safeguarding and developing the kind of rigidity that is protecting them*" (emphasis added). Ibid., 193.
16. *Ch'in-ting li-pu tse-li* (Peking, 1749), 16.11b, 23.1, 38.24b.
17. Charles O. Hucker, *The Censorial System of Ming China* (Stanford: Stanford University Press, 1966), 57.

18. On the organization of the Ch'ing Censorate see H. S. Brunnert and V. V. Hagelstrom, *Present Day Political Organization of China* (Shanghai: Kelly and Walsh, 1911), 75–79; and Kao I-han, *Chung-kuo yü-shih chih-tu ti yen-ko* (Shanghai: Shang-wu yin-shu-kuan, 1926), 77–96. Both these works are entirely normative and are based on the *Collected Statutes*. We still lack an archival study of how the Ch'ing Censorate actually functioned.

19. Ma Ch'i-hua, *Ch'ing Kao-tsung ch'ao chih t'an-ho an* (Taipei: Hua-kang ch'u-pan-pu, 1974), 78–84.

20. Under general terms such as *k'ao-k'o*, *k'ao-chi*, and *san-nien ta-pi*, periodic evaluation of officials appears in works as old as the *Rites of Chou (Chou-li)*, a text of the third century B.C. that purports to describe the institutions of China's ancient feudal monarchy, and in the dynastic histories of the Former and Later Han.

21. The early history of the system under the Ch'ing is in TCHTSL 78–80. The system underwent a number of minor changes during the first century of Ch'ing rule, but I am limiting my discussion here to the Ch'ien-lung reign. My own thinking about official evaluation has been stimulated by Thomas A. Metzger's fundamental study, *The Internal Organization of Ch'ing Bureaucracy* (Cambridge, Mass.: Harvard University Press, 1973), especially chapter 4.

22. A parallel system (called *chün-cheng*) was used for military officials.

23. This system is to be seen in the numerous surviving yellow registers of routine examinations in the First Historical Archives, Peking. See, for example, the rosters of the *ching-ch'a* for 1753, *Huang-ts'e*, vols. 3861-3-5.

24. *Ta-chi-ts'e* for 1751/52, CL 16, vol. 3860; these are county-level officials.

25. *Li-k'o shih-shu* CL 25.12 (1761), vol. 1076; these are prefectural- or county-level officials.

26. TCSCSH 91.4 (1742). The young emperor was still formally under the tutelage of the four regents appointed by his dying father. This edict, like many others of this early period, was "heard" (that is, probably drafted) by the regents. Yet its tone is quite consistent with Hungli's later edicts on the same subject, and there is no reason to assume that it does not reflect his views. For a similar complaint by Hungli's grandfather, see TCHTSL 80.10b (1697).

27. TCSCSH 93.1 (1750).

28. CSL 295.1b (1747).

29. TCSCSH 92.3b (1748).

30. TCSCSH 92.6 (1749).

31. Save in quotations, I shall use the term "governors" to cover both governors-general *(tsung-tu)* and governors *(hsun-fu)* in this discussion; the problems we are concerned with here affected them identically.

32. That is, those positions that bore all four of the "post designations" for difficulty; see G. William Skinner, "Cities and the Hierarchy of Local Systems" in Skinner and Elvin, eds., *The City in Late Imperial China*, 314–321, on the post-designation system.

33. The Ch'ien-lung edition of the TCHT does not categorize posts

according to their method of appointment, but that of the succeeding Chia-ch'ing reign does. One category listed in TCHT mixes some posts that were within governors' reach with others that were not, so I have not included that category in the 30 percent figure. TCHT, Chia-ch'ing, *chüan* 4–6, sections on Board of Civil Office. On the categories of posts, see Fu, *Ch'ing-tai tu-fu chih-tu chih yen-chiu,* 91–94. Early in his reign, Hungli had to issue a special prohibition against provincial patronage networks based upon regional or classmate ties—a conventional theme, but no doubt heartfelt: "How can Our Dynasty's official posts be [reserved for] the peaches and pears [that is, the clients] of private patrons?" Wang Hsien-ch'ien, *Tung-hua hsu-lu,* in *Shih-erh-ch'ao tung-hua-lu* (reprint; Tainan: Ta-tung shu-chü, 1968), 2.8, CL 2.2.13.

34. TCSCSH 94.4 (1757).
35. TCSCSH 94.3 (1755).
36. TCSCSH 91.4b (1744).
37. CSL 153.21b (1741).
38. CSL 816.7b (1768).
39. The nominal salary was but a small fraction of an official's total salary, which consisted mostly of the "incorruptibility allowance" *(yang-lien).* The ratio of *yang-lien* to nominal salary in the case of a circuit-intendant could be more than forty to one, depending on the jurisdiction. See Chang Chung-li, *The Income of the Chinese Gentry* (Seattle: University of Washington Press, 1962), 12–14.
40. *Ch'in-ting li-pu tse-li,* 1749 ed., 3.15.
41. KCSY CL 31.1.13.
42. CPTC *nei-cheng, chih-kuan,* file 2, no. 118, CL 31.2.9 (G'aojin and Mingde); CSLC 21.37.
43. TCSCSH 93.1b (1750).
44. TCSCSH 92.3b (1749), 97.3b (1769).
45. The special character of the Ch'ing regime, as Hungli saw it, was its superiority to the faction-riven government of its Ming predecessors. He was outraged when one governor suggested in 1769 that a special minimum-security prison be built for "official criminals" (to afford greater comfort to those imprisoned for crimes in office). Far from deserving favors, these men were actually worse than commoner-criminals. "Yet you do not scruple to follow the defunct Ming regime's hateful practice of officials' protecting each other." KCSY CL 33.12.15.
46. CSL 15.30 (1736).
47. TCSCSH 90.4 (1738).
48. TCSCSH 95.1 (1759).
49. CSL 628.6b (1761).
50. KCSY CL 31.6.17. I have not recovered the censor's original memorial.
51. Hungli was disgusted when an elderly brigade-general from a Yunnan garrison, evidently struck dumb by the awesome moment, "uttered not a word from beginning to end." The man's superior, Governor-general Aibida, shortly memorialized that the general was "old and sick" and should be retired. Hungli was furious at Aibida for disclosing such

information only when he knew that the imperial eye would have spied out the man's infirmity. TCSCSH 95.2b (1760).

52. Injen's audience comments have recently been published: Ku-kung po-wu-yuan, comp., *Ch'ing-tai tang-an tzu-liao ts'ung-pien* (Peking: Chung-hua shu-chü, 1983), vol. 9, 44–157.

53. TCSCSH 92.2b (1747). The official in question was, by the way, not some rough Manchurian trooper reeking of the saddle but a Han bureaucrat in mid-career, whom Hungli had certainly interviewed before.

54. I have seen what are probably all the surviving examples of Hungli's audience comments, jotted in vermilion on the official *vitae* prepared for him by the Board of Civil Office. These are in *Kung-chung tang-an, lü-li-tan,* two boxes; First Historical Archives, Peking. The imperial comments are not dated, but as a matter of convenience I have indicated the latest date that appears on the candidate's *vita.* Evidence for imperial personnel evaluation is not limited to audience notes. In addition, Hungli jotted evaluations on "gratitude" *(hsieh-en)* memorials from officials who had just received appointments. I noted a few dozen of these in the Peking palace memorial collection under the category "Civil government, officials in service" *(nei-cheng, chih-kuan),* but there are probably hundreds of them, if not thousands. An example shows that the tone and content are not markedly different from the audience notes. On the "gratitude" memorial of a recently appointed prefect, Hungli noted in vermilion, "He really does know a lot about river conservancy. He should still be used in that specialty. Sacai says he is not as good as Han Huang. His field of appointment *(chü-mien)* should be river conservancy." CPTC, *nei-cheng, chih-kuan* CL 45.2.5, T'ang Shih-pi. Besides specifying areas for future specialization, these comments sometimes indicated the top level that Hungli expected the man to attain: "An average talent. Will do only for an easy posting *(chien-chih)"*; "seems all right for prefect, but rather a minor posting *(chü-mien hsiao-hsieh)."* CPTC, *nei-cheng, chih-kuan* CL 45, boxes 63–65.

55. TCSCSH 93.1 (1750).

56. TCHTSL 78.8.

57. This contrasts with his father's instinct for regularity; at the outset of his reign, Injen reinstituted the Capital Investigation, which had been suspended since 1685, and decreased the interval from six years to three. The self-evaluation requirement remained in effect. TCHTSL 78.8.

58. R. Kent Guy has begun to explore the appointment process as it affected governors-general and governors: "The Appointment of Provincial Governors in Qing China: a Preliminary Analysis" (typescript).

59. TCSCSH 91.4 (1742).

60. CPTC, *nei-cheng, chih-kuan* CL 34.1.27.

61. In one example from 1768, twenty-three lines of an official's reply follow sixty-six lines of an imperial edict. CPTC 860.11, CL 33.9.15 (Funihan).

62. One memorial, for instance, dutifully quoted five separate scoldings, all quite humiliating. CPTC 815.13, CL 33.8.15 (Feng Ch'ien).

63. CPTC 861.6, CL 33.8.11 (Asha).

64. CSL 814.27, CL 33.7.11. In vermilion, inserted into a later court-letter

draft: "How can you not impeach such negligent subordinates?" KCTC CL 33.7.15.

65. CPTC 862.2, CL 33.7.14 (Jangboo).
66. KCTC CL 33.7.15.
67. CPTC 863.2, CL 33.7.21.
68. The execution of Chang Kuang-ssu, for allegedly botching the military campaign against the Chin-ch'uan aborigines in 1749, was notorious. In the Burma campaign of 1767, Hungli had two officials put to death for mendacious reporting from the field. On these cases, see Chapter 3. In the case of the Bogus Memorial of 1751, Hungli jailed the Shantung governor, Juntai, and confiscated all his property for failing to report material evidence. KCTC CL 16.8.27.
69. CPTC 862.4, CL 33.7.20.
70. See, for example, CPTC 853.6, CL 33.7.21 (Jangboo).
71. KCTC CL 16.8.27 (October 15, 1751). This edict does not appear in CSL. On the Bogus Memorial case, see Chapter 3.
72. CSL 780.23b, CL 32.3.7. Wu was also said to be in ill health. When the monarch queried Governor-general G'aojin, however, G'aojin said he had heard nothing about Wu to justify alarm. G'aojin promised a follow-up report later, which I have been unable to unearth. In any event, Hungli believed Wu to be an experienced official with "a sincere character" and kept him on the job.
73. Biographies of Wu and his sons are in CSK 327.10777–79.
74. CPTC 856.7, CL 33.8.22 (Wu Shao-shih).
75. CPTC 862.26 CL 33.10.7.
76. Wu T'an's original memorial has not been recovered, but it is summarized by Governor Jangboo, to whom Wu sent an urgent report, as well as in Hungli's edict in response. CPTC 862.15, CL 33.8.26, and CSL 817.36, CL 33.8.29. For the background of this case, see David E. Kelley, "Temples and Tribute Fleets: The Luo Sect and Boatmen's Associations in the Eighteenth Century," *Modern China* 8.3 (1982): 361–391; also his "Sect and Society: The Evolution of the Luo Sect among Qing Dynasty Grain Tribute Boatmen, 1700–1850" (Ph.D. dissertation, Harvard University, 1986), esp. chap. 3.
77. CPTC SLHK 281, CL 33.10.1 (Jangboo).
78. KCTC, CL 33.8.29, CSL 817.36, CL 33.8.29. The caution about "seditious writings" was added to the court letter with the vermilion brush. In the end, Jangboo recommended that the Soochow sectarian leaders be sentenced to strangulation with execution deferred (i.e., jailed indefinitely under sentence of death) and that followers suffer heavy beatings and exile. CPTC SLHK 281, CL 33.10.1 (Jangboo).
79. The routine-channel memorials that handled the impeachment, submitted in April and June of 1769, are *Li-k'o t'i-pen*, packet 71, CL 34.3.23; and packet 52, CL 34.5.14.
80. The date from which accountability was calculated differed from place to place, depending on when the sect was known to have been transmitted to a particular jurisdiction.
81. CPTC 865.19, CL 33.9.11 (Dingcang).

82. On one occasion when Governor-general G'aojin personally interrogated a soulstealing suspect, he brought along Feng Ch'ien, governor of Anhwei, who happened to be in Nanking on other business. CPTC 862.21, CL 33.9.12 (G'aojin).
83. Karl Mannheim, *Ideology and Utopia: An Introduction to the Sociology of Knowledge* (New York: Harcourt, Brace and Company, 1936), 118.
84. CPTC 862.10, CL 33.8.15 (Jordai).
85. CPTC 862.9, CL 33.8.13 (G'aojin). G'aojin was, however, authorized to carry out the re-registration in Kiangsu.
86. Hungli accepted this for discussion and referred it to the Board of Rites. CPTC 864.12, CL 33.9.2 (Tseng Yueh-li).
87. CPTC 866.1, CL 33.8.18 (Surde).
88. CSL 819.16b, CL 33.9.24. Surde has completely dropped out of the biographical record, perhaps for reasons that seemed good at the time.

10. Theme and Variations

1. Roger Chartier uses "representation," in one of its aspects, to mean "the operation of classification and delineation that produces the multiple intellectual configurations by which reality is constructed in contradictory ways by various groups." *Cultural History: Between Practices and Representations*, trans. Lydia G. Cochrane (Ithaca: Cornell University Press, 1988), 9.
2. SYT CC 15.5.22.
3. Shen Pao-chen, *Shen Wen-su-kung cheng-shu*, 1880 ed. (reprint, Taipei: Wen-hai ch'u-pan-she, 1967), 6.67; CSL.Kuang-hsu 34.2, KH 2.6.1; CSL.Kuang-hsu 38.17, KH 2.8.14; CSL.Kuang-hsu 39.10b, KH 2.8.23; *Chiao-wu chiao-an tang*, 3rd ser., 3 vols., comp. Chung-yang yen-chiu yuan, Chin-tai-shih yen-chiu-so (Taipei: Academia Sinica, 1967), 627. See also de Groot, *The Religious System of China*, V, 489–490, for a discussion of this episode. In the 1870s the "evil arts" were associated, in the official mind, with gangs of armed outlaws, so that prosecuting sorcery was really part of a general repression of public disorder. Christian converts were immune from prosecution, not only because the treaties guaranteed them freedom of worship, but also because foreign powers (particularly France) looked for excuses to send gunboats to protect their co-religionists.
4. On these campaigns, see Chuang Chi-fa, *Ch'ing Kao-tsung shih-ch'üan wu-kung yen-chiu* (Taipei: National Palace Museum, 1982), chaps. 4 and 6. We have already seen how Hungli dealt with the commanders of the Burma campaign after receiving the report of his advisor Fulinggan; see Chapter 3.
5. For example, a report from Jangboo that certain criminals had been clipping queues drew from Hungli the marginal vermilion comment: "How?" CPTC 853.5, CL 33.7.18. The documents contain other hints of this sort that suggest a morbid curiosity about the techniques of sorcery as such.
6. Richard Kieckhefer, *European Witch Trials: Their Foundations in Popular*

and Learned Culture, 1300–1500 (Berkeley: University of California Press, 1976), 36–37. On diabolism, see also Keith Thomas, *Religion and the Decline of Magic* (New York: Penguin Books, 1985), 521–525.

7. Hsiao, *Ch'ing-tai t'ung-shih,* II, 1–13.

8. Recent Chinese history has seen an abundance of such fantasy-power injected into society. I am reminded of a 1982 conversation in Peking with a former Red Guard, then a low-paid service worker. Mao's "Cultural Revolution," he said wistfully, was a wonderful time for people like him who lacked the formal qualifications to advance in society through conventional channels, but whose ambitions were well served by the sudden access of power from the top, in the form of Mao's summons to the young to make revolution. Now, he complained, society was so "exam-ified" *(k'ao-shih-hua)* that he had no hope of rising above his dead-end job.

9. Edwin M. Schur describes the social function of "labeling": "Through deviation . . . we construct the social meaning of conformity and delineate the boundaries of the social system." *Labeling Deviant Behavior: Its Sociological Implications* (New York: Harper and Row, 1971), 147.

10. Lester C. Thurow, *The Zero-Sum Society: Distribution and the Possibilities for Economic Change* (New York: Basic Books, 1980).

11. I am advisedly not speaking of "the elite" here, for the archives of soulstealing bear not a trace of those literati not in office, the "local gentry" whose presence became so visible a century later. These gentlemen stayed discreetly out of sight throughout the soulstealing crisis. Local gazetteers, which reflected gentry interests, breathe scarcely a word of it. Certainly nobody in government asked the gentry to lend a hand, and they stuck their necks out for nobody—whether as pursuers of sorcerers, as protectors of innocents, or as mediators. The days of "gentry" activism were yet to come.

12. CPTC 861.10, CL 33.9.11 (Asha). Asha's complete list of soulstealing suspects arrested in Honan over a three-month period is as follows:

Hsiang-fu County: A roving monk from Hu-kuang who sold medicinal ointments.

Nan-yang County: a roving monk from Kiangnan, who had been "begging" by intimidating people. Though no outright criminal activity could be found, he deposed that his "elder brother" monk had the same dharma-name and native place as a suspect named by the Shantung criminal Ts'ai T'ing-chang.

Hsin-yang County: A Kiangnan beggar accused of clipping women's lapels, along with his wife and four other beggars. Also, a criminal from Kiangnan who was reported to be carrying a queue-end and a knife, presently being sent to the provincial capital for further interrogation.

Lu-shan County: A roving monk from Kiangnan whose name sounded something like that of a monk implicated in one of the Shantung confessions.

Pi-yang County: Two roving monks from Hu-kuang.

Feng-ch'iu County: A roving monk from Hu-kuang.

Nan-yang Prefecture: A wandering stranger who turned out to be Honanese; also three wandering monks and a lay Taoist from Hu-kuang.

Ku-shih County: A monk from the Kuan-yin Temple who had been implicated by the Shantung criminal monk T'ung-kao.

Chang-te Prefecture: Three wandering monks from Shantung, and a Shantung beggar.

Yen-ling County: Two lay vagrants from Shantung.

Hsu-chou Sub-prefecture: Two criminals from Hu-kuang who were carrying medicinal charms.

13. Twenty-one million was the official count from the census of 1787, which probably represented considerable underreporting. See Ho, *Studies on the Population of China,* 281–283. A comparison with witchcraft prosecutions in England, though it can be only suggestive, provides a reference point for the scale of state effort. In the county of Essex, where the population may have been in the neighborhood of 100,000, in the peak years of witchcraft prosecution the courts produced 35 convictions in 1584, and 50 in 1645. For population estimates, see William Hunt, *The Puritan Moment: The Coming of Revolution in an English County* (Cambridge, Mass.: Harvard University Press, 1983), 25; and J. A. Sharpe, *Crime in Seventeenth-Century England: A County Study* (Cambridge: Cambridge University Press, 1983), 15; and on witchcraft prosecutions, Macfarlane, *Witchcraft in Tudor and Stuart England,* 26–27.

Bibliography

Bracketed numbers after romanized Chinese and Japanese titles refer to Part II of the Glossary.

Archival Sources

The archives on which this study is based are, unless otherwise noted, held in the First Historical Archives of China, Peking. The principal classes of documents are:

Chu-p'i tsou-che, CPTC [1]. Imperially rescripted palace memorials. These are reports sent directly to the emperor by officials in provinces and capital. They bear the emperor's comments and instructions in his own hand, written in vermilion ink. Unless otherwise noted, the document numbers in the notes refer to memorials currently classified under "Peasant Movements, Anti-Ch'ing Struggles" *(nung-min yun-tung, fan-Ch'ing tou-cheng).*

Kung-chung shang-yü, KCSY [2]. Imperial edicts in the palace collection. Often edited and augmented in the emperor's vermilion, these are open-channel imperial pronouncements drafted by the grand councillors.

Kung-chung t'ing-chi, KCTC [3]. Court letters in the palace collection. Drafted by the grand councillors and often emended in the emperor's vermilion, these are confidential instructions to specific provincial officials, sent to the field and later returned to the palace.

Lu-fu tsou-che, fa-lü, ch'i-ta, LFTC/FLCT [4]. Grand council file copies of memorials, legal affairs, miscellaneous. When a memorial had been read by the emperor, it was copied out by Grand Council clerks before being returned to the sender. The copy was filed along with any enclosures (such as lists, exhibits, or courtroom confessions) that had been sent to Peking with it. For my purposes, the enclosures are the most useful. They include not only the confessions of sorcery suspects but also detailed reports on local management of soulstealing cases. These materials have to be used with care. The "confessions," for example, are not necessarily verbatim transcripts of what a suspect said. They must be considered government documents and viewed with due skepticism. Most can be checked against other evidence (the findings of a lower court against those of a higher court, or facts reported in memorials from other quarters).

Shang-yü-tang fang-pen, SYT [5]. Grand Council record book of imperial edicts, square volumes. These volumes include copies of both open-channel edicts and confidential court letters. They also include confidential memoranda from the Grand Council to the Throne, which are not available from any other source, except an occasional unrescripted memorial from a grand councillor in the *lu-fu tsou-che* collection.

Hsing-k'o shih-shu [6]. Chronological summaries of routine memorials relating to "Punishments."

Li-k'o shih-shu [7]. Chronological summaries of routine memorials relating to Civil Office.

Hsing-k'o t'i-pen and *Hsing-pu t'i-pen, hsu-fa* [8]. Routine memorials relating to "Punishments: Retention of Hair." These memorials, which came up through the open channel, bear the red rescripts of imperial decisions drafted by the Grand Secretariat and sanctioned by the Throne. They are sometimes referred to as *hung-pen* (red [rescripted] memorials).

Li-k'o t'i-pen, li, chiu-ts'an ch'u-fen [9]. Routine memorials of the Board of Civil Office, official personnel, impeachment, and sanctions. These memorials are of the same type as those described in the preceding entry.

Huang-ts'e [10]. Yellow Registers.
  Ta-chi-ts'e [11]. Registers of Grand Accounting.
  Ching-ch'a-ts'e [12]. Registers of Capital Investigation.

Sui-shou teng-chi [13]. Chronological register of documents handled by the Grand Council.

Printed Documentary Collections

Chiao-wu chiao-an tang [14], 3rd ser., 3 vols. Compiled by Chung-yang yen-chiu yuan, Chin-tai-shih yen-chiu-so. Taipei: Academia Sinica, 1967.
Ch'in-ting li-pu tse-li [15]. Peking, 1749.
Hsing-an hui-lan (HAHL) [16]. Shanghai: T'u-shu chi-ch'eng chü, 1886.
Hsueh Yun-sheng. *Tu-li ts'un-i* (TLTI) [17]. Edited by Huang Ching-chia. Taipei: Ch'eng-wen ch'u-pan-she, 1970.

Kung-chung-tang Ch'ien-lung-ch'ao tsou-che (KCT) [18]. Compiled by Kuo-li ku-kung po-wu-yuan. Taipei: Kuo-li ku-kung po-wu-yuan, 1984.
Shih-liao hsun-k'an (SLHK) [19]. Palace Museum, Wen-hsien-kuan, 1930–31. Reprint. Taipei: Kuo-feng ch'u-pan-she, 1963.
Ta-Ch'ing hui-tien (TCHT) [20]. 1818.
Ta-Ch'ing hui-tien shih-li (TCHTSL) [21]. 1899 ed.
Ta-Ch'ing li-ch'ao shih-lu (CSL) [22]. Shenyang, 1937. Reprint. Taipei, Hua-wen shu-chü, 1964.
Ta-Ch'ing lü-li hui-t'ung hsin-tsuan (TCLL) [23]. Edited by Yao Yü-hsiang. Peking, 1873. Reprint. Taipei: Wen-hai ch'u-pan-she, 1964.
Ta-Ch'ing shih-ch'ao sheng-hsun (TCSCSH) [24]. Kuang-hsü ed. Reprint. Taipei: Wen-hai ch'u-pan-she, 1965.
Wang Hsien-ch'ien. *Tung-hua hsu-lu* [25]. In *Shih-erh-ch'ao tung-hua-lu*. Reprint. Tainan: Ta-tung shu-chü, 1968.

Articles and Books

Ahern, Emily. *The Cult of the Dead in a Chinese Village.* Stanford: Stanford University Press, 1973.
——— "Sacred and Secular Medicine in a Taiwan Village." In Arthur Kleinman et al., eds., *Medicine in Chinese Cultures,* 93–113. Washington, D.C.: Fogarty International Center, 1975.
Allom, Thomas. *China: Scenery, Architecture, Social Habits, & c., Illustrated.* 2 vols. London: London Printing and Publishing Company, [18–?].
An Shuang-ch'eng, "Shun-K'ang-Yung san-ch'ao pa-ch'i ting-e chien-hsi" [26]. *Li-shih tang-an* 10.2 (1983): 100–103.
An-chi hsien-chih [27]. 1874.
Atwell, William S. "Notes on Silver, Foreign Trade, and the Late Ming Economy." *Ch'ing-shih wen-t'i* 3.8 (1977): 1–33.
——— "International Bullion Flows and the Chinese Economy circa 1530–1650." *Past and Present* 95 (May 1982): 68–90.
——— "Some Observations on the 'Seventeenth-Century Crisis' in China and Japan." *Journal of Asian Studies* 45.2 (1986): 223–244.
Averill, Steven C. "The Shed People and the Opening of the Yangzi Highlands." *Modern China* 9.1 (1983): 84–126.
Bartlett, Beatrice S. "Ch'ing Palace Memorials in the Archives of the National Palace Museum." *National Palace Museum Bulletin* (Taipei), 13.6 (1979): 1–21.
——— "The Vermilion Brush: The Origins of the Grand Council System." Ph.D. dissertation, Yale University, 1980.
Bennett, Steven J. "Patterns of the Sky and Earth: A Chinese Science of Applied Cosmology." *Chinese Science* 3 (1978): 1–26.
Bodde, Derk. "Prison Life in Eighteenth-Century Peking." *Journal of the American Oriental Society* 89.2 (1969): 311–333.
Bodde, Derk, and Clarence Morris. *Law in Imperial China, Exemplified by 190 Ch'ing Dynasty Cases.* Philadelphia: University of Pennsylvania Press, 1967.

Brunnert, H. S., and V. V. Hagelstrom. *Present Day Political Organization of China*. Shanghai: Kelly and Walsh, 1911.

Butterfield, Fox. "New Yorkers Turning Angry with More Beggars on Street." *New York Times*, July 29, 1988, 1.

Chang Chung-li. *The Income of the Chinese Gentry*. Seattle: University of Washington Press, 1962.

Chao Shu-ch'iao. *T'i-lao pei-k'ao* [28]. 1893.

Chartier, Roger. *Cultural History: Between Practices and Representations*. Translated by Lydia G. Cochrane. Ithaca: Cornell University Press, 1988.

Ch'en Tung-lin and Hsu Huai-pao. "Ch'ien-lung-ch'ao i-ch'i t'e-su wen-tzu-yü: 'wei Sun Chia-kan tsou-kao an' k'ao-shu" [29]. *Ku-kung po-wu-yuan yuan-k'an*, no. 1 (1984): 3–10.

Chi-ch'i hsien-chih [30]. 1755 ed. Taipei: T'ai-pei shih Chi-ch'i t'ung-hsiang hui, 1963.

Chiang-su an-ch'a-ssu lu-ch'eng Ch'ang-chou-hsien na-huo ch'i-kai Ch'en Han-ju teng i-an ch'üan-chüan ch'ao-ts'e [31]. LFTC/FLCT CL 33 (1768). First Historical Archives of China, Peking.

Ch'ien Shih-fu. *Ch'ing-tai chih-kuan nien-piao* [32]. 4 vols. Peking: Chung-hua shu-chü, 1980.

Ch'ing-shih lieh-chuan (CSLC) [33]. Shanghai: Chung-hua shu-chü, 1928. Reprint. Taipei: Chung-hua shu-chü, 1962.

Ch'ing-tai ti-hou hsiang [34], series 2. Peiping: National Palace Museum, 1935.

Chu, Raymond W., and William G. Saywell. *Career Patterns in the Ch'ing Dynasty: The Office of Governor-general*. Ann Arbor: Center for Chinese Studies, University of Michigan, 1984.

Chuang, Chi-fa. *Ch'ing-tai tsou-che chih-tu* [35]. Taipei: National Palace Museum, 1979.

——— *Ch'ing Kao-tsung shih-ch'üan wu-kung yen-chiu* [36]. Taipei: National Palace Museum, 1982.

Ch'ü T'ung-tsu. *Local Government in China under the Ch'ing*. Cambridge, Mass.: Harvard University Press, 1962.

Ch'üan Han-sheng. "Ch'ien-lung shih-san-nien ti mi-kuei wen-t'i" [37]. In Ch'üan Han-sheng, *Chung-kuo ching-chi-shih lun-ts'ung*. Hong Kong: Hsin-ya yen-chiu-so, 1972.

Cohen, Myron L. "Souls and Salvation: Conflicting Themes in Chinese Popular Religion." In James L. Watson and Evelyn S. Rawski, eds., *Death Ritual in Late Imperial and Modern China*, 180–202. Berkeley: University of California Press, 1988.

Crossley, Pamela K. "*Manzhou yuanliu kao* and the Formalization of the Manchu Heritage." *Journal of Asian Studies* 46.4 (1987): 761–790.

Crozier, Michel. *The Bureaucratic Phenomenon*. Chicago: University of Chicago Press, 1964.

Crozier, Michel, and Erhard Friedberg. *Actors and Systems: The Politics of Collective Action*. Chicago: University of Chicago Press, 1980.

De Groot, J. J. M. *The Religious System of China*. 6 vols. Leiden: E. J. Brill, 1882–1910.

———— *Sectarianism and Religious Persecution in China*. Amsterdam: Johannes Muller, 1903–1904.

Dennys, N. B. *The Folk-lore of China, and Its Affinities with That of the Aryan and Semitic Races*. London: Trübner and Co., 1876.

Dore, Henry (Henri Doré). *Researches into Chinese Superstitions*. Translated from the French with Notes, Historical and Explanatory, by M. Kennelly, S.J. Shanghai: T'usewei Printing Press, 1918.

Entenmann, Robert E. "De Tonsura Sino-Tartarica: The Queue in Early Ch'ing China." Unpublished seminar paper, Harvard University, 1974.

Evans-Pritchard, E. E. *Witchcraft, Oracles, and Magic among the Azande*. Oxford: Clarendon Press, 1937.

Fairbank, John K., and Teng Ssu-yü. "On the Transmission of Ch'ing Documents." *Harvard Journal of Asiatic Studies* 5 (1940): 1–71.

———— "On the Types and Uses of Ch'ing Documents." *Harvard Journal of Asiatic Studies* 6 (1941): 135–246.

Feng Erh-k'ang. *Yung-cheng chuan* [38]. Peking: Jen-min ch'u-pan-she, 1985.

Fortune, Robert. *A Residence among the Chinese: Inland, on the Coast, and at Sea*. London: John Murray, 1857.

Freedman, Maurice. "Ancestor Worship: Two Facets of the Chinese Case." In *The Study of Chinese Society: Essays by Maurice Freedman*. Selected and edited by G. William Skinner. Stanford: Stanford University Press, 1979.

Fu Tsung-mao. *Ch'ing-tai tu-fu chih-tu chih yen-chiu* [39]. Taipei: Kuo-li cheng-chih ta-hsueh, 1963.

Fuchs, Walter. "Die Reisen Kienlungs nach Mittelchina." *Nachrichten der deutschen Gesellschaft fur natur- und Volkerkunde Ostasiens* 74.1–3 (1953).

Gee, Nathaniel Gist. *A Class of Social Outcasts: Notes on the Beggars in China*. Peking: Peking Leader Press, 1925.

Guy, R. Kent. "The Appointment of Provincial Governers in Qing China: A Preliminary Analysis." Typescript.

Hallpike, Christopher R. "Social Hair." *Man* 4 (1969): 256–264.

Hang-chou fu-chih [40]. 1784 ed.

Hansson, Harry Anders. "Regional Outcast Groups in Late Imperial China." Ph.D. dissertation, Harvard University, 1988.

Harrell, Stevan. "The Concept of Soul in Chinese Folk Religion." *Journal of Asian Studies* 38 (1979): 519–528.

Hershman, Paul. "Hair, Sex, and Dirt." *Man* 9 (1974): 274–298.

Ho Ping-ti. *Studies on the Population of China, 1368–1953*. Cambridge, Mass.: Harvard University Press, 1959.

Hsiao I-shan. *Ch'ing-tai t'ung-shih* [41]. 5 vols. Taipei: Shang-wu yin-shu-kuan, 1967.

Hsu K'o. *Ch'ing-pai lei-ch'ao* [42]. Shanghai, 1928. Reprint. Peking: Hsin-hua shu-chü, 1986.

Hucker, Charles O. *The Censorial System of Ming China*. Stanford: Stanford University Press, 1966.

Hulsewe, A. F. P. *Remnants of Ch'in Law*. Leiden: E. J. Brill, 1985.

Hummel, Arthur W. *Eminent Chinese of the Ch'ing Period*. 2 vols. Washington, D.C.: U.S. Government Printing Office, 1941.

Hunt, William. *The Puritan Moment: The Coming of Revolution in an English County*. Cambridge, Mass.: Harvard University Press, 1983.

Kahn, Harold L. *Monarchy in the Emperor's Eyes: Image and Reality in the Ch'ien-lung Reign*. Cambridge, Mass.: Harvard University Press, 1971.

Kao I-han. *Chung-kuo yü-shih chih-tu ti yen-ko* [43]. Shanghai: Shang-wu yin-shu-kuan, 1926.

Kelley, David E. "Temples and Tribute Fleets: The Luo Sect and Boatmen's Associations in the Eighteenth Century." *Modern China* 8.3 (1982): 361–391.

———— "Sect and Society: The Evolution of the Luo Sect among Qing Dynasty Grain Tribute Boatmen, 1700–1850." Ph.D. dissertation, Harvard University, 1986.

Kieckhefer, Richard. *European Witch Trials: Their Foundations in Popular and Learned Culture, 1300–1500*. Berkeley: University of California Press, 1976.

Kluckhohn, Clyde. *Navaho Witchcraft*. 1944. Reprint. Boston: Beacon Press, 1967.

Kuang-te chou-chih [44]. 1881 ed.

Kuhn, Philip A. "Chinese Views of Social Classification." In James L. Watson, ed., *Class and Stratification in Post-Revolution China*, 16–28. Cambridge: Cambridge University Press, 1983.

———— "Political Crime and Bureaucratic Monarchy: A Chinese Case of 1768." *Late Imperial China* 8.1 (June 1987): 80–104.

Kuo-ch'ao ch'i-hsien lei-cheng, ch'u-pien [45]. 1884–1890. Reprint. Taipei: Wen-hai ch'u-pan-she, 1966.

Larner, Christina. *Enemies of God: The Witch-Hunt in Scotland*. Baltimore: Johns Hopkins University Press, 1981.

———— *Witchcraft and Religion: The Politics of Popular Belief*. Oxford: Basil Blackwell, 1984.

Leach, Edmund R. "Magical Hair." *Journal of the Royal Anthropological Institute* 88 (1958): 147–164.

Levack, Brian P. *The Witch-Hunt in Early Modern Europe*. London: Longman Group, 1987.

Li Kuo-ch'i. *Ch'ing-tai chi-ts'eng ti-fang-kuan jen-shih shan-ti hsien-hsiang chih liang-hua fen-hsi* [46]. Taipei: Chung-yang wen-wu kung-ying-she, 1975.

Lin Man-houng. "Currency and Society: The Monetary Crisis and Political-Economic Ideology of Early Nineteenth-Century China." Ph.D. dissertation, Harvard University, 1989.

Lin Yung-jung. *T'ang Ch'ing lü ti pi-chiao chi ch'i fa-chan* [47]. Taipei: Kuo-li pien-i-kuan, 1982.

Liu Shih-chi. *Ming-Ch'ing shih-tai Chiang-nan shih-chen yen-chiu* [48]. Peking: Chung-kuo she-hui k'o-hsueh ch'u-pan-she, 1988.

Lo Kuan-chung and Feng Meng-lung. *P'ing-yao chuan* [49]. Based on an 1830 edition. Shanghai: Ku-tien wen-hsueh ch'u-pan-she, 1956.

Ma Ch'i-hua. *Ch'ing Kao-tsung ch'ao chih t'an-ho an* [50]. Taipei: Hua-kang ch'u-pan-pu, 1974.

Macfarlane, Alan. *Witchcraft in Tudor and Stuart England: A Regional and Comparative Study*. London: Routledge and Kegan Paul, 1970.

Mannheim, Karl. *Ideology and Utopia: An Introduction to the Sociology of Knowledge.* New York: Harcourt, Brace and Company, 1936.

Marwick, Max G. *Sorcery in Its Social Setting.* Manchester: Manchester University Press, 1965.

Matignon, Jean-Jacques. "Le mendiant de Pékin." In *Superstition, crime, et misère en Chine,* 207–246. 4th ed. Lyons: Storck, 1902.

Metzger, Thomas A. *The Internal Organization of Ch'ing Bureaucracy.* Cambridge, Mass.: Harvard University Press, 1973.

Middleton, John, and E. H. Winter, eds. *Witchcraft and Sorcery in East Africa.* London: Routledge and Kegan Paul, 1963.

Mitchell, Brian R. *European Historical Statistics, 1750–1975.* 2nd rev. ed. New York: Facts on File, 1981.

Moore, R. I. *The Formation of a Persecuting Society: Power and Deviance in Western Europe, 950–1250.* Oxford: Basil Blackwell, 1987.

Mortier, Florent. "De la Mendicité en Chine." *Bulletin de la Société Royale Belge d'Anthropologie et de Prehistoire de Bruxelles* 59 (1948): 176–187.

Murray, Laura. "New World Food Crops in China: Farms, Food, and Families in the Wei River Valley." Ph.D. dissertation, University of Pennsylvania, 1985.

Nakagawa Chūei. *Shinzoku kibun* [51]. 1799.

Naquin, Susan. *Shantung Rebellion: The Wang Lun Uprising of 1774.* New Haven: Yale University Press, 1981.

Naquin, Susan, and Evelyn S. Rawski. *Chinese Society in the Eighteenth Century.* New Haven: Yale University Press, 1987.

Ocko, Jonathan K. *Bureaucratic Reform in Provincial China: Ting Jih-ch'ang in Restoration Kiangsu, 1867–1870.* Cambridge, Mass.: Council on East Asian Studies, Harvard University, 1983.

Overmyer, Daniel L. *Folk Buddhist Religion: Dissenting Sects in Late Traditional China.* Cambridge, Mass.: Harvard University Press, 1976.

P'eng Hsin-wei. *Chung-kuo huo-pi shih* [52]. Shanghai: Ch'ün-lien ch'u-pan-she, 1958.

P'eng Tse-i. "Ya-p'ien chan-hou shih-nien-chien yin-kui ch'ien-chien po-tung-hsia ti Chung-kuo ching-chi yü chieh-chi kuan-hsi" [53]. *Li-shih yen-chiu,* no. 6 (1961): 40–68.

Potter, Jack. "Cantonese Shamanism." In Arthur P. Wolf, ed., *Religion and Ritual in Chinese Society,* 206–231. Stanford: Stanford University Press, 1974.

Prip-Møller, Johannes. *Chinese Buddhist Monasteries: Their Plan and Its Function as a Setting for Buddhist Monastic Life.* Copenhagen, 1936. Reprint. Hong Kong: Hong Kong University Press, 1967.

P'u Sung-ling. *Liao-chai chih-i* [54]. Edited by Chang Yu-ho. Shanghai: Ku-chi ch'u-pan-she, 1978.

Rosenberg, Hans. *Bureaucracy, Aristocracy, and Autocracy: The Prussian Experience, 1600–1815.* Cambridge, Mass.: Harvard University Press, 1958.

Ruitenbeek, Klass. "Craft and Ritual in Traditional Chinese Carpentry." *Chinese Science* 7 (December 1986): 1–23.

Saso, Michael. "Orthodoxy and Heterodoxy in Taoist Ritual." In Arthur P.

Wolf, ed., *Religion and Ritual in Chinese Society*, 329–335. Stanford: Stanford University Press, 1974.

Sawada Mizuho. *Chūgoku no juhō* [55]. Tokyo: Hirakawa shuppansha, 1984.

Schak, David C. *A Chinese Beggars' Den: Poverty and Mobility in an Underclass Community*. Pittsburgh: University of Pittsburgh Press, 1988.

Schipper, Kristofer. "On Chinese Folk Religion." Typescript.

Schur, Edwin M. *Labeling Deviant Behavior: Its Sociological Implications*. New York: Harper and Row, 1971.

Shan Shih-yuan. "Ch'ing-tai Ch'i-chü-chu" [56]. *Ch'ing-tai tang-an shih-liao ts'ung-pien* (Peking, Chung-hua shu-chü), vol. 4 (1979): 259–271.

Sharpe, J. A. *Crime in Seventeenth-Century England: A County Study*. Cambridge: Cambridge University Press, 1983.

Shek, Richard. "Millenarianism without Rebellion: The Huangtian Dao in North China." *Modern China* 8.3 (1982): 305–336.

Shen Chia-pen, *Li-tai hsing-fa k'ao* [57]. In Shen Chia-pen, *Shen Ch'i-i hsien-sheng i-shu* (Kuei-an, n.d.), vols. 1–22. Reprint. 4 vols. Peking: Chung-hua shu-chü, 1985.

Shen Pao-chen. *Shen Wen-su-kung cheng-shu*. [58]. 1880 ed. Reprint. Taipei: Wen-hai ch'u-pan-she, 1967.

Shen Te-fu. *Wan-li yeh-huo-p'ien* [59]. Peking: Chung-hua shu-chü, 1980.

Skinner, G. William. "Regional Urbanization in Nineteenth-Century China." In G. William Skinner and Mark Elvin, eds., *The City in Late Imperial China*, 211–252. Stanford: Stanford University Press, 1977.

——— "Cities and the Hierarchy of Local Systems." In G. William Skinner and Mark Elvin, eds., *The City in Late Imperial China*, 275–352 Stanford: Stanford University Press, 1977.

——— "Marketing and Social Structure in Rural China (Part I)." *Journal of Asian Studies* 24.1 (1964): 3–43.

Skinner, G. William, and Mark Elvin, eds. *The City in Late Imperial China*. Stanford: Stanford University Press, 1977.

Spence, Jonathan D. *Ts'ao Yin and the K'ang-hsi Emperor: Bondservant and Master*. New Haven: Yale University Press, 1966.

Sun, E-tu Zen. "Sericulture and Silk Textile Production in Ch'ing China." In W. E. Willmott, ed., *Economic Organization in Chinese Society*, 79–108. Stanford: Stanford University Press, 1972.

Suzuki Chūsei. "Ch'ien-lung shih-ch'i-nien Ma Ch'ao-chu ti fan-Ch'ing yun-tung: Chung-kuo min-chung ti wu-t'o-pang yun-tung ti i-li [60]. In *Ming-Ch'ing shih kuo-chi hsueh-shu t'ao-lun-hui lun-wen-chi*, 698–714. Tientsin: Jen-min ch'u-pan-she, 1982.

Tanii Toshihito. "Kenryō jidai no ichi kōiki hanzai jiken to kokka no taiō: katsuben'an no shakaishiteki sobyō" [61]. *Shirin* 70.6 (November 1987): 33–72.

——— "Shindai gaishō no keisatsu kinō ni tsuite: katsuben'an o tameshi ni" [62]. *Tōyōshi kenkyū* 46.4 (March 1988): 763–787.

Te-ch'ing hsien-chih [63]. 1673 ed. Reprint, 1912.

Te-ch'ing hsien hsu-chih [64]. 1808 ed. Reprint, 1912.

Thomas, Keith. *Religion and the Decline of Magic*. New York: Penguin Books, 1985.

Thompson, Laurence G. *Chinese Religion: An Introduction*, 3rd ed. Belmont, Calif.: Wadsworth, 1979.

Thurow, Lester C. *The Zero-Sum Society: Distribution and the Possibilities for Economic Change*. New York: Basic Books, 1980.

Tien-shih-chai hua-pao [65]. Shanghai, 1884–1889. Reprint. Hong Kong: Kuang-chiao ching, 1983.

T'ien Chü-chien and Sung Yuan-ch'iang, eds. *Chung-kuo tzu-pen chu-i meng-ya* [66]. Chengtu: Pa-shu shu-she, 1987.

Topley, Marjorie. "Chinese Traditional Ideas and the Treatment of Disease: Two Examples from Hong Kong." *Man* 5 (1970): 429–436.

Ts'ao Sung-yeh. "Ni-shui mu-chiang ku-shih t'an-t'ao" [67]. *Min-su* (Kwangchow) 108 (April 1930): 1–7.

Vogel, Hans-Ulrich. *Central Chinese Monetary Policy and Yunnan Copper Mining during the Early Ch'ing, 1644–1800*. Cambridge, Mass.: Council on East Asian Studies, Harvard University, forthcoming.

Wakeman, Frederic Jr. "The Evolution of Local Control in Late Imperial China." In Frederic Wakeman, Jr., and Carolyn Grant, eds., *Conflict and Control in Late Imperial China*, 1–25. Berkeley: University of California Press, 1975.

—— "Localism and Loyalism during the Ch'ing Conquest of Kiangnan: The Tragedy of Chiang-yin." In Frederic Wakeman, Jr., and Carolyn Grant, eds., *Conflict and Control in Late Imperial China*, 43–85. Berkeley: University of California Press, 1975.

—— "China and the Seventeenth-Century Crisis." *Late Imperial China* 7.1 (1986): 1–26.

—— *The Great Enterprise: The Manchu Restoration of Imperial Order in Seventeenth-Century China*. Berkeley: University of California Press, 1985.

Wakeman, Frederic Jr., and Carolyn Grant, eds. *Conflict and Control in Late Imperial China*. Berkeley: University of California Press, 1975.

Wang Ch'i. *San-ts'ai t'u-hui* [68]. 1607. Reprint. Taipei: Ch'eng-wen ch'u-pan-she, 1970.

Wang Shih-to. *Wang Hui-weng i-ping jih-chi* [69]. 1936. Reprint. Taipei: Wen-hai ch'u-pan-she, 1967.

Watson, James L. "Of Flesh and Bones: The Management of Death Pollution in Cantonese Society." In M. Bloch and J. Parry, eds., *Death and the Regeneration of Life*, 155–186. Cambridge: Cambridge University Press, 1982.

—— "Funeral Specialists in Cantonese Society: Pollution, Performance, and Social Hierarchy." In James L. Watson and Evelyn S. Rawski, eds., *Death Ritual in Late Imperial and Modern China*, 109–134. Berkeley: University of California Press, 1988.

Watson, James L., and Evelyn S. Rawski, eds. *Death Ritual in Late Imperial and Modern China*. Berkeley: University of California Press, 1988.

Watt, John R. *The District Magistrate in Late Imperial China*. New York: Columbia University Press, 1972.

Weber, Max. *The Religion of China*. Glencoe: Free Press, 1959.

—— *Economy and Society: An Outline of Interpretive Sociology*. Edited by Guenther Roth and Claus Wittich. 2 vols. Berkeley: University of California Press, 1978.

Welch, Holmes. *The Practice of Chinese Buddhism, 1900–1950.* Cambridge, Mass.: Harvard University Press, 1967.

Weller, Robert P. "Bandits, Beggars, and Ghosts: The Failure of State Control over Religious Interpretation in Taiwan." *American Ethnologist* 12 (1985): 49–55.

Willeke, Bernward H. *Imperial Government and Catholic Missions in China during the Years 1784–1785.* Saint Bonaventure, New York: Franciscan Institute, 1948.

Williams, E. T. "Witchcraft in the Chinese Penal Code." *Journal of the North China Branch of the Royal Asiatic Society* 38 (1907): 61–96.

——— "The State Religion of China during the Manchu Dynasty." *Journal of the North China Branch of the Royal Asiatic Society* 44 (1913): 11–45.

Wolf, Arthur P. "Gods, Ghosts, and Ancestors." In Arthur P. Wolf, ed., *Religion and Ritual in Chinese Society,* 131–182. Stanford: Stanford University Press, 1974.

Wu, Silas H. L. "The Memorial Systems of the Ch'ing Dynasty (1644–1911)." *Harvard Journal of Asiatic Studies* 27 (1967): 7–75.

——— *Communication and Imperial Control in China: The Evolution of the Palace Memorial System, 1693–1735.* Cambridge, Mass.: Harvard University Press, 1970.

——— *Passage to Power: K'ang-hsi and His Heir Apparent, 1661–1722.* Cambridge, Mass.: Harvard University Press, 1979.

Wu Wei-p'ing. "The Development and the Decline of the Eight Banners." Ph.D. dissertation, University of Pennsylvania, 1969.

Yang, C. K. (Yang Ch'ing-k'un). *Religion in Chinese Society: A Study of Contemporary Social Functions of Religion and Some of Their Historical Factors.* Berkeley: University of California Press, 1961.

Yeh Hsien-en. *Ming-Ch'ing Hui-chou nung-ts'un she-hui yü tien-p'u-chih* [70]. Anhwei: Hsin-hua shu-chü, 1983.

Yü Ying-shih. " 'O Soul, Come Back!' A Study in the Changing Conceptions of the Soul and Afterlife in Pre-Buddhist China." *Harvard Journal of Asiatic Studies* 47.2 (1987): 363–395.

Yuan Mei. *Tzu pu-yü* [71]. Shanghai: Chin-chang t'u-shu-chü, 1914.

Yung-cheng-ch'ao chu-p'i yin-chien-tan [72]. In *Ch'ing-tai tang-an tzu-liao ts'ung-pien,* vol. 9, 44–156. Peking: Chung-hua shu-chü, 1983.

Yung-chia hsien-chih [73]. 1882 ed.

Zelin, Madeleine. *The Magistrate's Tael: Rationalizing Fiscal Reform in Eighteenth-Century Ch'ing China.* Berkeley: University of California Press, 1984.

Glossary

This glossary is in two parts. Part I gives the Chinese for all key terms and names in the text and notes. Omitted are names of persons whom the specialist can readily find in standard biographical references, and names that have no historical significance beyond this volume. Manchu names are listed with their Chinese transcriptions. Part II gives the Chinese or Japanese for authors and titles romanized in the Bibliography.

I.   Key Terms and Names

Aibida　愛必達
an-ch'a-ssu　按察司
Asha　阿思哈

ch'an-wei　讖緯
chao-hun　招魂
chao-kuei　招鬼
chen-hsieh　鎮邪
cheng-shih　政事
ch'eng-huang　城隍
chi-hsi　積習
chi-ssu　祭祀
ch'i-chü-chu　起居注
chia-kun　夾棍

ch'iang ching-shen　搶精神
chiao-hua-tzu　叫化子
chiao-hun　叫魂
chiao-kung　教供
chieh-shih　結實
chieh-yuan　結緣
chien　賤
chien-chih　間職
chien-kuai pu-kuai, ch'i-kuai tzu-pai　見怪不怪，其怪自敗
chien-kuei hsieh-o　奸宄邪惡
chien-seng　奸僧
ch'ien-t'i　乾惕
chih　旨
chih-chieh　肢解
chih-jen　紙人
chih-tao-liao　知道了
chih-tsao　織造
chin-fa　盡法
ch'in　勤
ch'in-wang　親王
ching-ch'a　京察
ching-kan neng-shih　精幹能事
ching-sui　精髓
ch'ing　清
ch'ing wang-ming　請王命
chiu-ch'ing　九卿
chiu-ho　糾劾
chiu-lao-hsien-tu chin-yin　九老仙都金印
chiu-lien-tsan　九蓮贊
cho-i　卓異
Chou-li　周禮
chou-shui　咒水
chu-lien ken-chiu　株連根究
chu-p'i　硃批
chu-tsu shang　祝詛上
ch'u-chia　出家
ch'u-fen　處分
chü-jen　舉人
chü-mien　局面
chü-mien hsiao-hsieh　局面小些

chueh-lo　覺羅
chün-cheng　軍政
chung-hou　忠厚

Dingcang　定長
Dorgon　多爾袞

erh-teng　二等

fa　法
fan　犯
fei shan-lei　非善類
fei ta-ch'i　非大器
feng-shui　風水
fu　復
Fuheng　傅恆
Fulin　福臨
Funihan　富尼漢

G'aojin　高晉

hao-ch'u　好處
hsia-ch'in　嚇親
hsia-ch'uang　榔牀
hsiang-huo shao-lei　香火燒類
hsiao-tao hsiao-hsi　小道消息
hsieh-en　謝恩
hsieh-shen　邪神
hsieh-shu　邪術
hsing　刑
hsing-ch'iu　刑求
hsing-ch'iu ch'ü-i　刑求屈抑
hsing-lü　刑律
hsun-fu　巡撫
hu-hu t'u-t'u　糊糊塗塗
hua-yu wei-wu　化有為無
hua-yuan　化緣
hui-pan　會辦
hui-pi　廻避
hun　魂

Hungli　弘歷
huo-chü tao-shih　火居道士
huo-chung　惑眾
huo-fu　禍福

i-chih　儀秩
I-ching　易經
i-ch'u　議處
i-kuo chih jen　異國之人
Injen　胤禛

Jangboo　彰寶
jen-ming　人命
jen-yao　人妖
Jordai　卓爾岱
Juntai　準泰

kai-fei　丐匪
kao-yin-chuang　告陰狀
k'ao-ch'eng　考成
k'ao-chi　考績
k'ao-k'o　考課
k'ao-shih-hua　考試化
k'ao-yü　考語
kou-hun　勾魂
kou-tao　勾到
ku-ming　沽名
ku-tu yen-mei　蠱毒魘魅
kua-t'a　掛搭
kuan-hsueh　官學
k'uan-ta　寬大
kuei　鬼
k'uei-nan wu-ti　愧赧無地
K'ung Ch'uan-chih　孔傳旺
kuo-chia kung-shih　國家公事

lan　覽
li　理
li-lü　禮律
li-pu　吏部

liang-min 良民
lien-hua-lo 蓮花落
ling-hun 靈魂
lü 律
lü-li-tan 履歷單

mai-pu 賣卜
mai-sang 埋喪
mai-sha 埋煞
Man-chou shih-p'u 滿洲世僕
mi-tsou 密奏
mi-yao 迷藥
mi-yu shan-liang 迷誘善良
mien-chih, shen-chih 勉之, 慎之
Mingde 明德
ming-fa shang-yü 明發上諭
ming-pai 明白
Mingšan 明山
mou-p'an 謀叛
mu-hua 募化

Necin 訥親
nei-cheng chih-kuan 內政職官
nei-wu-fu 內務府
nen (leng) 嫩(冷)
ni-ming 逆命
nien-li 年力

Ocang 鄂昌

pan-t'ien hsiu-ts'ai 半天秀才
pen-fen 本分
pen-kuo 本國
p'eng-min 棚民
pi-hsieh 避邪
p'i 匹
po 薄
p'o 魄
p'o feng-shui 破風水
pu-chih-en chih wu 不知恩之物

pu-i　捕役
pu-tao　不道
pu-tung sheng-se　不動聲色
pu-ying (wei), chung　不應(為)，重
p'u-fu yang hsien-te　普福養顯德
P'u-kuang lao-mu　普光老母

Sacai　薩載
san-nien ta-pi　三年大比
san-tung　三冬
seng-hui-ssu　僧會司
seng-kang-ssu　僧綱司
seng-lu-ssu　僧錄司
shen　神
shen-ch'u wan-shih　審處完事
sheng-li　生理
sheng-shih　盛世
sheng-yuan　生員
shih-ch'a　失察
shih-fu　師父
shih-kung　師公
shih-li　事例
shih-o　十惡
shih-wu　師巫
shou-yuan　収圓
shu　術
shu-shih　術士
ssu　似
ssu-chu-ts'e　四柱冊
sung-ch'ü nan-an　悚懼難安
Surde　蘇爾德
Syda　四達

ta-chi　大記
Ta-Ch'ing hui-tien　大清會典
Ta-Ch'ing lü-li　大清律例
ta-fa hsiao-lien　大法小廉
Ta-i chueh-mi lu　大義覺迷錄
ta-ni　大逆
Ta-sheng-chiao　大乘教

ta-tien　大典
tai-fa hsiu-hsing　带髮修行
tai-ling yin-chien　带領引見
t'ai-p'ing　太平
tao-chi　道紀
tao-chi-ssu　道紀司
tao-lu-ssu　道錄司
tao-shih　道士
Ti-mou-ching　地畝經
t'i-pen　題本

t'i-shen　替身
t'i-tu　提督
tieh-chao　牒照
t'ing-chi　廷寄
Toendo　託恩多
t'o-kuo　他國
tsai-an　在案
ts'ai-chü　才具
ts'ai-sheng che-ko　採生折割
tsao-ku　造蠱
ts'ao-shou　操守
tsei-tao　賊盜
tso-tao i-tuan　左道異端
tso-tao i-tuan chih shu　左道異端之術
tsou-che　奏摺
tsou-ma t'ien-kang　走馬天罡
tsu-shih　祖師
tsung-shih　宗室
tsung-tu　總督
ts'ung-ming　聰明
tu-ch'a-yuan　都察院
tu-tieh　度牒
t'u an-i　圖安逸
tuan yü-ts'ai　短於才
tzu-ch'en　自陳
tzu-chi　字寄

wan　卍
wan-hun-ch'iao　萬魂橋

wei-kao an　僞稿案

wu　巫

wu-hsing　五行

wu-ku　巫蠱

wu wang-yeh t'i-seng　五王爺提僧

wu-wei chiao　無為教

ya-i　衙役

yang　陽

yao-jen　妖人

yao-shu　妖書

yao-shu　妖術

yao-shu yao-yen　妖術妖言

yao-tao yin-seng　妖道淫僧

Yenjišan　尹繼善

yen-mei　魘魅

yin　陰

yin-chien-tan　引見單

ying-fu-seng　應付僧

ying-ho　迎合

yu　優

yu ch'u-hsi　有出息

yu-fang　遊方

yu-fang seng-tao　遊方僧道

yu liang-hsin　有良心

yü-mi chih hsiang　魚米之鄉

Yungcang　永常

Yungde　永德

Yungyan　顒琰

II.　Authors and Titles

The numbers below correspond to the bracketed numbers found after romanized Chinese and Japanese titles in the Bibliography.

1.　硃批奏摺，農民運動，反清鬥爭
2.　宮中上諭
3.　宮中廷寄
4.　錄副奏摺，法律，其他

5. 上諭檔方本
6. 刑科史書
7. 吏科史書
8. 刑科題本，刑部題本，蓄髮
9. 吏科題本，吏，糾參處分
10. 黃册
11. 大計册
12. 京察册
13. 隨手登記
14. 教務教案檔
15. 欽定吏部則例
16. 刑案滙覽
17. 薛允升，讀例存疑
18. 宮中檔乾隆朝奏摺
19. 史料旬刊
20. 大清會典
21. 大清會典事例
22. 大清歷朝實錄
23. 大清律例會通新纂
24. 大清十朝聖訓
25. 王先謙　東華續錄
26. 安双成　順康雍三朝八旗丁額淺析
27. 安吉縣志
28. 趙舒翹　提牢備考
29. 陳東林　徐懷寶　乾隆朝一起特殊文字獄偽孫嘉淦奏稿案考述
30. 績溪縣志
31. 江蘇按察使司錄呈長州縣拏獲乞丐陳漢如等一案全卷抄册
32. 錢實甫　清代職官年表
33. 清史列傳
34. 清代帝后像
35. 莊吉發　清代奏摺制度
36. 清高宗十全武功研究
37. 全漢昇　乾隆十三年的米貴問題
38. 馮爾康　雍正傳
39. 傅宗懋　清代督撫制度之研究
40. 杭州府志
41. 蕭一山　清代通史
42. 徐珂　清稗類鈔
43. 高一涵　中國御史制度的沿革
44. 廣德州志

45. 國朝耆獻類徵初編
46. 李國祁　清代基層地方官人事嬗遞現象之量化分析
47. 林咏榮　唐清律的比較及其發展
48. 劉石吉　明清時代江南市鎮研究
49. 羅貫中　馮夢龍　平妖傳
50. 馬起華　清高宗朝之彈劾案
51. 中川忠英　清俗紀聞
52. 彭信威　中國貨幣史
53. 彭澤益　鴉片戰爭後十年間銀貴錢賤波動下中國經濟與階級關係
54. 蒲松齡　聊齋志異
55. 沢田瑞穂　中國の咒法
56. 單士元　清代起居注
57. 沈家本　歷代刑法考
58. 沈葆禎　沈文忠公政書
59. 沈德符　萬曆野獲編
60. 鈴木中正　乾隆十七年馬朝柱的反清運動—中國民眾的烏托邦運動的一例
61. 谷井俊仁　乾隆時代の一広域犯罪事件と国家の対應——割辮案の社會史的素描
62. 清代外省の警察機能について——割辮案を例に
63. 德清縣志
64. 德清縣續志
65. 點石齋畫報
66. 田居儉　宋元強　中國資本主義萌芽
67. 曹松葉　泥水木匠故事探討
68. 王圻　三才圖會
69. 汪士鐸　汪悔翁乙丙日記
70. 葉顯恩　明清徽州農村社會與佃僕制
71. 袁枚　子不語
72. 雍正朝硃批引見單
73. 永嘉縣志

Index